D1429280

Edmund Nankivell

The JOWETT JUPITER

the car that leaped to fame

B.T. BATSFORD LTD, LONDON

To St Agnes and St Jude

© Edmund Nankivell 1981
First published 1981

Typeset in 9 on 10 pt Press Roman
by Tek-Art Ltd, London SE20
and printed in Great Britain by
Robert Maclehose & Co Ltd
Renfrew, Scotland
for the publishers B.T. Batsford Ltd
4 Fitzhardinge Street, London W1H 0AH

ISBN 0 7134 3835 5

Contents

Acknowledgments 5

Prologue : Gordon Wilkins and the R1 6

CHAPTER 1 The Jowett Jupiter 8
Introduction
A Jupiter chronology
The Jupiter experiment
The skin and beneath
Summary of road tests
Comparisons with other cars
Factory and good private speed and rally summary
Jowett records

CHAPTER 2 Le Mans and the R1 Jupiters: The Leap to Fame 32

CHAPTER 3 The Major Rallies : 1951 to 1953 43

CHAPTER 4 Races and Speed Events : 1950 to 1953 61

CHAPTER 5 Minor Rallies and All Other Events : 1951 to 1966 80

CHAPTER 6 Jupiters Yesterday and Today 93
25,00 miles in a Jowett Jupiter
The Jupiter in Concours d'Elégance
The Jupiter in historic racing
Current use

CHAPTER 7 History of the R4 Jupiters 101

CHAPTER 8 Special-Bodied Jupiters: The Coachbuilders 106

CHAPTER 9 Jupiter Register 117
Factory Jupiters
Numbering systems
Jupiters in California and the 'Bulletin 149' engines
The register

Epilogue: Sir Hugh Bell Remembers 140

Index 141

Acknowledgments

First and foremost thanks must be recorded to George Mitchell who suggested the book, supplied the factory records information, opened his customer files on Jupiters and contributed elsewhere – notably much of the section on engine numbers. Secondly, essential assistance was rendered in ways large and small by several former Jowett personnel, among whom particular mention should be made of Donald Bastow, Charles Grandfield, Phil Green, Cliff Howarth, Reg Korner, Ken Shackleton, Charles Philip Stephenson, and the drivers Marcel Becquart, Ted Booth, Bert Hadley, George Phillips, Bill Robinson.

The competition history would hardly have been possible without recourse to Pete Dixon's collection of relevant magazines of the period; and I would further like to thank Mr Dixon for his day-to-day help in this and other aspects of the contents, together with his part in arranging publication and coordinating funding.

I am grateful to *Autocar, Autosport*, and particularly *Motor Sport* for permission to reproduce certain extracts; to Malcolm Wood for permission to search through the records and to use the photographs of C.H. Wood (Bfd) Ltd; to the National Motor Museum for permission to inspect their material and for the use of photographs; to Jonathan Wood of *Thoroughbred and Classic Car* regarding aspects of company history.

It would not have been possible to complete this book, covering as it does so many aspects, without the help of many people too numerous to mention by name – Jupiter owners past and present – in many countries. My sincere thanks to all those who have lent photographs, searched their attics and their memories, and supplied information and I hope that they feel that they have played a part in the creation of this book. I must list, however, John Blazé for camerawork, draughtsmanship and encouragement; Malcolm Bergin for the New Zealand angle; Roger Gambell for information on the R4s; Ted Miller for superhuman feats of discovery in the USA, Bruce Polain (Australia), and Jacques Touzet (Portugal).

Finally, publication has only been possible thanks to the efforts of the Jupiter Owners Auto Club as a whole, of club committees over the years maintaining links with owners in many countries so tracing and reporting Jupiter history through the pages of the club's newsletter *By Jupiter*, and ultimately through the generous financial contributions towards the book's production costs by the following owner/members:
D. Banks (747), J. Blazé (743), E. Davis (840), R. Davis (521), K. Latham (866, 871, 999), J. Parker (505, 1032), D. Sparrow (253, 734).

Throughout this book, a number in parentheses indicates a Jupiter chassis number.

Prologue:
Gordon Wilkins and the R1

The Jowett Jupiter which Becquart and I had at Le Mans has excellent handling characteristics. Weight distribution is right and the steering is first class. Modifications to the tooth form of the rack and pinion and a revision of pivots for the steering and suspension have contributed to the quick, light and direct control. With tanks full or nearly empty, the R1 can be twitched into a slide and out again under perfect control; if anything it understeers slightly, but the control is always light and the response immediate.

At Le Mans we were repeatedly held up by bigger cars on the winding stretches and between Mulsanne and Arnage we several times had to re-pass cars which had overtaken us on the straight. There was nothing faster than the Jupiter through the corners.

The thick drifting mist brought a strange sense of isolation and unreality during the night hours, heightened by the fact that I found myself passing Ferraris, Talbots and other fast cars which loomed up suddenly and were left behind. An open car is undoubtedly an advantage in such conditions and one of the Jupiters passed a Mercedes; probably the car driven by Lang, who was losing 40 seconds a lap at the worst period. At one time the White House bends could be taken at 100 mph or more; two laps later the maximum speed would be nearer 50. Long practice in England's winters undoubtedly helps, and Briggs Cunningham said to me afterwards: 'I wished I had been born an Englishman last night. You fellows seem to go through the fog as though it wasn't there.'

Gordon Wilkins, after Le Mans 1952
Autocar, July 1952

1

The Jowett Jupiter

Bradford in Yorkshire had throughout the nineteenth century been considered the 'worsted capital of the world' and even in the 1940s and 1950s wool textiles were still a major industry there, although synthetic fibres were by then challenging its supremacy. Thanks to abundant coal and iron, Bradford developed as an engineering town too, and one engineering establishment that flourished was the business founded around the turn of the century by the Jowett brothers Willie and Ben. During the inter-war years Jowett Cars Ltd expanded into a new site near the village of Idle, just to the north of, and soon to be engulfed by, Bradford and it was at this factory at Idle that the Jupiters were developed, built, tested, and in the case of the factory cars, housed.

Bradford was far from the natural centre of the British motor industry, and this ensured for Jowett cars an interesting and sometimes quirky individualism not to be found in cars of other makes. For while Jowetts could attract clever engineers and designers such as Gerry Palmer, Frank Salter and Donald Bastow to the higher echelons, as regards the lower and middle levels of design and drafting they were forced to grow their own and, for better and worse, there was not the free interplay of ideas as at Coventry then.

2 Aerial view of the works 1) Experimental Department 2) Here Jupiter No.1 was photographed by C.H. Wood 3) Weighbridge – near where HAK 317 was pictured 4) Main offices 5) Production 6) Spion Kop 7) Here the group photograph was taken of Jupiter No.1 and Experimental Department: C.H. Wood

In 1939 car building was abandoned for the war's duration and the company quadrupled its size to about 2,000 people under the energetic management of Calcott Reilly, a man ambitious for further peacetime expansion through the spearhead of the Palmer-designed Javelin saloon car. Charles Clore as chairman came and went, buying the Jowett brothers' majority holding in 1945 and selling it to Lazard Brothers, the merchant bank, in 1947: Lazards then installed Wilfred Sainsbury as non-executive director, and George Wansborough in place of Clore. Two years later Jowetts were rocked by three high-level changes: Palmer returned to MG to be replaced by Roy Lunn, a young designer destined for great things in Detroit but at that time with only three years' experience in the motor industry; Calcott Reilly went to the Cyclemaster moped firm perhaps crucially taking Jowetts works manager with him; and in a move that was to result in the arrival of Arthur Jopling on the board, Wansborough, having given the green light to the Jupiter project left abruptly after some of his share dealings – unconnected with Jowetts – met with the disaproval of Lazards.

The actual conception of the Jupiter is attributed to the journalist Laurence Pomeroy, who after the war began promoting the idea of a sports car capable of standing up to the challenge of German and Italian machines in the medium-capacity field. Promising early competition results for the Javelin ensured that Pomeroy's idea was taken up, and when the famous Austrian engineer, Robert Eberan von Eberhorst, arrived in England in May 1949 plans were already underway for the construction of a chassis to be produced by ERA, using Javelin components. Eberhorst gave the Jowett programme new impetus and the course of the project was subjected to a number of radical changes before the ERA-Javelin was ready for the 1949 London Motor Show. Jowetts exhibited an

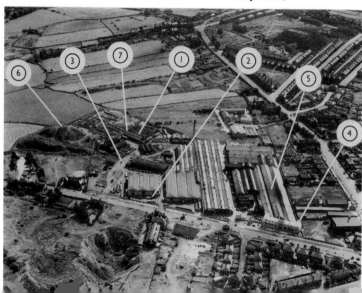

ERA chassis, on which anti-roll bars were visible front and rear, but were not attracted to the complete car.

The first Jowett Jupiter model had been a side-valve, flat-four-engined 10 hp saloon car, introduced in September 1935. It was not a success and was replaced the following March by the Peregrine model.

The concern of this book is only with the Jowett Javelin Jupiter (as it was called initially) sports convertible and its derivatives produced between 1949 and 1954, and in all 831 standard-bodied cars were made by the company during that time, of which 736 were Mk1 and 95 Mk1a. An additional 68 fully equipped rolling chassis* were supplied and a few of these received bodies closely resembling standard from the hands of various constructors. But at least 22 had bodywork fitted by well-known coachbuilders with national or international reputations such as Stabilimenti Farina of Italy, Beutler, Ghia Suisse and Warblaufen of Switzerland, and Abbott and Richard Mead of England. Some 15 or so attracted the attentions of the new breed of specialist constructor that in-

*Two rolling chassis reman unused at the time of writing (36,115) and a third may have been dismembered in 1958. One or more specials may, like 'Jehu', have been constructed around new, unnumbered Jupiter frames bought as spares, while the 'Ineson Special' apparently shares its chassis number with a standard car. Two unused, unstamped LHD Mk1 frames existed in 1980. The 'Appleton Jupiter Special' was a Jupiter-engined special as was that monstrous contraption, the rear-engined 'Fryer Scientific'.

habited the Thames Valley region in the early 1950s; Lionel Rawson, Coachcraft of Egham, Maurice Gomm, Charles Robinson and others, who tended to be strongly influenced by the work of the more advanced Italian designers. Another group, of whom the two Lancashire-based concerns KW Bodies and J.E. Farr & Son, with Harold Radford of London accounted for nine between them, were firms, often long-established, whose normal output might be Rolls-Royce bodies, hearses, utilities and such like for whom sports-car bodywork was a rarity that tended to be engaged in with more enthusiasm that concinnity. However, whereas in 1950 proprietary coachbuilders had been looked to for Jupiter chassis sales, when the production of complete cars began to get going in some quantity towards the end of the following year, Jowett's lower price made it impossible for outside constructors, the differential in Britain being commonly around £400.

Jowett's Experimental Department built three cars, known as the type R1, on slightly modified chassis for racing purposes (one survives) and three type R4 Jupiters – prototypes of what was to have been a faster but lower cost sports car – were built on a completely different chassis to the design of Roy Lunn and Phil Stephenson. Two survive. As far as is known a single Mk1a Jupiter was built up from new spares in 1956.

The Mk1 chassis was designed by Professor Dr Dipl Ing Robert Eberan von Eberhorst when chief engineer at ERA Ltd,

3 The drophead coupé by Richard Mead. The hood line anticipated the Jowett Mk1a Jupiter. An unusual feature is the trafficator in the door: Autocar

9

Dunstable. It is said that six chassis were built by ERA: one was shown (bodyless) at the London Motor Show in October 1949 while EO/SA/1R received the definitive Jupiter shape at Jowetts from the hand of chief bodywork designer Reg Korner and was first seen at the British Motor and Engineering Show in New York in April 1950.

Jowett-designed body panels were obtained unfinished from Western Manufacturing Co Ltd (formed from the ashes of the Miles Aircraft Co) at Woodley Aerodrome near Reading, thence to Jowett's Clayton plant where they were handfitted into sets on to their respective bodyframes, etched and primed, and transported to Idle behind a Bradford driveaway chassis: Jowetts built the chassis after the ERA frames had been used.

The factory records were obtained by George Mitchell in 1963 and in addition to the information listed at the end of this book they show the name of the agent or dealer making the sale and the original body and upholstery colours, together with the names and addresses of original owners in the cases of home sales. Any owner requiring these data should contact the Jupiter Owners Auto Club.

Every effort has been made to ensure accuracy throughout this work but no responsibility can be accepted for any errors or their consequences. Some of the minor events in particular presented many headaches due to the way they were reported: a Jowett in a saloon event could have been a Javelin or a saloon Jupiter, the same competitor might, like A. Wake, have at different times apparently appeared in a standard Jupiter, a Javelin, and a saloon Jupiter. The Javelin and Jupiter might be owned simultaneously or consecutively, and a Javelin owner might borrow a Jupiter for an event. Although one or two open Javelins exist, an open Jowett has been regarded as a Jupiter.

Period or up-to-date information on listed and unlisted Jupiters is always sought and will invariably be acknowledged. Please contact Edmund Nankivell, Downland, 4B South Way, Lewes, Sussex, England, or the Jupiter Owners Auto Club, 16 Empress Avenue, Woodford Green, Essex, England.

A Jupiter chronology

1947 Charles Clore replaced by Lazard Brothers, the merchant bankers, as majority shareholder of Jowett Cars Ltd. George Wansborough became chairman of Jowetts.

1948 January: ERA bought by Leslie Johnson from Humphrey Cook (with Raymond Mays one of its two founders in 1933).

1949 Leslie Johnson persuaded Jowetts to enter a Javelin in the Spa 24-Hour race claiming that as he ran his Javelin everywhere at 70 mph the car ought to win. Jowetts agreed if ERA paid for the entry; the Javelin was driven to the meeting trailing a spare engine in Horace Grimley's holiday trailer, and, with Tom Wisdom and Anthony Hume sharing the wheel, it won the 2-litre touring-car class at 65.5 mph.

January: Steel shortage hit Jowetts and some workers were laid off. (Steel allocation depended on exports.) Hume, Leslie Johnson, and Laurance Pomeroy (*Motor* technical editor) hatched a plan for ERA to design a sports car around the Javelin's mechanicals. Wansborough, on the lookout for a new, exportable, product, agreed. Pomeroy and Hume drove to Italy by Javelin to contact Pomeroy's friend, the Austrian-born Professor Dr Dipl Ing Robert Eberan von Eberhorst, at that time working for Cisitalia in Turin.*

May: Eberhorst came to England to work on the contract from Jowetts for six chassis powered by the Javelin engine, power raised to 60 bhp. David Hodkin assisted.

September: One of the chassis given a plump fixed-head coupé body by Harold Radford and a photo of it appeared in the *Daily Graphic* of the 28th. Jowetts, thinking of an open car were not enamoured.

October: London Motor Show. One of the ERA chassis was on the Jowett stand (chassis terminated at rear-axle support structure, 60 bhp achieved by special camshaft) and was received with rapture as a piece of advanced engineering by the

*In 1933 Auto Union had bought the Porsche-designed 'P-Wagen' after it had proved that it could lap a particular circuit at 120 mph. Professor Ferdinand Porsche then joined Auto Union and Eberhorst, under first Porsche then Dr Feureisen, was put in charge of racing engine work with two racing engineers under him and 200 men in the racing workshops. The first engine was the 4.25-litre V16 which grew to 5, 6, then 6½ litres. In 1938 a 3-litre, V12-engined car was produced, known as the D-type. This had torsion rod springing at both ends and a large-bore chrome-molybdenum tubular steel chassis. In 1939 Eberhorst began work on a 1½-litre V12 but the war intervened. During the war he was said to have been imprisoned at some time by Hitler for some aspect of tank design.

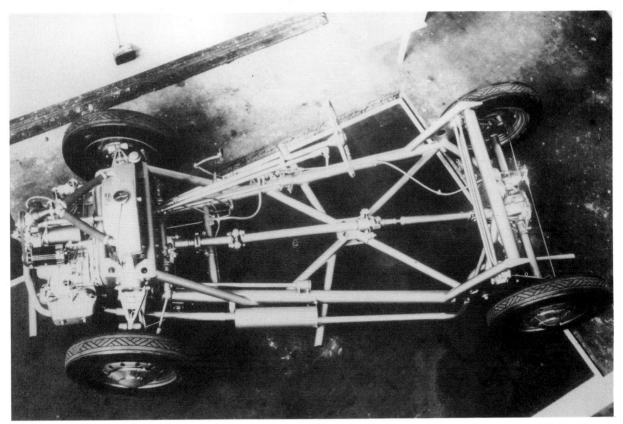

British motoring press. The 'ERA-Javelin' was elsewhere, probably Dunstable.

November: Wilfred Sainsbury (a Lazards man with much power in JCL) met L.J. and told him there would be no further contract as Jowetts intended to build the chassis themselves and design their own bodywork for it. Eberhorst was subsequently seen at Idle about twice.

Early December: Reg Korner Jowetts chief bodywork designer given four months to design a prototype Jupiter to be in the British New York Motor and Engineering Show the following April. This seems to have been the programme for five out of the six ERA frames:

1 First prototype car, for New York.
2 First exhibition chassis for Brussels, Geneva, etc.
3 Second exhibition chassis, for New York.
4 Entry for Le Mans 24-Hour race, required by June 1950.
5 The second prototype car for road testing.

The Hoffman Motor Car Co. was to buy both the USA machines.

1950   Mid-January: Brussels Motor Show had exhibition chassis (2) now with tail extension but otherwise as ERA made it.

March 8: The *Autocar* and *Motor* carried articles on the Jowett Javelin Jupiter, as it was christened, with photos of the chassis but artist's impressions of the car. 60 bhp with the modified camshaft was claimed and the price for the chassis was given as £495 before tax. The exhibition chassis was in the month's Geneva Motor Show.

March 27: First complete car finished on the Saturday after 14 weeks of effort. It was tested over 22 miles on the Sunday, a somewhat foggy day, photographed and released to the local press on the Monday (29th), and delivered to Liverpool for shipping to the USA on the Tuesday with the other exhibition chassis (3). The brochure for the Jupiter had colour drawings by Roy Nockolds.

The second complete car (5) went on a 3,000-mile tour of Britain and France driven by Charles Grandfield and Horace Grimley, where it averaged 46 mph at 31 mpg: whatever else it was, a Jowett had to be economical to run.

April: The Le Mans car, GKW111, the responsibility of Grandfield, Korner, and Grimley, was ready for road testing.

April 18: The New York Show a success for the Jupiter in its colour (metallichrome

copper, fawn hood) new for the show. Cameron Peck the president of the Sports Car Club of America bought a Jupiter at £910 and an Aston Martin DB2 at £1,963, out of more than 100 exhibits. There was heady talk of selling 1,000 Jupiters a year to the USA in reports of '90 mph car sold out a year ahead and not even in production'. UK prices given as £495 (chassis), £795 (car), pre-tax.

May or early June: It is thought, the second prototype (5) appeared in the Silverstone paddock, long returned from its continental tour. (In July it was shipped to Canada where at the time of writing it still is.)

June 24–25: Jupiter won its class, Le Mans 24-Hour race.

August 11: First production chassis (6) shipped to Sweden and the second (7)

5 Some of the Experimental Department staff, shown here with the prototype, have been identified. From the left: (1) Horace Grimley, chief experimental engineer; (2) Margaret Haspell, secretary to Charles Grandfield; (3) Bill Poulter, body foreman; (4) R. Brayshaw, trimmer; (5) Johnny Bromhan, machinist; (9) A. Hudson, trimmer; (12) W. Brogden, joiner; (14) Teddy Fannon, fitter; (17) Bill Eglestone, bodymaker under Bill Poulter; (18) Arthur Illingworth (in white coat), supervisor under Horace Grimley; (19) F. Schonn, labourer; (22) C. Rogers

6 Horace Grimley (left), Roy Lunn and Charles Grandfield (right) pose with the 1950 Le Mans contender on 16 June: C.H.Wood

7 The Jowett stand at the British New York Motor and Engineering Exhibition. The prototype Jupiter (centre) stayed in the USA and was later raced there

went to Stabilimenti Farina three days later. Chassis 6 to 16 were all fully equipped rolling chassis, hydromechanically braked with the hydraulic tappet engine of the period little altered.

October 6: Surprise last-minute entry to the Paris Motor Show was the Stabilimenti Farina Jupiter Fixed Head Coupé (7) clearly to the design of Pininfarina. The car appeared at the London Motor Show two weeks later where it was quite a centre of attraction.

November: First production batch of complete cars (17 to 21) straked but otherwise normal; no louvres in the bonnet. No 17 went to M. Thévenin, the owner of a garage in Bordeaux; Nos 19 and 21 were demonstrators with No 20 the showroom car. No 18 was intended for Plissons the Paris

importer but the sale was cancelled for Frenchmen could buy foreign cars only with foreign money: this car went to France anyway, class-winning the Monte Carlo Rally.

A further batch of five Jupiters (strakes discontinued to save money) were completed before the end of the year, four for export, with another two dozen rolling chassis among which may have been, in rebuilt form, the sixth ERA frame* and the USA show chassis. (Max Hoffman had changed his mind about buying it.)

December 7: Sir Hugh Bell's Jupiter, body by Lionel Rawson (builder of the Healey Sportsmobile), on the road. Alf Thomas followed with a similar car in February.

1951   January: Standard-bodied Jupiters

*See (3) page 125, (48) page 126.

8 Stabilimenti Farina Jupiter pictured near the factory's weigh-bridge in October 1951. It had been registered HAK317: C.H.Wood

now being produced for overseas, the braking full hydraulic and the tappets solid. No bonnet louvres yet, throttle pedal still Javelin type.

January 31: Jupiters first and second in class in Monte Carlo Rally.

February: LHD prototype delivered to Angell Motors of Pasadena. Rolling chassis still only available to British customers with four exceptions: Bill Skelly, L.J. Roy Taylor, Godfrey Imhoff and W.J. Tee of *Motor Sport*. British prices now £540 and £875 before tax. Reports of steel allocation cuts affecting Javelin and Jupiter production. It was announced that 'Javelin' was to be dropped from the Jupiter's name.

April: Production LHD Jupiters available, price $2,850 f.o.b. New York, $700 more than the Morgan Plus 4 and the MG TD but a similar amount less than the Simca 8 and Porsche.

June/July: Last batch of rolling chassis, about 22, delivered. Standard cars now have four-louvre panels let into bonnet, rear lamps cast-aluminium-housed rather than formed in to the rear wings.

June 23–24: Jupiter again won its class, Le Mans 24-Hour race.

August: Film comedian Red Skelton came to England, bought four Jupiters for himself and his entourage and returned to California with them where three still remained in 1978.

September 15: Jupiters first and second in class, RAC TT Dundrod.

September 28: R1 Jupiter won Watkins Glen race for 1½-litre cars.

October: Paris Salon has the fourth Farina Jupiter (109). At the London Motor Show, Jupiters released to the home market but a long wait existed. Price now £895 + £498 14s 5d tax. The exhibition chassis interestingly had rubber-bushed front suspension, a feature not available on production Jupiters for another 12 months. Bonnet louvres still let-in panels, now in groups of seven smaller ones, although the show car had the old louvre arrangement, plus an instrument layout and metal fascia that would later be used on the Mk1a. Sales now in the upper 30s per months.

1952 January: Power of Jupiter engine now 62.5 bhp at 4,500 rpm with compression ratio 8:1. Jupiter price raised to £1,518 3s 4d. Javelin deliveries began to slip from the 110 per week of the previous three years to around 75.

January 29: Becquart finished a difficult

Monte Carlo Rally in fifth place overall, second in class, in his Farina Jupiter.

February 11: The Mk1a prototype HKW197 delivered to the Experimental Dept. Ford began takeover negotiations with Briggs, the supplier of Javelin and Bradford van bodies.

February/April: Jupiter production hits peak of 208 over these three months; the Jupiter was now in its classic pre-series III form with late radiator, engine-mounted oil cooler etc.

April: Design study for the 'Jupiter Mk2' carried out by Phil Stephenson, incorporating the 'attenuated Eberhorst frame', R1-type scuttle, and coachwork close to the R4 design of 1953. (In the event, the 1952 R1s were little altered from the 1951 version.)

April 5: Becquart switched to Javelin for RAC Rally to beat all other closed cars.

April 7: JCL AGM statement recorded '1951 a very good trading year for Jowetts, but exports fell away badly at the end of 1951[with the] closure of export markets like Australia. Javelin production at Idle cut to 50 per week.

June 14–15: R1 Jupiter in third consecutive class win, Le Mans 24-Hour race, but other two cars broke cranks. After the race Jopling, Jowett's managing director, told the drivers there would be no more Jowetts raced.

August 15: Jupiter price cut to £1,284 16s 8d. Delivery now 'months rather than years'.

September: The eminent engineer Donald Bastow, MIMechE, BSc (Eng), MSAE, MSIA, former assistant to W.O. Bentley (1947 to 1950), joined JCL from the BSA Engines and Mechanisms Laboratory, in the newly created post of chief engineer.

October: London Motor Show. Mk1a announced where it won a silver medal for coachwork design. Almost all export cars (except personal export) and all LHD cars were henceforth Mk1a. Prices were £825 + £459 16s 8d = £1,284 16s 8d for the Mk1 and £895 + £498 14s 5d = £1,393 14 s 5d for the Mk1a; the Mk1 was available until October 1953. All versions were to have the newly released series III engine.

November: Three Javelins and a Jupiter (76) circulated around the MIRA track at constant speed for three weeks to demonstrate the reliability of the series III power unit. Javelin sales sank to 22 per week.

December 1: Jopling suspended his order,

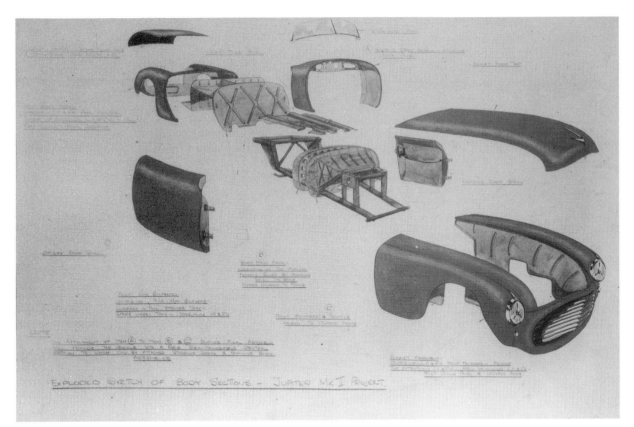

EXPLODED SKETCH OF BODY SECTIONS - JUPITER MkI PROJECT

*9 The Jupiter Mk2,
the forerunner of the R4
design of 1953, would
have incorporated
lessons learnt from the
Le Mans Jupiter type
R1: C.H.Wood*

*10 How the Mk2 would
have looked : C.H.Wood*

placed on Briggs in May, for 5,000 CDs,
now tooled for and due for imminent production. He requested that Javelin production should cease and that CC Bradford
body assembly should continue but at half
the 1952 rate: this last request was refused,
thus sealing Jowett's fate. Jupiter deliveries
hit low of 12 in the last quarter of 1952.

1953 January: Briggs ceased delivery of
Javelin and Bradford bodies.

February: Ford takeover of Briggs effected.
Crash programme to design and build a
new Jupiter sports car began – Experimental
Department told that, if in the October
Motor Show, such a car might save Jowetts.

March 5: Phil Stephenson completed
colour sketch of the 'Jupiter 100', later
called the 'R4'. Stephenson left Jowetts
three months later.

11 The Mk1a has an externally accessible boot and a hood line of increased rake. This is the prototype HKW197, hence the front strake: C.H.Wood

12 One of the first photographs of the prototype R4, taken in July 1953. The bonnet emblem here is an RAC badge. The bonnet of this car was later louvred: C.H.Wood

April: Grandfield, moving spirit behind the works competition effort, left JCL. Jupiter price lowered to £795 + £332 10s.

May: The continuing assembly of stored Javelin bodies enabled the debt to Briggs to be paid, permitting Jopling to reopen negotiations with Briggs – now under new management – regarding Javelin (at 40 per week) and CD

June: Briggs refused to resume Javelin production, CD production considered but a hard line taken and no agreement could be reached. The Jupiter enjoyed a mini-boom with 28 cars sold. The first R4 Jupiter, JKW537, with all-metal body, ready for trials.

July 7: Jopling reported a 'heavy overall loss for 1952, leaving an adverse balance, since liquidated, of £286,353. Exports dropped 75% in 1952 and sales fell at home'.

July 10: JKW537, with aeroscreens as only weather protection, photographed with 148 miles on its odometer. No overdrive yet.

August 22: JKW537, after its continental proving run, had overdrive, 4,766 miles on its odometer, hardtop but no front screen ready.

September 16: At a press conference Jopling explained that there could be no further Javelin production.

October: London Motor Show. Two Javelins, a LHD Mk1a Jupiter (now listed at £725 + £303 4s 2d) and new glass-fibre-fronted R4 on the Jowett stand. JKW537 gave demonstration drives through London's street. . . 'Thousands could be sold.' Roy Lunn approached by Fords who made an offer he could not refuse.

December: International Harvester began to move their production planning department into the Experimental Department buildings.

December 24: The Motor Show R4 had its last photographic session in Bradford, now with full-width screen and soft top.

1954 Thanks to George Green (general sales manager, formerly service manager), who correctly believed that if Jupiters were built they could be sold, two small batches were constructed in 1954 – body parts were largely in stock as the manufacture of a second 1,000 had been sanctioned the previous year. Negotiations continued with IH and Blackburn & General Aircraft Co. Jopling was on the baord of the latter company and a flow of subcontract work resulted.

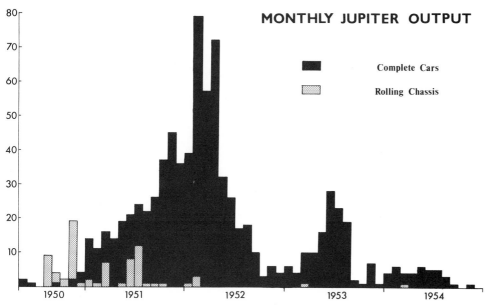

MONTHLY JUPITER OUTPUT

■ Complete Cars

▒ Rolling Chassis

13 Production chart showing monthly Jupiter output, 1950 to 1954

March: Jowett's Albermarle Street showroom sold.

May 11: The end is close. Partially built and complete Jupiters were photographed at Idle. Price now down to £1,028 4s 2d.

September: Harvesters now in full control of the Idle factory. Subcontract work phased out in favour of their new light tractor, the B250, to be entirely constructed within the factory confines, apart from a few proprietary items, at the rate of 50 per week. The last all-new Jupiter (1032) completed. Spares operation set up at Birstall with commitment to supply components for nine years, although its main function soon became aircraft parts.

November: Last Jupiter (1033), the last Jowett-built car, completed using the show chassis (2), in a corner of the Idle factory.

December 17: Announcement that the sale of the Idle factory and plant to IH enabled the 5% mortgage debenture stock to be repaid at 102% plus accrued interest; it was expected that the following February more surplus cash would cover preference shares, plus an interim payment on ordinary shares.

1955 September: The rump of Jowett Cars Ltd, at Birstall, bought by Blackburn & General. This enabled Jowetts financial affairs to be wound up leaving no debts and shareholders were paid pound for pound. The oval webbed crankshaft put into production about this time.

1958 July 10: The Jupiter Mk 1a built up from new parts by Robert Townend, a friend of George Green, ready for the road.

August: Jowett Cars Ltd at Birstall changes its name to Jowett Engineering Ltd.

1960 Blackburn & General taken over by Hawker-Siddeley.

1962 Jupiter Owners' Auto Club formed.

1963 December: Jowett Engineering closed, due to contraction in the aircraft industry, which obliged HS to bring all manufacture into its main factories. Spares manufacture ceased as it no more than paid its way.

1964 January: Saloon Jupiter 538KOR (246), with body by Maurice Gomm finally finished off and registered – believed the last all-new Jupiter.

1973 Ron Davis completed probably the first total 'kit of parts' Jupiter rebuild (521).

1981 First book on the Jupiter published.

14 Production returns to Idle at the end of 1955: International Harvester

*15 This 1/5 scale
model by Cyril Sweet
actually works; it won a
silver medal*

chased so their sentiments can probably be taken as genuine.

A man insistent upon the lack of humbug of his reports was the retired racing driver John Bolster, who road-tested for *Autosport*. About the day, also teeming with rain, that he borrowed his test Jupiter he wrote (18 January 1952) that he did not anticipate much excitement as for him 'the luxuriously equipped and solidly constructed body had more of the American convertible than the British two-seater . . . and with only 1½ litres of engine it did not seem likely that this would be a brilliant performer. A conscientious tester should discover what happens in extreme driving conditions . . . accordingly whenever it was safe to do so I flung the spray-enveloped Jupiter through the curves to the best of my ability. I was utterly dumbfounded by the result for the machine simply stuck to the road, and followed the road with complete accuracy. Here was a challenge, so I turned off the radio, sat up straight, and entered the next corner at an entirely impossible speed. A very gentle four-wheel drift was the result, and the course was held without any appreciable correction on the steering'. He later reflected (*Autosport*, 26 December 1952) '. . . it has roadholding and steering of great merit. Even on wet roads it can be cornered at the highest speeds and I soon acquired the most abundant confidence in its behaviour. I have driven many faster cars but something intangible about this one made it appeal to me very much and I returned it with regret.'

The opposite view was reported by Tom McCahill in *Mechanix Illustrated* (British edition, November 1951) in stating that '. . . this little pancake-powered eggbeater . . . corners and steers *worse* than any Detroit family bus' and continued 'The manufacturers in Merry Albion have us tagged for a bunch of dopes who wouldn't know a good sports car if it ran over us.' But *Road and Track* (March 1953) looked at two Jupiters and disagreed, as did Dick Hayward writing in *Motor Sports World*: 'Seldom have I read a more unjust evaluation of the handling behavior of an automobile . . . this little beauty not only cornered superbly but recovered straight as an arrow out of four wheel slides, hands off!' Encouraged by Newton Small, Hayward sold his TD, bought a Jupiter, and continued: 'She is all I expected and more. She has better manners than anything I have driven and that includes a couple of Tom's Top Ten.'

Eberhorst was one of the Jupiter's severest critics, remarking once to his

The Jupiter experiment

William Boddy, in his road test of GKY106 (*Motor Sport*, December 1950), after remarking that the Jupiter's performance figures were not very different from the prewar 1½-litre, Meadows-engined HRG, found himself pleasantly surprised at the handling of the car in the teeming rain that prevailed on the day of the test, and noted the high average speed he was able to maintain on a 400-mile round trip to the West Country. There was comment on 'the steering and suspension with cornering that builds up confidence' and the balance between over- and understeer was liked. 'The tail breaks away first, tail skids, easily corrected, seemed to occur rather frequently, probably because fallen leaves made the wet roads more than usually slippery and the rear Goodyears were rather worn. This tendency kept the driver alert.' Three months later *Motor Sport* bought a Jupiter (98) and further articles praising the handling, long-distance high-average-speed capabilities, coupled with low driver fatigue and good fuel economy followed. In 1953 a Mk1a (972) was pur-

friend L.J. Roy Taylor (51) 'Don't hold the car against me, it's not one of my best efforts.' This, though, should be received in the light of the professor's unhappiness with the poor facilities at ERA to develop a new car, and the need, always a restriction for a designer, to use existing components.

Bert Hadley commented 25 years later 'I found the Javelin a fantastic car to drive in 1951–2, it was a credit to its designers way back in 1948. The road-holding was incredible and it would easily have contained a power unit with 50% more power. The Jupiter – well the road-holding was again quite amazing and a credit to the chassis designed by Eberhorst. I can recall driving the Jupiter flat out in the 1952 RAC Rally in conditions of snow, ice, and slush. It never put a foot wrong.'

In Bill Robinson's view 'the Jupiter's handling was really outstanding in tight street racing, and particularly on adverse surfaces. A mug could drive one faster than other cars, the grip was uncanny in snow: the tyres seemed to burn in, and on black ice while other cars were skidding around one could pass them effortlessly.'

The last word shall come from George Phillips. Offered the 1952 Silverstone Production Sports Car drive by Charles Grandfield, he visited Idle, was shown over the car, and reported 'I had always looked upon the Jupiter as a bit of a giggle – until I drove one.' He had a high regard for his MG TC and could happily throw it about, but felt he did not do the Jupiter full justice because 'the built in oversteer of the TD was hard to forget. The Jupiter was so much better than a TD I could have done better with more experience . . . every swerve I went throught I thought "Christ I could do better than that." '

If in its day the Jupiter could arouse such enthusiasm it is worth enquiring why this should have been so. But apart from its Javelin inheritance it had no pedigree visible to the naked eye. Jowett's Experimental Department, enlarged in 1948 by Charles Grandfield, had done a lot of good work with the Javelin suspension system, its response, front-to-rear interaction, and the like. Woodhead-Monroe, the shock-absorber people, had been very helpful and the Javelin handled well, having a good coordinated system.

For the Jupiter, Jowetts seem to have divined a market gap for a comfortable, reasonably quick touring car and mounted thick (16 g) aluminium panelling on a sturdy steel bodyframe. This was then fitted to a chassis designed up to a particular, calculated, value of torsional stiff-

16 Bert Hadley at the start of the Prescott Hill Climb, 1952

ness, and other factors, rather than down to a minimum weight. But if there was such a market gap, time quickly ran out, for initially the supply of panels, made on aircraft presses, depended upon pauses in demand from the industry. So it was not until the early part of 1952 that the delivery of Jupiters was reduced to months rather than years.

The Jupiter experiment may be regarded as having been promising, not wholly successful, but one that has not yet been concluded. The car remains something of an enigma: touring car or sports car? A sports car it was not, although its engine was quite highly tuned for the period, and any less power would have been unacceptable. It does, of course, require competent handling in spite of what has been said, but it was more congenial than inveterate oversteerers such as the contemporary Porsche or, notwithstanding its massive chassis, the TD MG, or the HRG whose good handling was at the expense of its bodywork – efforts to provide the HRG chassis with a modern enveloping shape resulted in even shorter coachwork life.

The experiment began in 1949 with the unique chassis design of von Eberhorst. By all accounts a charming and cultured man, an academic, reared in the money-no-object racing workshops of Hitler's Germany, engineering for economic production in post-war Britain must have been a new experience for him. He took the suspension units and power train from the Jowett Javelin and to them added a chassis

17 *Eberhorst* (left)
at Silverstone in 1952:
Guy Griffiths

frame of which the front structure (crucial to the car's special properties) was only made possible by the adoption of the horizontal opposed-four-cylinder engine from the Javelin, short in length the low in weight and centre of gravity.

Gerry Palmer, the Javelin's designer, had not been against a relatively large amount of body roll and, to maintain that car's good handling qualities, had had to provide it with an extra front suspension adjustment – track-rod-ball height – that when correctly set eliminated steering geometry changes as the suspension deflected under cornering. The Jupiter rolls rather less than the Javelin but the adjustment was retained. Also inherited from the Palmer design was the all-round, torsion-rod springing, a form that minimises unsprung weight, and a well-located rear axle for which von Eberhorst again produced a suitably rigid structure. But his special contribution was the chassis front structure, which, with its trailing diagonal struts, provided a far more rigid anchorage for the front suspension than can ever be normally possible as the usual vertical in-line engine would have intruded here.

The chassis turned out to be less torsion-ally stiff than might have been expected, taking into account its more than adequate weight, but the front structure did ensure that the twisting would not upset steering geometry. It was this lack of torsional stiffness that led Korner to mount the coachwork in the way he did, a method not entirely successful, in that sticking doors and scuttle shake were encountered with early cars. A rarity for production cars in those days, the rack-and pinion steering unit was a good example of the type and well-secured to the front structure which thus served a double function.

The construction of the chassis frame was from straight lengths of largely two sizes of tube and this was pivotal to the future of the car for, although it meant that it could be built relatively simply by Jowetts, it could never be cheap. It could never be anything like as cheap as the £20 or so of a pressed-steel frame; so it would never be built in high volume and it would never be built by Briggs.

The car was found to be lacking the twin vices of chassis steering, where under cornering a chassis may twist to alter the steering geometry to oversteer, and suspension steering where suspension deflection

20

can produce a similar destabilising effect under cornering. Certain MG models for one example suffered from the first, and the second was commonly countered in sports cars by having a suspension with hardly any travel – for this reason the HRG was sometimes known as the 'Springless Wonder'. The Jupiter's excellent road manners were not at the expense of riding comfort and it was therefore possible to conceive a car with a certain amount of luxury.

There are compromises in the design of all cars and the Jupiter was no exception. The position of the engine, close to but forward of the front-axle line has two disadvantages. Its mass does not contribute to the weight over the driven wheels, indeed actually subtracts from it, and in this position its inertia contributes less to opposing or slowing the onset of a spin, should the tail break away. The Achilles' heel was however the engine, inherited from the Javelin. This power unit is integral to the design and experimenters have generally found to their chagrin that alternative engines destroy the car's handling qualities. The chassis, rigid but heavy, carried relatively heavy coachwork and an engine that reasonably reliably produced 50 bhp for the Javelin was unreliable above 60 bhp, faults which Jowetts were fatally slow to eliminate. Leao Padman and others have shown that reliable power up to 90 bhp is possible and the limit is probably not yet known – reliability is a relative term and more than the usual measure of skill and care will always be a necessary ingredient in the assembly of a successful Jupiter engine: perversely this original unreliability and the demands on skill may have firstly contributed positively to the excellent survival rate of the Jupiter and secondly form part of its appeal today. Jowetts, however, in solving the crankshaft and liner-sinkage problems rather late could not contemplate much increased power for their R1 design and therefore developed its handling character to its maximum, further stiffening the chassis by a subtle alteration to the central cruciform bracing and by the perforated pressed-steel stiffening arch or stress panel that formed the bulkhead. This may have been the first instance of consequence of the use on a racing car of a technique that was common aircraft practice at the time. Five years later Len Terry, no doubt independently, adopted it and it became his trademark on Formula 1 designs (Lotus 16 etc) up to the introduction of the monocoque.

The stillborn CD range of vehicles

would have incorporated a fabricated chassis front end, based very closely on the Jupiter front structure and probably as rigid; the R4 design continued the experiment but efforts were made to reduce the size of the engine bay by a back-sloping radiator, and the use of the electric cooling fan (thrown in for good measure on the CD but essential to the R4 layout). The R4 front structure was weaker as a result of these changes, a weakness that might lead to oversteer under heavy cornering loads; regrettably there was no room in such a small car for the stiff but space-hungry

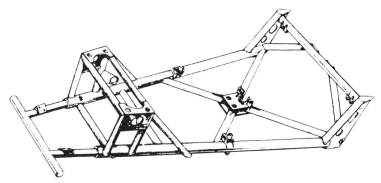

18 The basic Eberhorst frame, showing the front structure on the left

19 Detail of perforated stress panel

rear-torsion-bar structure and one may speculate that the semi-elliptic-sprung rear axle, together with the very short crab-tracked wheelbase, could explain the apparent accident-proneness of this otherwise promising design – Jowetts fastest model.

The skin and beneath

The general style of Korner's Jupiter can be traced to a series of dropheads by Pininfarina on Alfa Romeo chassis and a few others such as a Lancia Aprilia drophead coupé around the years 1939 to 1941. Here were to be found the flowing front wing line, taken high and deep across the door to intersect the leading edge of the rear wing; in spite of the difficulty of hanging such doors, these elegant designs were repeated for a time in the later 1940s, again on Alfa Romeo and Lancia chassis, strongly influencing the XK120 of 1948. London-born Reg Korner's brief was to

design a body with similarities to the Jaguar: the result was generally, although not universally, liked but those who did, as today, were often most enthusiastic. That it *was* liked is borne out amply by the amount of space photographic editors allotted it – so helpfully for historians – in magazines of the period, often in considerably greater measure than can have otherwise been warranted: a good example is *Motor Trend*'s review of the 1950 British New York Show. Out of over 100 models, 14 photographs were shown of which three were of the Jupiter; only one other car was pictured even twice. Stylistically therefore the Jupiter seems to have been well received. So what else is there to the car?

Chassis

The frame is entirely formed from straight lengths of chrome molybdenum steel tubing, 3 inch diameter 16 swg for the main sidemembers and 2 inch 18 swg for the

20 The first Jupiter with Jowett's chairman and the design team. Left to right: Harry Woodhead, Charles Grandfield, Horace Grimley, Reg Korner. Mr Woodhead retired in 1951: C.H.Wood

struts and torsional stiffness members, electric welded with $2\frac{1}{2}\%Cr/\frac{1}{2}$-1%Mo electrodes. At chassis 940 modifications at the rear were required to accommodate the revised boot/petrol tank arrangements and at the front for the modified rack housing fixing.

Front suspension

By unequal length arm, transverse link, with longitudinal silicon manganese steel torsion rods. Total wheel movement is $4\frac{1}{2}$ inch (metal bushed), 7 inch (rubber bushed): up to the introduction of the Mk1a there was a pressed-steel upper link assembly which employed bronze bushes at both ends and at the outer end of the lower link. The inner end of the lower link (the spring arm) has rubber bushes bonded to inner and outer sleeves and pressed on to the link trunions and into brackets bolted to the chassis. The Mk1a, and the 1953 Mk1 from about 865 on, have a forged upper link assembly pivoted on sets of conical 'Metalastic' rubber bushes at both ends, as has the outer end of the lower link. Shock absorbers are Woodhead Monroe telescopic units, not interchangeable between the two types of front suspension.

Steering

The Javelin front hub units are reversed, left to right, bringing the steering arms out at the rear of the hub, enabling the ERA-designed helical rack-and-pinion steering unit to be solidly attached to the unyielding chassis front structure above the gearbox. A revised rack housing and fixing was evolved for the R1s in 1952 and this appeared on the Mk1a, although not on the 1953 Mk1s as it would have required a minor chassis alteration. The following adjustments are provided: camber angle may be set by shimming behind the upper link bracket; tracking by adjustment of steering rod length and, by varying the height of the steering ball above the steering arm, changes in tracking as suspension defects can be eliminated. Front ride height is controllable by torsion-rod-tension adjusters. There is no adjustment for castor angle.

Brakes

For 1950 the Girling hydromechanical system was adopted with hydraulically operated twin leading shoes at the front and mechanical leading-trailing shoes at the rear, the total friction area being $88\frac{1}{4}$ sq inch for the car. From about chassis 51 the braking became hydraulic front and rear

and the friction area was increased to 122.8 sq inch.

Rear axle

Conventional live, Salisbury 2HA (hydromechanical) or 3HA (full hydraulic) ratio 4.56:1, located by a rubber bushed transverse stay – the Panhard rod – and parallel trailing arms of equal length. Torsion rods are as for the front but transverse running the full width of the chassis, damped by Woodhead Monroe telescopic shock absorbers. The total wheel movement is $7\frac{1}{4}$ inch. Tyres are 5.50 x 16 on ventilated disc wheels giving 16.9 mph/1,000 rpm in top gear.

21 A LHD Mk1a Jupiter, April 1953: C.H.Wood

Mk. I Body Frame Assembly

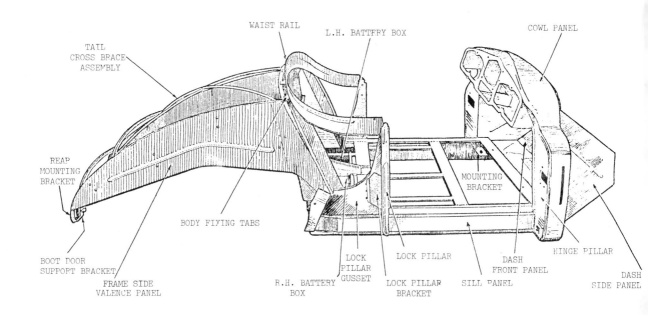

TAIL CROSS BRACE ASSEMBLY

WAIST RAIL

L.H. BATTERY BOX

COWL PANEL

REAR MOUNTING BRACKET

BODY FIXING TABS

MOUNTING BRACKET

BOOT DOOR SUPPORT BRACKET

FRAME SIDE VALENCE PANEL

R.H. BATTERY BOX

LOCK PILLAR GUSSET

LOCK PILLAR

LOCK PILLAR BRACKET

DASH FRONT PANEL

SILL PANEL

HINGE PILLAR

DASH SIDE PANEL

22 Mk1 body-frame assembly

Coachwork

The body-work is supported by a complex sheet-steel body-frame assembly, itself mounted at three points on each side on bonded rubber 'Silentbloc' units, bolted to chassis frame brackets. The body frame is best understood by reference to Figure 22: it comprises a dash panel – firewall or bulkhead – to the front, a cowl panel subassembly which is the only visible part of the bodyframe, supporting as it does the bonnet and door hinge systems, the windscreen, and through which the trafficator arms project when energised (not LHD USA models). From this the door sills run aft to the door lock pillars, floor support channels, tail frame, side valances, tail cross-brace assembly and so forth. This whole assembly, largely hidden except for the cowl panel, is the chief area for corrosion as the chassis frame material shows good resistance to such attack.

The main modification was to the Mk1a, and the 1953 Mk1 after about 861, when a tubular cross-brace structure was integrally fitted, running from the rear face of the front structure to the dash panel, and thence to behind the door top hinges; a

recommendation from the factory to combat steering kick with front-end vibration suggested replacement of the four silentbloc front and centre bodymount bushes by hardwood blocks, thus with other extra parts providing a more rigid attachment of the bodyframe to the chassis frame, while flat strips of steel were to cross-brace the firewall to the top of the front structure. The floor itself is plywood but the door frames include some steel.

The body is made from eleven panels formed from 16 swg aluminium. Four one-piece wings are brass-bolted to the main panels and separated by anti-squeak piping, visible externally; to the front, a bonnet centre section hinged at the bodyframe and incorporating an inner tubular steel stiffening framework and support mount has openings for the three grilles and two headlamps. Both bonnet hinges and their mounting boxes are fully adjustable. Doors are of aluminium skin and feature winding windows with fixed quarterlights.

The tail section is one large aluminium panel, running from the cockpit down to the sills immediately behind the doors and to the tail extremity itself, supported at its

front edges by being turned over and riveted to steel inner panels. The main length of the tail panel rests over the tail cross-brace assembly, with a foam rubber overlay affording only anti-drumming support. On the Mk1 model there is at the rear a small aluminium spare-wheel access door which carries the number plate, the spare wheel being supported in a cradle beneath the fuel tank. The steel-framed removeable windscreen has a V of two separate pieces of glass, usually laminated, set in a three-piece chromed brass surround (Mk1 only). The duck hood, which *Motor Sport* quoted as their standard of excellence* for a number of years, features a permanent frame, consisting of two main hinged and double-jointed oak side pieces which meet the window edges and top, and three steel-tube hoops running from there across the

*As late as September 1966 Bill Boddy terminated a lengthy correspondence in *Motor Sport* on the pros and cons of open/closed cars and the hoods of cars such as Morgans and Sprites with the words 'What is wanted is a really quick to erect hood giving coupé comfort when it's up. Which was best in this respect? Perhaps the late lamented Jowett Jupiter.'

width. As original the hood would be fitted with a small rear glass window in a metal frame. However this is often replaced with flexible clear plastic quarterlights and larger rear light. The hood front lip is of metal and timber, and latches down on to the top of the screen. To prevent undue strain on the duck, there are two zip-fasteners running horizontally from the rear door edge position (Mk1 only). To fold, the fasteners around the waist rail and the catches at the screen top are released, and the hood may be then lowered in one operation and stowed behind the seat: when erected it is normally water and wind proof.

Within the car there is a leather-covered bench seat, shaped over Dunlopillo foam, capable of accommodating two in comfort and occasionally three. The seat back tilts forward for access to the aluminium box boot void beneath the tail – in its time a pair of fitted suitcases were available for this – and seat adjustment in a fore-and-aft plane is provided.

During the model life bonnet louvres were not provided until chassis 162, when they took the form of two panels of four

23 Another view of Jupiter 1: hood raised, the profile of the Mk1 is as singular as that of the Mk1a variant: C.H.Wood

24 Top LHD production for the USA, March 1952; Jupiters were built on a simple line by lifting chassis from boxes until wheels were fitted: C.H.Wood

25 Body on chassis. Earlier each body-panel set, hand-fitted to the body frame, had been sprayed as a unit: C.H. Wood

large louvres, the panels let in to bonnet cut-outs. Later they became panels of seven smaller louvres, and around the beginning of 1952 the louvres were formed in. The Mk1a version had a different tail panel with a larger tonneau, and external access to the boot volume and spare wheel through a boot door cut in the tail panel. The walnut-veneered instrument panel of the Mk1 gave way to a symmetrical metal fascia and to match this the door tops, hitherto woodcapped, were given aluminium tops.

The hood top catches had been ring-pull telescopic type, left and right, with an overcentre toggle at the centre; the toggle remained but screw clasps and claw brackets now replaced the telescopics. These hood clips and metal doortop trims were also fitted to the 1953 Mk1 cars after about chassis 853. The Mk1a also benefited from a simpler system of bonnet fixing, and a modified and less upright rear hood line.

Engine

The die-cast, aluminium-alloy engine and cylinder block is split vertically down its centre-line and held together by six large bolts on either side of the main bearings and five smaller bolts along the top flange. The four semi-wet liners are an easy push-fit into the crankcase and have a bore of 72.5 mm which, with the 90 mm stroke, gives 1,486 cc. The overhead valves are push-rod-operated from a central cast-iron camshaft. The cylinder heads are cast iron, gas-flowed, exhausting into a system somewhat more efficient than the Javelin's, the heads also carrying the twin-carburettor system, initially 30VIG, but, following competition experience, from about chassis 657 the 30VM type was introduced in abandonment of the troublesome accelerator pump. It is believed that Jupiters leaving the works after about September 1952 would have been fitted with the series III engine, an improvement in numerous small ways on previous units. Sundry other changes include mounting the SU fuel pump low down amidships, following vapour-lock experience in hot climates from chassis 481; the single air cleaner of the Vokes type mounted, behind the radiator, being replaced at 590 with individual air cleaners mounted above the carburettors and receiving the benefit of cold air thereby; the sometimes leak-prone chassis-mounted oil cooler, another legacy from ERA, became a conventional type, mounted off the engine at around the same time.

Gearbox

Synchromesh on 2nd, 3rd, and top. A well-engineered steering column gearshift was provided on all Jupiters (except the R4s).

Colours

The Jupiters were invariably upholstered in hide, usually beige, although red began to come in, very sparingly at first, towards the end of 1951 when cars finished in copper commonly had red leather trim. Ivory as a body colour was required from time to time in 1951 but increasingly when Angell Motors started ordering them around April 1952. It was always accompanied by red hide. Jupiters could be had in any colour, including primer, although the most popular colours seem to have been red, copper, blue, turquoise blue, ivory, and various greens including bottle, Connaught, and British racing. The 1953 brochure listed these standard colours: metallichrome turquoise with red or beige leather and beige hood; metallichrome Connaught green with beige leather and beige hood; ivory with red leather and black hood; scarlet with beige leather and beige hood.

Dimensions

Wheelbase: 93 inches
Track, front: 52 inches
Track, rear: 50½ inches
Ground clearance: 8 inches
Overall length: 168 inches
Width: 62 inches
Height: 56 inches
Turning circle: 31 feet
Kerb weight: usually given as 1,895 lb (17 cwt) but 2,100 lb would be closer to the weight of a typical production Jupiter.

Summary of road tests

Performance

MAGAZINE	CAR	WEIGHT (lb)	BEST GEAR ACCELERATION (mph, secs) 10-30	20-40	30-50	STANDING START ACCELERATION (mph, secs) 0-30	0-50	0-60	0-70	STANDING QUARTER MILE	TOP SPEED (mph)	FUEL CONSUMPTION (miles/gal)
Motor Nov 1950	GKY106 (Mk1)	2,462 (as tested)		5.8	7.8	5.1	11.7	18.0	29.6	20.5	86.1	25.1
Autocar Dec 1950	GKY107 (Mk1)	2,107 (Curb)	5.5	5.1	7.6	5.7	13.1	20.4	30.3		90	27-30
Motor Sport Dec 1950	GKY106 Mk1					5.0	11.9	17.0	29.0		88	25-28
Mechanix Illustrated Sept 1951	early Mk1					5.4	11.9	15.3	21.3		89	
Country Life Dec 1951	Mk1		6.8	5.8				18.5			87.8	26.2
Autosport Jun 1952	HKU56 (Mk1)	2,075 (Curb)					10.5	14.2	21.0	21.0	88	23
Autocar Jun 1953	HKW197 (Mk1a)	2,535 (as tested)	4.9	7.4	7.6	4.9	11.7	16.8	24.5	20.7	85	21-26
Road and Track March 1953	Mk1	2,382 (as tested)				4.1	10.4	15.1	22.9	20.44	86.2	31
Autocourse Spring 1953	Mk1a	2,072						18.5			88.3	25.8
Measham 1954	HKW197 (Mk1a)			8.0	8.0	4.8	11.0	15.5	21.0		92.5	21-23 driven hard
McAuley 1976	NXH709 Mk1a	2,027 (as tested)	4.2 3rd	4.4 3rd	6.0 top	4.5	8.2	11.0	14.4	18.4	95.5	28-32

Comparisons with other cars

Comparisons cannot be made with precision as prices and specifications fluctuated yearly or more frequently, so this inexhaustive list should not be seen as a retrospective buyers' guide. These comparative data from various sources may, however, help the reader to place the Jupiter in the scheme of things.

YEAR	CAR	ENGINE CAPACITY (litres)	MAX POWER (bhp)	DRY WEIGHT (cwt)	ESTIMATED TOP SPEED (mph)	OVERALL LENGTH (ft)	TURNING CIRCLE (ft)	UK PRE-TAX PRICE £
1951	AC Sports Tourer	2.0	76	25	85	$15\frac{1}{2}$	39	1,098
	Austin A40 Sports	1.2	50	19	80	$13\frac{1}{2}$	37	565
	HRG Type 1500	1.5	60	$14\frac{1}{2}$	84	12	32	895
	Jupiter	1.5	60	19	90	$13\frac{1}{2}$	31	895
	MG TD	1.25	54	$18\frac{1}{2}$	83	12	$31\frac{1}{4}$	470
	Morgan Plus 4	2.1	68	$15\frac{1}{2}$	85	$11\frac{2}{3}$	33	535 or 590
	Porsche 356	1.3	44	$14\frac{1}{2}$	90	13	29	
	Singer Roadster	1.5	58	$16\frac{1}{4}$	73	$12\frac{2}{3}$	33	
1952	Allard Palm Beach	1.5	47	$16\frac{1}{2}$	85	13	28	800
	Allard Palm Beach	2.25	68	17	90+	13	28	865
	Austin A40 Sports	1.2	50	19	80	$13\frac{1}{3}$	37	586
	HRG Type 1500	1.5	62	$14\frac{1}{2}$	84	12	32	895
	Jupiter Mk 1	1.5	62.5	19	90	$13\frac{1}{2}$	31	825
	Jupiter Mk 1a	1.5	62.5	19	90	$13\frac{1}{2}$	31	895
	MG TD	1.25	54	$18\frac{1}{2}$	83	12	$31\frac{1}{4}$	530
	Morgan Plus 4	2.1	68	$15\frac{1}{2}$	85	$11\frac{2}{3}$	33	565–620
	Simca Sport	1.22	50	$18\frac{1}{2}$	85	$13\frac{2}{3}$	31	
1953	AC Ace	2.0	85		100+			915
	HRG Type 1500	1.5	62	$14\frac{1}{2}$	84	12	32	895
	Jupiter Mk1a	1.5	62.5	19	90	$13\frac{1}{2}$	31	725
	Jupiter R4	1.5	64	14	110	$11\frac{1}{2}$	31	545
	Porsche 356	1.5	55	$14\frac{1}{2}$	95	13	29	FHC 1,260
	Porsche Super	1.5	70	$14\frac{1}{2}$	100+	13	29	–
	Singer Roadster	1.5	58	$16\frac{1}{4}$	73	$12\frac{2}{3}$	33	519
	Triumph TR2	2.0	90	$17\frac{3}{4}$	100	$11\frac{3}{4}$	32	625
1978	Triumph Spitfire (USA version)	1.5	57	$15\frac{1}{2}$	94	$12\frac{1}{2}$	24	

Factory and good private speed and rally summary

Le Mans 24–25 June 1950	GKW111	Wise/Wisdom	Class 1st
Production sports cars up to 2-litre, Silverstone, 26 August 1950	GKW111	Grimley	Class 5th
RAC TT Dundrod, 16 September 1950	GKW111	Wisdom	Retired when leading
Monte Carlo Rally, 23–31 January 1951	GKY106	Wise/Grimley	Class 13th
	GKY107	Wilkins/Baxter	Class 2nd
	GKY256	Ellison/Robinson	Class 1st
Tulip Rally, 23–28 April 1951	GKY256	Robinson/Leck	Class 7th
Lisbon Rally, 2–7 May 1951	E1SA74R	Nogueira	Overall 1st

Event	Car	Driver	Result
BRDC 1-hour production sports car race, Silverstone, 5 May 1951	GKW111	Hadley	Retired when leading
Morecambe National Rally, 25–26 May 1951	GKW111	Wise	Best closed car
	HAK117	Imhoff	
RAC Rally, 4–9 June 1951	GKY256	Becquart/Lunn	Class 5th
	HAK117	Imhoff/Wick	Class 4th
	LHR 2	Booth/Bowes	Class 12th
Swiss production sports car race, Bremgarten, May 1951		Gurzeler	Class 1st
Rheineck/Walzenhauzer Hill climb		Gurzeler	Class 1st
Le Mans, 23–24 June 1951	HAK364	Wise/Wisdom	Retired
	HAK365	Becquart/Wilkins	Class 1st
	HAK366	Hadley/Goodacre	Retired
Alpine Rally, 13–21 July 1951	GKW111	Wise/Wilson	Retired
	GKY256	Robinson/James	Retired
Rallye de l'Iseran, 18–19 August 1951		Armangaud	Overall 1st
RAC TT Dundrod, 15 September 1951	GKW111	Wise	Class 2nd
	HAK365	Wisdom	Still running at end
	HAK366	Hadley	Class 1st
Queen Catherine Monteur Cup, Watkins Glen, 15 September 1951	HAK364	Weaver	1st
Monte Carlo Rally, 22-29 January 1952	E1SA59R	Becquart/Ziegler	Class 2nd
	MTJ300	Ellison/Mason	Retired
RAC Rally, 31 March–5 April 1952	GKW111	Wise	Retired
	GKY107	Hadley/Butler	61st
	LHR 2	Booth/Bowes	15th
	NNK560	Still/Still	36th
BRDC production sports car race, Silverstone, 10 May 1952	HAK366	Phillips	Class 3rd
British Empire Trophy, Isle of Man, 29 May 1952	GKY256	Robinson	Class 3rd
	E1SA120R	Kelly	Class 6th
Volta a Portugal (National)	E1SA74R	Nogueira	Overall 1st
Prix de Monte Carlo, 2-litre sports car race, 2 June 1952	HAK364	Becquart	Class 4th
Le Mans, 14–15 June 1951	HAK364	Gatsonides/ Nijevelt	Retired
	HKW48	Hadley/Wise	Retired
	HKW49	Becquart/Wilkins	Class 1st
Alpine Rally, 11–16 June 1952	GKW111	Wise	Retired
	HAK365	Gott/Gillespie	Retired
Monte Carlo Rally, 20–27 January 1953	E1SA59R	Becquart/Ziegler	Class 15th
	LOL 1	Grounds/Hay	Class 4th
RAC TT, Dundrod, 9-hour race, 5 September 1953	GKY256	Lund/Robinson	Retired
MCC/Daily Express Rally, 11–14 November 1953	NLX909	A.D.C. Gordon	Class 3rd

Jowett records

Le Mans	1950	GKW111	1,819.725 miles in 24 hr	Wisdom/Wise
Le Mans	1951	HAK364	6 mins 2.0 secs 83.373 mph	Wisdom
		HAK365	6 mins 13.7 secs 80.60 mph	Hadley
		HAK366	6 mins 19.0 secs 79.633 mph	Becquart

26 Memories of Churchill fresh in 1950: Wise (left) *and Wisdom toast their first Le Mans victory while Roy Lunn (far right)* waits his turn: Louis Klemantaski

Le Mans	1952	HAK364	5 mins 51.4 secs 85.86 mph		Gatsonides
		HKY 48	6 mins 5.7 secs 82.50 mph		Hadley
		HKY 48	957.3 miles in 12 hr		Hadley/Wise
		HKY 48	1,000 miles in 12 hr 33 mins 1.8 secs		Hadley/Wise
Monaco	1951	GKY256	2 mins 31 secs 47.2 mph		Robinson/Ellison
	1952	HAK364	2 mins 12.1 secs 54.0 mph		Becquart
Rest and be	1951	GKY256	82.1 secs		Becquart
Thankful	1951	JGA123	81.89 secs		K.B. Miller
	1952	GKY107	81.6 secs		Hadley
Dundrod	1950	GKW111	6 mins 28.0 secs		Wisdom
	1951	GKW111	6 mins 17.0 secs		Wise
	1951	HAK366	6 mins 21.0 secs		Hadley
Willarton	1951	EOSA37	4 mins 19 secs 53.92 mph		Robinson
(Isle of Man)	1952	GKY256	3 mins 55 secs		Robinson
	1952	E1SA120	3 mins 55 secs		Kelly
Winfield	1951	GKW111	1 min 46 secs		Wise
Silverstone	1952	HAK366	2 mins 29 secs *Full circuit*		Phillips
	1957	JKW537	1 min 24 secs *Club circuit*		A. Thomas (R4)
	1976	FVG332	1 min 26 secs		P. Dixon
Prescott	1952	HAK366	53.77 secs		Hadley
	1952	E2SA748	59.5 secs		Seivwright
Bo'ness	1952	GKW111	46.9 secs		Brearley
Goodwood	1952	E2SA718	2 mins 16.8 secs	av. of 5 laps st. start	Lewis

Standing km	1952	–	37.3 secs	Hackney
Standing	1950	GKY106	20.5 secs	*Motor*
$\frac{1}{4}$ mile	1953	–	20.1 secs	Hackney
	1965	E1SA182	19.43 secs	Morrison
	1967	E1SA72	19.5	Wolf
	1976	E3SC947	18.4	McAuley

2 Le Mans and the R1 Jupiters: The Leap to Fame

The modest sum of £12,000 reputed to have been paid to Leslie Johnson for the design, development, and construction of the half-dozen ERA-Jupiter chassis, brought Jowetts the basis for a far better sports car than they could have produced themselves. It appealed to some quite respectable international drivers, amongst whom were George Weaver, the American Le Mans veteran, Tom Wisdom, Marcel Becquart, and Bert Hadley, the latter passing up Jaguar drives (including the 1951 Le Mans where Bill Lyons wanted to pair him with the emergent Stirling Moss) for the $1\frac{1}{2}$-litre outsider.

Money was never plentiful at Jowetts, thanks to the failure of the Javelin – for all the many and varied reasons – to break even except in 1951 and it is enduringly to Charles Grandfield's credit that he was able to get the competition programme going and to sustain it at the level he did. Indeed, without his organisational skills, the best results could not have been possible. He personally would translate the complex Le Mans regulations, and ensure that everyone concerned had a copy of sections relevant to him; in the RAC rallies mechanics and caches of spares and tyres would be concealed in suitable woodland

along the routes in a form of rule-avoidance that was indulged in by all the teams with a real chance of collecting the top honours. Generally it was tyres that were required as Javelins and Jupiters driven hard had quite an appetite for road rubber. If the Javelin lost money, and the good old Bradford van made it, the financial contribution of the Jupiter could only be negligible, for what could fewer than 900 cars do among 63,000 except announce the existence of the marque and this they did.

The Jupiter leaped to prominence with its record-breaking 1950 Le Mans class win and, seven months later, thanks to some rather quick laps of the Monaco Grand Prix circuit, took first and second in class in the Monte Carlo Rally. Bearing in mind the Javelin's first-time-out rally and race victories in the Monte and at Spa in 1949, Jowetts may be forgiven for feeling that to enter was to win.

In 1951, the design of the ambitious CD range of vehicles – van, utility, pick-up, and car on a common chassis – was begun, but did not interfere with the second Le Mans victory, the hill-climb and sports car race firsts for Gurzeler in Switzerland, the RAC Tourist Trophy 1 and 2, or George Weaver's run-away win at Watkins Glen, where for once a Lester-MG and an HRG were condemned to inferior placings.

In British production sports car racing, Jowetts' main rivals were initially the works and quasi-works MGs; although of slightly less capacity, their engines were 'staged' to about the same power as the Jupiter's. In the USA by contrast, there was available to the sporting MG owner a wider range of tuning options that could bring 80 bhp within reach, at least for the duration of a race or two, and an increase in capacity to 1440 cc was possible by fitting Lincoln pistons. Compared with the Jupiter, the HRG offered a little more power at a little less weight.

Jowetts did not have a policy of providing support for private entrants, thus narrowing the room for error, and the

27 The Jupiter that was to win its class at Le Mans in 1950. Later in the year it was rebuilt to match the first production Jupiters, with strakes and concealed door hinges: C.H.Wood

28 *The works Jupiters were prepared for any eventuality in the 1951 Monte Carlo Rally*

rather greater expertise of the established opposition was to prove a little too much for them, whereas the need, perhaps, was the more. Likewise in the USA, where George Weaver and Bill Lloyd had provided a glimpse of what was possible, the novice drivers, who more usually raced Jupiters, tended to find their efforts at engine tuning counterproductive; later Hunter Hackney, who seemed to understand the Jupiter power unit, was able to win there also.

The Jupiter's flying start in international rallying continued when the Lisbon was won outright by Joaquim Nogueira in his own car, sponsored by the Portugese importer. Tommy Wise then received an important award in the Morecambe National Rally, just before the RAC International, where Jupiters were placed fourth and fifth in a large class. A stroke of miserable luck on the final day of the Tulip Rally had prevented a higher place than 7th and in the Alpine, the only other international attempted in 1951, neither Jupiter finished this most arduous of trials, although the Frenchman, Armangaud, victor of the National Rallye de l'Iseran, took the Monza class award whilst Wise took those for the Falzarego and Stelvio ascents.

The Jupiter's last good international rally result was Becquart's hard-fought class second, overall fifth, in the 1952 Monte at the start of a year when the Jupiter was probably still a better rally car than for example the Porsche, although the profusion of that make was beginning to tell. Nogueira was to win outright the Volta a Portugal event and Becquart's Javelin performance in the RAC Rally of that year demonstrated what he or Hadley might have done with properly prepared Jupiters. Not perhaps the best car for swinging into or out of boxes, but first rate for rallies in bad conditions.

Regrettably, a certain uneveness of Jowetts' usually high standard of factory preparation meant that Hadley, for example, had to retire from the lead of the 1951 Silverstone 1-Hour race after 38 minutes whilst driving the car that had run 24 hours the previous year; his 1952 RAC Rally car, moreover, he could only describe as "just a member of the staff, and in a bit of a mess". Wise's Jupiter retired through engine failure in the same event, which coincided with the round-the-clock development driving programme on the prototype CDs, for much was at stake here and Experimental resources were stretched.

Although 1952 had started well, with Jupiter production peaking at 80 in February and exceeding 70 in April, the previous year's optimism was beginning to look premature. It was one thing to race to improve the breed, but the delays in implementing some of these lessons tempted fate. Hardly noticed at first outside the accountant's office, the company was slipping into troubled water, and there was no largesse to be dispensed to any but a select few, and increasingly these were Javelin drives, as it was by the Javelin that Jowetts would stand and ultimately fall. The emphasis in sports car racing, was in any case, moving away from true production cars to specials disguised as production cars, and in Britain Lester-MGs and Cooper-MGs, not at all comparable, now existed in sufficient numbers to assure for themselves first and second places in the important production sports car events. It was particularly galling to those racing MGs to have to compete against cars which were permitted to use, in nominally the same engine, a higher capacity and a considerably higher state of tune: MGs even had difficulty in having the use of aeroscreens permitted!

The R1 was stymied by the crankshaft problem, for there was no point in tuning for the extra 10 to 15 bhp that would have brought parity with the Lesters and Coopers, or the 15 to 20 bhp for the faster continentals, while crankshafts were snapping like carrots in the test bed. Therefore 1951's four major class wins in four countries from five races was not the sort of success that could be expected the following year, and indeed the four main efforts produced two thirds, a fourth, and the Le Mans hat-trick victory. Jowetts reacted by designing a new car, the R4 Jupiter, again a production car; however the technology behind its plastic body, necessary if Jowetts were to build it themselves in quantity, may have been a little too experimental for Jowetts in 1953 - 4. For the Jupiter, and even more for Jowett Cars Ltd, striving to slough off its image of staid pre-war side-valvers, the 1950 Le Mans result was therefore a very good one indeed. Bathed in the brightest glare of publicity, in its first and best race, the Jupiter leaped to fame. Then Jowetts became addicted to the event and had to rely increasingly on superior reliability, itself an elusive quality, and luck, in order to retain their grip on the class. This, though, they did and their three in a row was a feat that had been achieved surprisingly infrequently over the decades, until more recent times.

Before considering the three races 1950-2 in detail, the $1\frac{1}{2}$-litre class winners of the 1935-49 races may be reviewed. In 1935 the third-placed car overall was a 1494 cc Aston Martin, which covered 1805.437 miles at 75.226 mph. There was no race in 1936 or in the period 1940-8.

YEAR	CAR	DISTANCE	SPEED
1937	1493 cc Aston Martin	1,720.378m	71.682 mph
1938	1495 cc Adler	1,718.111m	71.587 mph
1939	1496 cc HRG	1,619.380m	67.307 mph
1949	1496 cc HRG	1,700.181m	70.841 mph

There were normally 60 starters, and the finishers of the 24-Hour Grand Prix d' Endurance were classified in three ways. First there was the general classification, on total distance covered in the 24 hours, the winner being awarded the Long Distance Cup. Second came the index of performance, a classification (effectively on a handicap basis) according to the degree by which competitors improve upon a minimum distance calculated from the engine size, the winner receiving the Index of

Performance Cup. Third was the Biennial Cup on an index basis but confined to entrants who qualified by exceeding their minimum performance in the previous year's race. And competitors who achieved their minimum stipulated performance qualified for automatic invitation to the next years race.

The rules are many and complex and in part are designed to encourage manufacturers to improve all aspects of their products, hence the night racing that places the maximum demand on electrical components. Refuelling can take place only in the pits, using official fuel and only after a certain minimum distance has been covered. On entering the pits, the engine had to be switched off immediately and only restarted with the electric motor, the starting handle hole being sealed just before the start. A push start led to instant disqualification.

In 1949 a lightened but basically correct Javelin driven by Tommy Wisdom and Anthony Hume won the 24-Hour race at Spa, 2-litre touring class, so Jowetts were tempted to try their luck with a Jupiter at Le Mans in 1950, at a time when only three complete cars were in existance. Their good pit work owed more to wartime fire drill than competition experience and earned the applause of those in a position to observe. The car for 1950 was the development model GKW111, about 3 cwt lighter than the production car was to be, with special free-running wheel bearings, an aero screen and bucket seats. It was transported to Le Mans by a lorry which had to be reversed into a bank somewhere near Le Mans as the only means of extrication for the car.

This was the year that Louis Rosier won in a 4483 cc Talbot, after changing a rocker shaft himself and driving for 23 hours of the 24, and a team of three XK120s made up Jaguars first appearance at Le Mans, Leslie Johnson and Bert Hadley maintaining third place for 21 hours in one of them.

The $1\frac{1}{2}$-litre class-winning Jupiter had been nicknamed *Sagacious II* after its drivers Tom Wisdom and Tommy Wise. Wisdom, in addition to being a very quick driver much in demand, was the motoring editor of the *Daily Herald*, the *Sunday People* and *Sporting Life* (which accounts for that paper's excellent coverage of motor sport in those days) while his No.2 had much pre-war trials experience and five rallies behind him. It finished 16th overall out of 29 finishers with a record-breaking 220 laps - 1819.725 miles

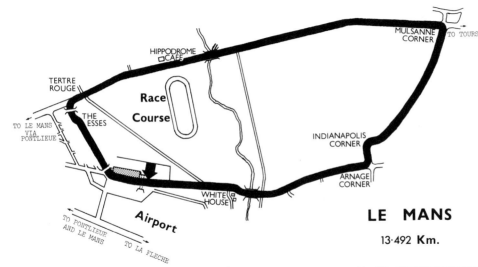

HIPPODROME CAFÉ

MULSANNE CORNER

TO TOURS

TERTRE ROUGE

THE ESSES

Race Course

TO LE MANS VIA PONTLIEUE

INDIANAPOLIS CORNER

ARNAGE CORNER

WHITE HOUSE

TO PONTLIEUE AND LE MANS

TO LA FLECHE

Airport

LE MANS

13·492 Km.

30 *Tom Wisdom at the wheel of GKW111, Le Mans 1950:* Louis Klemantaski

31 *Elation from the chef d'équipe: Charles Grandfield* (far left), *Wise, Wisdom, Lunn, Grimley:* Louis Klemantaski

covered at 75.821 mph – ahead of a 2443 cc Riley, the George Phillips/Eric Winterbottom 1224 cc MG TD (class 2nd nine laps behind), a 2443 cc Healey, a 1970 cc Frazer Nash and the clockwork mice. The Jupiter's fastest lap was said to have been 80 mph; it had led the 1½-litre field of five for most of the race – only briefly falling behind the MG when delayed at around 9 pm with a broken fuel pipe – with the 1491 cc Simca-Gordinis of Gordini/Simon and Loyer/Behra out after 14 and 50 laps, and the Fiat retiring after 75. The Jupiter made four pit stops, all routine, only the fuel line problem costing as long as eight minutes. It was placed 11th in the index of performance but, perhaps significantly, by the time Wise returned the car to Idle it was suffering from a failing head gasket.

The 1951 race was run in the wettest after-dark conditions the event had seen, with seven hours of night driving to frighten the most courageous; it was also the race where many British competitors were troubled by the lower-than-expected octane rating of the official fuel. As a consequence some considerable improvisation took place in certain camps. The event of course was to see the first outright win by a Jaguar.

The 1½-litre class contained four extremely rapid 1.4-litre, 85 bhp Simca-Gordinis, entered by Amédée Gordini; the TD Mk II MG, streamlined in prototype MGA bodywork entered by George Phillips; and against these were pitted the new R1 Jupiter HAK364, driven by the sagacious two and a brace of light-weight standard Jupiters HAK366 for Bert Hadley/Charles Goodacre (two former works Austin drivers) and HAK365 for Becquart/Wilkins. The latter car was sixth reserve and lucky

35

to get in. All three cars were specially built for the race with slightly tuned engines – the R1's more so than the other two, at 67.5 bhp at 4,750 rpm from a compression ratio of 9.25:1.

The Simcas immediately set up a murderous pace, three of them lapping at over 90 mph (as fast or faster than the Aston Martins, Frazer Nashes and even some Ferraris) and were not expected to last the distance, while the MG settled down to about $82\frac{1}{2}$ mph average, hitting 107 mph down the pit straight. The R1 accelerated to match. Retirements came quickly, the Hadley/Goodacre Jupiter being the second out of the race after 19 laps at 78.5 mph with a broken valve collar, soon to be joined by the first Simca retirement. After 3 hours the R1

32 Sketch of proposed R1 by Phil Stephenson for the Le Mans entry application

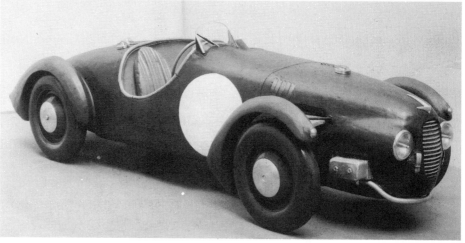

33 The design moves to the plasticene-model stage: C.H.Wood

34 The R1 as prepared for Wisdom and Wise, Le Mans 1951: C.H.Wood

35 Becquart and HAK365 at the scrutineering. Standing: *Jowett employee* (left) *and the man from Zenith Carburettors*

and the MG were still on the same lap but then the MG made two pit stops in quick succession, thereafter continuing at a much reduced 67 mph. After 5 hours the R1, which had exceeded 105 mph down the Mulsanne straight, having averaged 80.68 mph for its 45 laps, suddenly developed a thirst for water and retired with a blown gasket, and the MG, with a melted piston, was soon to follow at around nightfall.

The second Simca was already out and the third was soon to follow, leaving the Veyron/Monneret Simca well placed eight laps ahead of Becquart/Wilkins and the Veuillet/Mouche 1100 cc Porsche at nightfall. At daybreak Becquart, by now nine laps behind the Simca and three laps behind the Porsche, did not have long to wait for $1\frac{1}{2}$ hours after the headlights were switched off he passed the Simca slowly making its way back to the pits – all the highly tuned Simca engines had failed and Becquart toured to finish: thus it was that in the closing hours the very rapid and reliable DB of Bonnet/Bayol passed the Jupiter, which therefore finished 22nd out of 29 finishers, its class win secured at 1707.580 miles, 71.15 mph.

FASTEST LAPS

Simca	37	5 mins 35.8 secs	89.88 mph
	38	5 mins 20.8 secs	94.08 mph
	39	5 mins 20.3 secs	94.23 mph
	40	5 mins 27.4 secs	92.19 mph
MG	43	6 mins 00.1 secs	83.81 mph
R1 Jupiter	41	6 mins 02.0 secs	83.373 mph
Hadley	42	6 mins 13.7 secs	80.6 mph
Becquart	66	6 mins 19.0 secs	79.633 mph

Jowetts could be reasonably satisfied with the way the R1 had matched the more highly tuned MG and accordingly it was shipped to the USA when Grandfield was satisfied that the New York and Chicago based importer Max Hoffman could arrange a good enough driver for it.

In July the car appeared at the pre-race Concours d'Elégance of the second annual Pebble Beach (California) road race, and on 28 September, with Horace Grimley as mechanic in charge, it was driven in the $1\frac{1}{2}$-litre sports car race for the Queen Catherine Monteur Cup on the Watkins Glen road circuit. The 33 starters were parked diagonally: two MGs were the first to move out, followed by a 1400cc Siata, but George Weaver (HAK364) caught

36 Becquart driving the sole Jupiter survivor, 1951: Louis Klemantaski

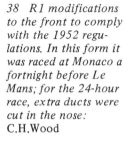

37 George Weaver airborne at a level crossing, Watkins Glen 1951

them at the first bend and pulled clear of the pack, finishing the 11-lap event 1 min 55 secs ahead of the second-placed Lester-MG; an HRG was third. Weaver's speed, 68.96 mph, was an improvement of 5 mph on the previous year's winning speed.

It was not until Christmas Eve that Grimley reappeared in the Experimental Department, just in time to help demolish a barrel of beer thoughtfully provided by Wisdom and Wise.

Following this success, Jowetts put out a leaflet on the R1 to see if there might be the possibility of overseas sales: 70 bhp at 5000 rpm was quoted from a cr of 9.25:1 and a special camshaft with higher lift and increased overlap – but no demand materialised.

For 1952 a further two R1s were built with all-enveloping frontal treatment to comply with the new regulations. Tom Bradley built up the chassis (although a welder from the production line did the actual chassis welding), together with Donald Wade, an AJS works rider in his spare time who later joined the Jaguar competition department. Bill Poulter and Bill Eglestone constructed the bodies and the early car was updated as they proceeded. As usual, close attention to detail

was required by Charles Grandfield, entailing perhaps 30 hours polishing the moving internals of the engine to stress-relieve the crank and reduce oil drag. Phil Green drove GKY107 to Wolverhampton to collect four 10-gallon airflow tail tanks, four water and four oil radiators, beautifully made in aluminium to aircraft standards by Marston Excelsior and donated by them to Jowetts – so much for remarks by the ignorant that the Jupiter barely has room for a toothbrush!

Maurice Gatsonides had co-driven van Nijevelt's Javelin in the Tulip Rally two months earlier (where they were robbed of possible victory by a stuck radiator blind causing boiling); now the practice R1, HAK364, was accepted for Le Mans as fourth reserve for the Dutch pair but first Becquart was to drive it in the Prix de Monte Carlo race for sports cars of up to 2 litres on 1 June 1952, the event to be run over 65 laps of the Monaco Grand Prix circuit, a distance of about 127 miles. Stirling Moss took pole in his Frazer Nash at 2 mins 4.7 secs with Becquart on the fourth row at 2 mins 12.1 secs, 54.0 mph. His Jupiter finished a very creditable fourth in the $1\frac{1}{2}$-litre class, 9th overall – 61 laps, 2 hr 14 mins 38.9 secs, 53.1 mph, on this exacting circuit, ahead of two Ferraris (one of them driven by Castelotti), a BMW, a DB, a Veritas and others. Of the Jupiter's performance, Becquart later remarked: "On such a twisty circuit I had no problem for road-holding, just wishing at the moment the car could have been faster!" The winner was a 1.9-litre Gordini at 57.12 mph.

The Le Mans 24-Hour Grand Prix d'Endurance on 14-15 June 1952 contained a drama undimmed by the passage of time. The Jaguars, having been too hastily fitted with untried bodywork to meet the threat posed by Mercedes' post-war return to

38 R1 modifications to the front to comply with the 1952 regulations. In this form it was raced at Monaco a fortnight before Le Mans; for the 24-hour race, extra ducts were cut in the nose: C.H.Wood

racing, quickly excluded themselves through overheating. The 2.3-litre Gordini led a Talbot for nine hours (French cars, French drivers!) but retired shortly before dawn, leaving the $4\frac{1}{2}$-litre Talbot of Pierre Levegh to uphold French honour four laps ahead of the highest-placed Mercedes. The German car was unable to close the 21-minute gap as Levegh circulated relentlessly on, fanatically determined to drive the entire 24 hours himself, even though at his last refuelling stop after 21 hours he was utterly exhausted and barely able to stand. With little more than an hour to run, and to the dismay of the partisan crowd, the Talbot's engine put out a con-rod, allowing the Mercedes (German cars, German drivers) through to their one – two racing come-back. A mere seven years after the war's end, the crowd did not take the German victory well and no recording of their national anthem was played.

In opposition to the Jowetts in the $1\frac{1}{2}$-class was a 1491 cc Gordini, a 1484 cc Porsche and a 1342 cc OSCA, all faster than the Jupiters. Veuillet and Mouche were back with a factory-entered 1086 cc Porsche and also in the 1100 cc category was a very fast and short lived (4 laps) Simca.

Thanks to last-minute withdrawals all the reserves were called up, including therefore Maurice Gatsonides, who hurriedly matt-painted his R1 (the practice car HAK364) a bright orange, distinguishing it from HKY48 – green – for Hadley/Wise and HKY49, the blue car for Becquart/Wilkins. There was no sagacious pair this year for Wisdom co-drove with Leslie Johnson the American Nash-engined Healey to overall third.

Jowetts had solved the gasket-blowing problem and had raised compression ratios but as the crankshaft weakness was not yet understood and, although the R1s were capable, it was said, of 115 mph on tow down the Mulsanne, Jowetts had to be content with lower average speeds than they knew their competitors would use. The OSCA, designed by the Maserati brothers with Vignale coachwork (said to have been built in only ten days) and developing 93 bhp for an all-up weight of only 1450 lb, regarded the Loyer/Rinen Gordini and the Lechaise/Martin Porsche as the real opposition. Extra air intakes were cut in the bonnet noses of the Yorkshire cars to allow plenty of cool air to reach the carburettor intakes. Fortuitously, as it turned out, the Becquart/Wilkins car missed the last practice session for the fitting of a new engine, following a blow-up.

39 Power unit of the R1. Even the dynamo pulley is light-weight: C.H.Wood

At 4 pm as usual Charles Faroux flagged off the 57 starters and Gatsonides initially set the Jowett pace. An exhilarating third lap was completed by him for the history books in 5mins 51.4 secs (85.86 mph) but thereafter he settled into circulating with Hadley on his tail for $3\frac{1}{2}$ hours and averaging over 81 mph.. The $1\frac{1}{2}$-litre Gordini, for the glory of France, led the class at nearly 94 mph for its 134 minutes, retiring after 25 laps, leaving the OSCA just ahead of the $1\frac{1}{2}$-litre Porsche on lap 22, Gatsonides and Hadley on lap 21 and Becquart already in the pits with but 20 laps completed and the engine of his R1 not running properly.

*40 The 1952 Le Mans,
seconds after the start.
Behind Hadley in the
leading R1 Jupiter is the
Dennis Poore/Pat
Griffith Aston Martin
DB3, followed by
Gatsonides and
Becquart:* Louis
Klenmantaski

At nightfall the OSCA was 11 seconds ahead of the Porsche on lap 57 while Hadley (lap 53) was keeping up with the 1.1 Porsche of Veuillet/Mouche; Gatsonides was two laps behind Hadley, and Becquart (the fault temporarily cured after several pit stops, having completed a 15-lap spell at $82\frac{1}{2}$ mph and his fastest lap in 6 min 1.75 secs) was on his 44th lap and about to come in for a half-hour stop for a complete clear-out of the carbs, fuel lines, and tanks. Water and sand in the official petrol supplied were confirmed and officially admitted as the cause of the trouble.

After 7 hrs 18 mins 51.1 secs, 68 laps, at 77.9 mph the orange R1 broke its crankshaft. Hadley was on his 70th lap, three laps behind the $1\frac{1}{2}$-litre Porsche, which in its turn was now over a lap behind the OSCA. Becquart had completed 59 laps. At half time, 4 am, the race between the OSCA and the Porsche intensified when the OSCA made a pit-stop after 120 laps, allowing the Porsche into the lead. Hadley, 15 laps ahead of Becquart, having completed 115 laps was taking it easy as he knew that if he drove harder the car would certainly break. When the usual early morning fog developed, drifting across the road in heavy swathes, especially from Mulsanne to Arnage and from Arnage to the pits, Hadley found he could best get round by following Becquart, an unparalleled driver in foggy conditions sometimes so thick that the Mercs had to drive with their gull-wing doors open and flapping.

Disaster again struck the Jowett team,

for after nearly 16 hours the Hadley/Wise Jupiter broke its crankshaft near Arnage. The green R1 had completed 149 laps at 78.6 mph, at which point it was six laps ahead of the 1.1 litre Porsche and a certain speeding 851 cc Dyna-Panhard, and 14 laps ahead of the remaining Jowett. Hadley's fastest lap had been 6 mins 5.7 secs.

The $1\frac{1}{2}$-litre Porsche still led the class at 158 laps but the OSCA was pressing hard and closing and nearly an hour later was to set its fastest lap – 89.7 mph – to snatch the class lead. Soon, though, the German car made two unscheduled pit-stops on consecutive laps, thereafter proceeding at a speed reduced (by 10 mph) to about 77 mph. The Porsche, like the Jowett, was now forced to play a waiting game. The wait was short for after 168 laps at 83.4 mph the OSCA broke its clutch and its driver vainly took an hour to push it unaided the two miles back to the pits. Becquart, although no threat with a deficit of 21 laps, was slowly gaining on the Porsche when, with $4\frac{1}{2}$ hours of the race remaining, Eugene Martin pit-stopped the Porsche and, failing to switch off his engine, was disqualified. He went off to find the clerk of the course, explaining that the engine was suffering from running-on, but it was a waste of time.

Meanwhile, in the Jowett pit, a check of the records of the two engines that had failed revealed that the known 48-hour life of crankshafts on test-bed simulation of racing conditions was reduced to precisely 24 of the real thing! While the pit staff

41 Hadley at the wheel of the green *R1:* Louis Klemantaski

42 The race is over for the $1\frac{1}{2}$-litre survivor: the clock by Becquart's left shoulder reads ten minutes past four: Louis Klemantaski

endured the tortures of Tantalus, Becquart once again toured to finish, the class win of 1,751.586 miles having been achieved at an average speed of 72.94 mph, unsurprisingly a lowly 15th in the index of performance, and 9th and last in the Biennial Cup. About 19 laps had been lost through no fault of the car or drivers, but Jowetts had their third consecutive class victory. The successful Jupiter was transported to the Albermarle Street showroom in London where it remained on view for two weeks, still covered in Le Mans grime, and it was then driven back to Bradford very carefully by Phil Green, who remembers stopping at the Ram Jam Inn, 8 miles to the north of Stamford for lunch. On strip-down the crankshaft was crack-detected and found to be literally cobwebbed by fatigue cracks. The oval webbed shaft was overdue.

There were no Jowetts entered for the 1953 Le Mans Grand Prix d'Endurance; the $1\frac{1}{2}$-litre class was taken that year by two Porches at over 86 mph.

Jowetts never raced the R1s again, although they survived 1953, stored in the Experimental Department. International Harvester began moving their planners into the Experimental area near the end of 1953 and when there began to be a shortage of space the R1s, hand-built in the Experimental shop at a reputed cost of £5000 each, had to go. They were stripped down to their bare frames and the main parts put on the factory scrap pile with the chassis sawn through, management probably playing safe in avoiding the possibility of responsibility if anything happened to a subsequent owner. Employees often bought parts from the scrapheap and two apprentices took a fancy to the remains of the R1s: Tony Lockey paid about £5 for a bare frame for a V8 special he had in mind (never built; chassis probably scrapped), whereas about £30 brought Eric Price enough parts to reassemble a complete car, with the exception of the engine – these were scarce. The car was given a Vauxhall engine and re-registered YKU761 in 1962. Some years later the car acquired a Javelin engine and on the discovery that the frame was from Becquart's 1952 Le Mans class-winner, it received its original registration of HKW49. It was also found that, of the special hubs, one carried traces of orange paint, one of blue, and two of British racing green.

3 The Major Rallies: 1951 to 1953

Jowetts had a longer association with the Monte Carlo Rally than with any other international event, extending from the first post-war Monte in 1949, through the Jupiter years, and on into the mid-1950s, an association that was to be rewarded by two class wins, an overall fifth, and several other high placings. It began with Raymond Mays's suggestion to Jowetts that they should have a go at the Monte; Charles Grandfield had had some useful experience of the preparation side of rallying with the pre-war works Austin teams, and so it came to pass that Jowetts first rally with the Javelin was their first success when T.C. Wise and Cuth Harrison finished overall tenth and class first to take the Riviera Cup. Gerry Palmer had gone along for the ride and had paid his way by helping the AC de Monte Carlo with their arithmetic, for initially they had placed the Javelin third.

Success eluded the team of three works Javelins entered in the 1950 event, where again the organisers had difficulties with their sums. One of the three Javelins had as drivers Captain John Minchin of the Police Driving School at Hendon, and Louis Klemantaski: Eason Gibson was with them. On the last leg the screen wipers failed and John drove the Javelin as fast as he could over the Col des Leques, in falling snow, with his head out of the window; Klemantaski drove the last flat-out blind from Nice to Monte Carlo to arrive apparently 15 seconds outside the time limit. The following year it was learned that there had been another error and the car had been officially classified as a finisher.

For 1951, Grandfield replied with a team of three Jupiters for the 21st International Monte Carlo Rally which took place from the 23–31 January 1951 and was filmed by Shell. Out of an unprecedented 362 entries accepted, 337 started, 65 of them – including four Jupiters – from Glasgow. For this year a new mountain section in France had been added for all competitors, as had been the regularity/

speed test on the Monaco Grand Prix circuit, devised to decide the finishing order if more than one car should reach Monte Carlo without penalty.

There were six starts – Glasgow, Oslo, Stockholm, Lisbon, Palermo and Monte Carlo itself – each route being about 2,000 miles in length and the cars having to average between $31\frac{1}{2}$ and 41 mph to avoid penalisation, at 10 marks per minute for cars early or late at controls.

At Monte Carlo all competitors underwent the acceleration/braking test (200 metres standing start; cross a line; reverse over it; accelerate 50 metres to flying finish). The best of these, if having lost no road marks, took part in the regularity/speed test, the last four of six laps being timed on the 1.98 mile Grand Prix circuit, which had to be lapped as fast as possible with as little variation as possible between the four laps. This formula was applied:

$$R = \frac{t + 1.2(E_1 + E_2 + E_3)}{10}$$

where t = the best time on any one of the 3rd, 4th, 5th or 6th laps, and E_1, E_2, E_3, = the difference between the time, t, and

43 Tommy Wise, every inch the motor trader, and the Javelin's designer Gerry Palmer pose at the factory with the car prepared for the first post-war Monte in 1949: C.H.Wood

44 *The Robinson/ Ellison Jupiter on the Digne–Grasse section.*

the time taken to cover each of the three other laps. An additional penalty accrues for any lack of regularity between the first two laps.

It was his knowledge of this circuit that enabled local man Louis Chiron to improve the position of his Delahaye from 44th to 6th, for example. However one error such as a missed gear change in the 250 metre A/B test could nullify over 3,000 km of faultless driving, for the time taken was counted at half a mark per second – at 30 marks to the minute easily the most burdensome test.

The rally was strictly confined to standard series-built passenger cars that had to correspond exactly to a model built by a recognised firm, described in that manufacturer's catalogue and offered for sale through normal commercial channels; at least 30 had to have been completed and be ready for delivery to the public by 1 November 1950 and the Jupiter qualified thanks to the rolling chassis ordered by accredited coachbuilders. Drophead and 'allweather' bodywork was accepted provided the bodies were closed before crossing the finishing line at Monaco and kept closed until after both the acceleration/braking and speed/regularity tests had been completed. Few deviations from the catalogued specification were permitted and there were penalties for faults and damage upon arrival: for example a mudguard wrenched off or no longer having the required dimensions owing to a crash entailed a 5-point penalty; no headlamps working 50 points; an all-weather body not closed on arrival 20 points.

No less than 15 Gordini-tuned Simcas were Jowett's main threat in the $1\frac{1}{2}$-litre category, several with top-line French racing drivers at their wheels.

A 'flu epidemic was raging in Britain when on Tuesday 23 January the Glasgow starters, among them four Jupiters, were flagged away from Blythswood Square. The three works cars were GKY106 for T.C. Wise and Jowett's chief experimental engineer Horace Grimley; GKY107 for Gordon Wilkins, the motoring journalist (*Autocar*) and the BBC's Raymond Baxter, and GKY256, driven by R.F. Ellison and W.H. Robinson, both Lancashire Jowett agents who had come to notice the previous year after some useful rally efforts in their Javelins. The ill-fated private entry JGA123 (41) of K.B. Miller and F.D. Lang soon blew a head gasket and retired before the Carlisle control, whereas the three others crossed the Channel from Dover on the SS *Dinard* and followed the circuitous route northward through Belgium, Holland, then through Paris (where the rally crews were well entertained), arriving after relatively untaxing motoring at Clermont-Ferrand in the Massif Central on the Thursday. That night the Jupiters travelled the last 430 miles, through the new section over the Auvergne Mountains up 1 in 8 gradients to the 3,400 foot Col du Pertuis, then descending to Valence in the Rhone valley, followed by a climb through the southern Alps to Gap, encountering a snow storm along the severely hilly and winding road to Digne, again with 1 in 8 gradients, then over the 3800 foot Col des Leques to Grasse, on to Nice and Monte Carlo.

Robinson and Ellison shared the driving of GKY256. There was a bag of cinders at each driving position, needed about twice, typical of their thoughtful rally technique.

Robinson tended to drive the mountain and snow sections: the crossing of the St Julien Pass on the Le Puy–Valence section had seen them blaze the trail for other competitors as the previous control had warned them to avoid the more direct route over the pass, where the snowdrifts were known to be up to 13 feet deep. A wrong turning, however, found the Jupiter headed over the pass following a track made by a farm cart but, by rushing some of the worst parts in order to keep going, the car was brought safely through. The fresh firm snow gave way to 6 inches to a foot of icy slush on the Digne–Grasse section and it was difficult even to keep moving; on one occasion they passed a competitor cutting his way out of an entanglement of fallen telegraph wires. They could hear the wires snapping as they forced 256 through but fortunately there was no damage.

By contrast the route down the treacherous lower slopes from Grasse was in tropically heavy rain: the cars refuelled in Nice with only the tortuous run through the lower Corniche between them and Monte Carlo; the Baxter/Wilkins Jupiter clocked in with a bare minute in hand, thanks to the need to send radio reports to the BBC. Tired crews, including the penalty-free Jupiter team, began to check in at the famous 'Arrivée' arch in the Boulevard Charles III to immediately commence the A/B test on the quayside. Early arrivals found the course swimming with rainwater and it was felt that the later arrivals, principally the Lisbon starters, would have the advantage, for the water gradually disappeared as the day wore on. GKY107 and 256 did well at 24.5 and 24.6 secs (although nearly 2 secs outside their practice time back home), being among only a dozen cars to have broken 25 seconds before the middle of the afternoon when the course began to dry.

Wise broke a petrol pipe (suction side of the pump) on one of the inevitable jerks in this test and his Jupiter spluttered across the line to record 28.1 secs and was therefore not among the best 50 to take part in the regularity/speed trial, – which meant

that the Jupiter team was out of the Charles Faroux Challenge Cup.

Tough though the road section undoubtedly was, of the 337 starters, 307 reached Monte Carlo, of whom 194, including six Javelins, were penalised, whereas 113, including two Javelins and our three Jupiters had escaped penalty.

Saturday was given over to an examination of the cars and on Sunday the roads were closed for the regularity speed trial over the Monaco Grand Prix circuit. Robinson had no racing experience, had not expected to match the Simcas and was surprised therefore to clock his first flying lap at 2 secs quicker than their best up to that point. Ellison counselled caution but Robinson, catching sight of the $4\frac{1}{2}$-litre Delahaye that had started half a minute before the Jupiter, stunned the French spectators – and the Simca drivers – by closing the gap and cheekily passing it on the last corner of the last lap just past the Hotel de Paris.

Lap times on the Monte Carlo Grand Prix circuit were:

45 Robinson is the passenger for the acceleration/braking test on the quay: the inward facing auxiliary lamps are a Robinson speciality

	LAP 3	LAP 4	LAP 5	LAP 6
GKY256 (Robinson)	2 mins 32 secs	2 mins 33 secs	2 mins 31 secs	2 mins 31 secs
M. Scaron (best Simca)	2 mins 36 secs	2 mins 35 secs	2 mins 35 secs	2 mins 34 secs
GKY107 (Wilkins/ Baxter)	2 mins 35 secs	2 mins 36 secs	2 mins 38 secs	2 mins 35 secs
John Marshall (Les Odell's Javelin)	2 mins 51 secs	2 mins 50 secs	2 mins 50 secs	2 mins 50 secs

46 Robinson in the
'Round the Houses'
test, Monte Carlo

The Javelin had lost no road marks and recorded 25.2 secs in the A/B test. The fastest British competitor 'around the houses', Bill Robinson, with Ellison beside him handling the stopwatches, drove GKY256 to fourth best performance behind Louis Chiron, G. Gautriche and Pierre Levegh* to clinch the class win and sixth place in the general category.

Wilkins fluffed his third timed lap to come 12th in this test, making him class 2nd at 10th overall and, with Les Odell's Javelin class 4th (overall 26th) behind a Simca Grand Sport, Jowetts took the Manufacturers Team Prize. Luck had been with GKY 256 for, as Robinson engaged first gear and accelerated away to start the first of his six laps, a clonk had been heard from the gearbox – but as all seemed well this was ignored. After the test (the rally being effectively over) the car was parked with all the others in the gas-works yard and as Robinson was a stranger to the circuit

*4,485 cc Delahaye, 2,867 cc Citroen, 4,482 cc Talbot respectively.

there were suggestions from the Simca camp that the Jupiter must have had a racing engine fitted. The referee ordered the car to a garage in Monaco for inspection but it could not be driven – the gearbox had locked up! The car had to be towed to the garage and a day and a half was spent dismantling, inspecting and measuring the engine components; as hydraulic devices had been anticipated the solid tappets caused some difficulty, resolved by assurances from Horace Grimley, and eventually it was agreed that the engine was a standard production unit which of course it was, producing a shade over 60 bhp at 4,500 rpm. Horace then removed the gearbox coverplate and chipped out a broken half tooth to free the transmission – such is sometimes the margin between victory and defeat.

The car was entirely driveable again and was to return to Bradford via the Albermarle Street showroom with no further attention.

Robinson shared 6th place in the general category with Ken Wharton, the 1950 British trials champion; Ken scored 23.8 secs in the A/B test but his meagre, for a $3\frac{1}{2}$-litre car, 15.86 points in the speed/regularity test brought him equality with the Jupiter at 27.76 points overall.

Robinson and Ellison won the following: The $1\frac{1}{2}$-litre class and with it the Riviera Cup (for $1\frac{1}{2}$-litre cars only), class win of the Coupes Cibié, the Calculateur Roadex Award and, equal with Ken Wharton/J.D. Sleeman ($3\frac{1}{2}$-litre Ford Pilot), the Stuart Trophy and the Tyresoles Challenge Cup (awarded irrespective of tyres used) for best performance of a member of the Monte Carlo Rally British Competitors Club.

R. Thévenin with R. Campuon were in a Jowett starting at Lisbon, finishing class

47

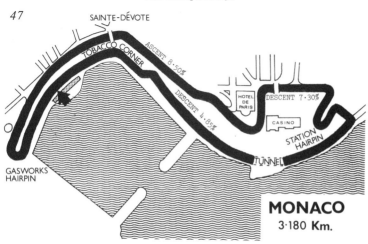

MONACO
3·180 Km.

43rd, 146th overall. This Jowett could have been a Jupiter as EO/SA/17R was booked to R. Thévenin on 4 December 1950.

If the driving part of the rally ended in the gasworks yard on Sunday, the social side was only beginning. The inspection of the prize-winning cars on Monday was followed by cocktails given by the municipality at the Jardins Exotique with a ball for the competitors in the evening. On Tuesday there took place the 'Concours de Confort' competition and for British crews a dinner at the Hôtel Metropole (the Jupiter team's hotel), while on Wednesday there was the parade of cars and the distribution of the 50 or more prizes culminating in the dinner given by the International Sporting Club (CSI).

There was one Jupiter among the 281 starters and 196 finishers of the Third International Tulip Rally 23–28 April 1951, for which there were nine starts in eight countries. GKY256 was entered for Bill Robinson and his friend Towers Leck navigated, competing in the 1.1 to 1.5-litre category II against 90 others, including 13 Javelins and four MGs. In addition to four categories based on engine size, a distinction was made between touring cars 'A' and sports cars 'B', based on weight/power ratio; category II cars had to have a ratio above 18.5 kg/bhp to be considered a touring car. On this basis the Jupiter was a 'B' car and therefore its average speed on the special stages had to be 8 per cent higher than for 'A' cars. Similarly, in the final eliminating tests, 'B' cars had their

48 A solemn moment for the 1.5-litre class winners. The manually, operated screen wiper arm can just be made out on the drivers side

49 The mood of surprised elation is well captured by this menu for the celebratory dinner held in Leeds on 21 February 1951. Lord Calverley of Bradford was among the guests. Identified signatures are 1 Jopling; 2 Gordon Wilkins; 3 H.Woodhead; 4 R.F.Ellison; 5 Lord Calverley; 6 Raymond Baxter; 7 Wilfred Sainsbury; 8 Mike Wilson; 9 L.Clegg; 10 Tommy Wisdom; 11 A.H.Grimley; 12 J.Hepworth of the firm of piston makers; 13 Roy Lunn–the drawing may be a reference to his knowledge, apparent even then, of the key to eternal youth; 14 N. Snell, company secretary; 15 Dr Thomas Smallhorn: Phil Stephenson

50 Bill Robinson and Towers Leck at the final control after an unpenalised run

was now sealed and any repair except a supervised wheel change was penalised by exclusion. Robinson managed to change the throttle cable without opening the bonnet as there was a spare taped in place but of course this was without the desired effect and the tests had to be carried out at full choke with an engine producing plenty of smoke but unable to rev: he scored 30,151 points to come 7th in his category. An MG was 6th at 29,917, the best Javelin (9th) scored 30,422 and the ubiquitous John Gott (HRG) made 33,284 to place 24th. Robinson's time was less than 5 per cent slower than his category's winner; Ian Appleyard won the rally; ten out of 113 in category I scored less than GKY256 and none in the categories III or IV.

The Fifth International Lisbon Rally was run from 2–7 May 1951 over nearly 2,000 miles from ten starting points in nine countries, attracting 69 starters, the two best-known of whom were Ken Wharton ($3\frac{1}{2}$-litre Ford Pilot), the winner in 1947 and 1949 and the runner-up in 1950 (and the best all-round British race, rally, hill-climb and trials exponent at that time) and Godfrey Imhoff (Allard), a driver who by contrast confined himself solely and frequently successfully to rallying. They both started from Frankfurt and if these two failed the rally was expected to be won by a Portuguese.

Following the road section (requiring 50 km/hr to be averaged between controls) were three complementary tests, at Figueira da Foz, Gradil, and Estoril and for these the cars were divided into five groups by engine capacity: in this way a general category could be calculated which took into account differences in engine size. These divisions were such that the lone Jupiter (BF-17-18, E1/SA/74R) of Joaquim Filipe Nogueira, starting from Lisbon, had as company mainly Simcas, Volvos and Lancia Aprilias, whereas the three 1100 cc Porsches ran in another group.

By the Estremoz control 15 competitors including Imhoff had been eliminated at the effective end of what was considered a notably difficult road section, and from here the cars made their way to Figueira da Foz, 120 miles to the north of Lisbon for the first of the penultimate day's three tests – the timed 3 km sprint through streets closed to traffic. Nogueira had to repeat his run as during the first attempt he suddenly encountered a cart that had somehow slipped on to the course. In this and the next test the winner of each group was allotted zero penalty marks and the others

times augmented by 5 per cent and open cars had to run with their hoods closed. Between the special stages, all cars had to average between 50 and 65 km/hr to avoid penalties.

The 2,000 mile routes included four special stages which were: the 115 km Circuit du Pay de Dôme around Clermont-Ferrand in the Massif Central; the 140 km Route of the Fifteen Mountains in Alsace above the west bank of the Rhine; the similar Parcours du Bonhomme of 105 km nearby; and the Route of the 1000 curves through Luxembourg and east Belgium, 140 km in length. Neither the routes of these special stages nor the speeds to be maintained were disclosed until the start of the relevant stage, when a hieroglyphic route card was handed to the car's navigators. Robinson, Ian Appleyard (Jaguar NUB120) and Goff Imhoff (Allard) formed the BARC team to compete for the club team award, and as all these three cleaned the road and stage sections they were awarded the trophy – all other teams entered collecting penalties. Sixty-two category II cars finished of which 32 were unpenalised.

Friday 27 April was given over to the eliminating tests at Noordwijk and Robinson in his third Tulip in a Jowett was confident of a win. He collected the Jupiter from the Parc Fermée in the morning and although it started easily, unknown to him the tachometer drive cable had detached itself from the dynamo drive and had lodged in the position of jamming the carburettor chokes fully open. The engine was clearly running rich but the bonnet

in the group were marked in the proportion that they were slower than the group's best time; the penalties incurred, however, were small in relation to the marking of the rest of the rally and counted only a little towards the final result.

The first test was fast but somewhat dangerous due to the poor road surface that evidently suited the Jupiter for Nogueira class-won at 1 mins 33.7 secs (about 72 mph), compared with 1 mins 40.4 secs, Aprilia, 2nd, the 1 mins 41.6 secs, Simca, 3rd, and the best Porsche time of 1 mins 38.4s. The Simca's penalty amounted to 140 points.

The second test, at Gradil, was another timed street course, over 3.3 km but here the Jupiter did not feature in the first five of its group, none of whom were penalised thanks to the closeness of their times – all within 0.6 secs in three minutes. Indeed this was the experience of the top five competitors in four out of the five groups.

The cars then headed south for Lisbon where they began to arrive a little after midday, and then on to Estoril, the elegant, glamorous resort to the west of the capital, where an improvised circuit had been constructed for the acceleration, regularity, and braking test.

Drivers had to accelerate along a 100 metre straight, the last 25 metres being timed, then lap the circuit four times as fast as possible and with as little as possible difference, and then stop in the shortest distance after crossing a line. Nogueira again led his group with 9,196 points (the same Aprilia 2nd, 9,411 and the Simca 3rd with 9,449), lower than any other car in the rally except for the 3½-litre Ford Pilot of Clemente Meneres. This placed Nogueira second in the general category up to this point which read:

1 Meneres
2 Nogueira
3 da Fonseca, Simca
4 Ernesto Mattorell, Porsche

The Ford Pilot of Ken Wharton was lying 7th.

On the final day of the rally there were at Estoril a series of decisive tests and trials performed in front of crowds which were large once the early morning downpour had moved away. It was here that Nogueira showed that he was a great driver: resourceful, methodical and with the will to win Jowett's only outright victory in international competition. The final order in the general classification was as follows:

Six competitors were eliminated in the two

POSITION	DRIVER	CAR	PENALTIES	GROUP
1	Joaquim Nogueira	Jupiter	16,296	3
2	Manual Meneres	Ford Pilot	16,398	1
3	Conde Passanha	Allard	16,759	1
4	Emilio Christillin	Lancia Aurelia	16,918	2
5	Ernesto Mattorell	Porsche	17,132	4
6	Ken Wharton	Ford Pilot	17,407	1
7	Carlos da Fonseca	Simca	17,409	3

days of tests, leaving 48 finishers of whom 28 were Portuguese. Nogueira was awarded the Automovél Club de Portugal Cup for the best-placed Portuguese driver.

May 25–26 1951 saw the first National Morecambe Rally as a full-scale event, with substantial support from the front-ranking rally specialists (possibly practising for next month's RAC) with a 231-car entry and six starts. On the first day 250 miles were covered, culminating in tests at Morecambe, while on the second day an 80-mile road section through part of the Lake District included the timed ascent of Tow Top, followed by more driving tests on the return to Morecambe. The outright winner was Ian Appleyard in NUB120, his already famous XK120.

The talented rally specialist Godfrey Imhoff – normally associated with Cadillac-engined Allards – was beginning a brief flirtation with Jowetts: he drove his Jupiter HAK117 (E1/SA/77R) to do particularly well in the driving tests, finishing second in class B.

Tommy Wise in GKW111 sensibly chose to keep its hood raised and was rewarded by 11th place in the general category. As all above him were open cars he not only won the 1,300 to 3,000 cc class for closed production cars but carried away the award for the best performance in a closed production car.

Ted Booth with his special-bodied Jupiter LRH 2 EO/SA/1OR, also took part. In the final driving test, the gear change jammed in reverse and the unexpected direction of movement so alarmed some marshals standing nearby that they leaped over the sea wall on to the sands beyond!

The First International RAC (The 'Festival of Britain') Rally, 4–9 June 1951, comprised four starts, 1,700 road miles, tests at Silverstone, the Rest and Be Thankful hill-climb, a timed section embracing the up to 1 in 3.5 gradients of the Hard Knott and Wrynose passes in the Lake District, driving tests at Blackpool, a speed trial at Eppynt in Wales and the final test at Bournemouth. There was no general category or first prize and the four classes were for open and closed cars of greater and less that 1½-litre.

A team of three Jupiters had been mustered: GKY256 for Marcel Becquart (his only rally in a standard Jupiter) with Roy Lunn navigating; Goff Imhoff/Cyril Wick in HAK117; and Ted Booth in LHR2, Derek Bowers with the maps. Becquart was once described by a contemporary as the Scarlet Pimpernel of rallying, for 'no matter how hard one drove he was always at the next control ahead of one'. In 1948 his friend and usual co-driver in continental events, Henri Ziegler, had taken the Geneva Jowett agency and at the Geneva Show that year Becquart tested the Javelin demonstrator in a most electrifying manner along the lakeside to show how the car could be handled. But Hotchkiss had finished 1st and 2nd in the 1949 Monte and he started his rally career in a 1939 Hotchkiss Grand Sport, giving that marque its sixth Monte win in 1950. Roy Lunn had joined Jowetts – from Aston Martin where he had worked with Claude Hill the man responsible for the DB1 – to take over Gerald Palmer's position as chief designer.

The class opposition comprised five HRGs, eight MGs and four of the new Jensen designed and built open Austin A40s.

For the 229 cars involved, the Silverstone test was more like a half-hour high-speed trial and on the short club circuit too: a set number of laps (dependent on class) had to be covered in 30 minutes, one mark to be deducted for every second over the half hour. The track rapidly became slippery with rubber dust, hot tarmac, and spilled petrol. Alec Gordon's HRG slid happily at Stowe, while Booth's Jupiter once had a double slide there. Becquart had his Jupiter going so fast that Imhoff had all his work cut out screaming his tyres and hooting at the slower stuff to catch him. The test was later annulled thanks to a muddle about the exact position of the finish line and

this had the effect of dropping Becquart two places in the final order.

He was unable to match the HRGs on the 'Rest' returning a 3rd place 82.1 secs behind J.V.S. Brown and Nancy Mitchell. Goff Imhoff recorded 9th place, 85.3 secs, picked up places by cleaning the Hard Knott to Wrynose timed stretch, and came third behind a TD and another MG at the Blackpool driving test. The similarly powered but lighter if primitive HRGs were quicker on the hills whereas the Jupiter's superior handling was overwhelming on the zig-zag 1.9 mile Eppynt speed trial for, on Army property, this was ideal Jupiter territory with an abundance of corners and switchbacks to make it interesting.

The class results here were:

1 Becquart	2 mins 14.2 secs
2 Imhoff	2 mins 15.4 secs
3 Best HRG	2 mins 17.4 secs
4 Booth	2 mins 18.4 secs
5 and 6 HRGs	

Javelins had filled the first five places in the $1\frac{1}{2}$-litre closed class on the 'Rest' with a best of 90.8 secs and now at Eppynt they took the first six.

At the final driving tests on the Bournemouth promenade, Imhoff opened the proceedings in light drizzle to return 84.05 secs. Becquart, however, won his class with a perfect display of sliding into and out of chicanes with the minimum of breaking to record 78.92 secs.

Maurice Gatsonides, co-driver in van der Mark's Dutch Javelin drove the LHD car to a $1\frac{1}{2}$-litre closed class equal 3rd, scoring 86.22, having got his gears mixed up and missing a foul line. Dr Spare's 2nd place Javelin recorded 84.05 behind a $1\frac{1}{4}$ MG saloon's 83.41 secs.

Overall results placed Imhoff 4th in class behind two HRGs and an MG, Becquart 5th and Booth in his everyday car a creditable 12th; the Dutch Javelin finished 2nd in its class behind an MG with Javelins 4th and 5th.

The Second Swedish Rally to the Midnight Sun, 14–16 June 1951 included the Jupiter of K.V. Andersson, who finished class 6th out of 36 finishers in his category.

The Single-Start 14th International Alpine Rally, 13–21 July 1951, was regarded as the toughest of the European trials and had at times much of the character of a road race. Generally only a small number of cars would complete unpenalised (on time and condition of coachwork) the 2,000 miles and 20 or more of Europe's highest moun-

51 The Jupiter team near Loch Ness after the 'Rest and Be Thankful'. Left to right: *Roy Lunn, Godfrey Imhoff, Cyril Wick, Ted Booth, Derek Bowers:* Becquart

tain passes. All who did received Coupes des Alpes, with a final eliminator at Cannes to decide ties within classes. In addition, there were four separate tests with their own awards but whose results did not contribute to the overall rally position. These four were the $13\frac{1}{2}$ mile Mont Ventoux regularity run and the standing start km speed test at the Monza Autodrome on the first stage, the 10 mile Falzarego hill climb on the third stage and the 9,000 feet Stelvio Ascent ($8\frac{3}{4}$ miles) on the penultimate stage.

The rally traditionally attracted strong British teams: 31 of the 65 cars had British crews and among them was GKW111 (travelling with three spare wheels strapped to the Jupiter's tail luggage rack) of T.C. Wise and Mike 'The Laugh' Wilson, longtime chairman of the BARC Yorkshire centre. Even in his slimmest form he weighed $18\frac{1}{2}$ stone so it was a tight fit in the Jupiter, for TCW was no midget. W.H. Robinson, with W. James was driving GKY256, probably by now owned by Robinson, and also entered was the high-mileage Javelin of Dr Smallhorn, the car in which he made his doctor's rounds.

A French entrant, J. Armangaud, was to distinguish himself with his Jupiter. Also in the 1.1 to 1.5-litre class were 6 MGs, 2 HRGs, 3 Simcas and a Lancia. The start, in tropical heat, was at 8.30 am from the quayside at Marseilles, and the first-stage, 450-mile run took the competitors through the Mont Ventoux regularity test, then NE into Italy via the Turin Autostrada to Monza and on to Milan. Robinson was unpenalised but Wise, with electrical problems, and Armangaud were both late at controls. The Jupiters were not very successful in the regularity test, where the HRG of those two famous motoring policemen J.A. Gott and G.W. Gillespie, in their third Alpine with the same car headed the class, with Wise 4th and Armangaud 9th. At Monza, Armangaud's Jupiter was on form, winning the class in the standing km at 40.4 secs, 0.6 faster than the 2nd-placed MG and Wise (5th) recorded 42.0 secs, just 0.2 secs slower than Gott with Robinson class 8th at 42.4 secs.

The second stage included the difficult Dolomite road from Bolzano to Cortina and only four of the $1\frac{1}{2}$-litre cars reached Cortina unpenalised, amongst which was GKY256. Armangaud had a good run, incurring no penalty points for the day.

The third day's motoring covered 200 miles through the Dolomite mountains, starting and finishing at Cortina and covered at higher speeds than the average for the rest of the rally: for the smaller cars this meant maintaining very high downhill speeds expecting a great deal from the brakes, too much in fact for the Alfin drums on the hitherto unpenalised GKY256 and they cracked right round from stud to stud. Robinson, the $1\frac{1}{2}$-litre favourite at that point, was therefore obliged to retire. Wise, however, electrical problems temporarily in abeyance, took GKW111 up the Falzarego pass in the class-winning time of 17 mins 2.8 secs (37.2 mph); Armangaud was 2nd in 17 mins 25.0 secs, with Gott 4th (17 mins 42.0 secs), behind a Simca. Armangaud again had a day without penalty, by now using the batteries out of Robinson's Jupiter as his car was having dynamo trouble.

The fourth day took the cars northward from the Italian Tyrol into Austria over four passes; Wise's electrical problems were again slowing him. At the end of the day, at Innsbruck, of the 16 $1\frac{1}{2}$-litre cars, 7 had retired and only one, the Gott/Gillespie HRG was unpenalised.

52 Ted Booth at the final test at Bournemouth, temporary screen fitted: Booth

53 Tommy Wise takes GKW111 through the Dolomites: Autocar

From Innsbruck, the 450-mile fifth stage brought the survivors back into Italy, through the Brenner Pass, easy in spite of the poor weather, to the Mont Giovo Pass, a very different and fitting prelude to the 9-mile, zig-zag climb (ten hairpins in a 2-km stretch) to the summit of the Stelvio, and the alarming, hurried, 14-mile descent to the Bonio time-check; then, briefly into Switzerland through the clouded St Bernard Pass – visibility virtually zero – and across the French border to Chamonix.

Wise was again running well and took the class for the Stelvio ascent (20 mins 53.0 secs), less than 2 mins slower than Tommy Wisdom in the ex-Le Mans 3-litre Aston. Armangaud recorded a 3rd place 21 mins 6.0 secs, behind an MG, and Smallhorn's Javelin, its high-altitude misfiring cured, 23 mins 31.4 secs, was one place ahead of Gott, a poor 6th with 23 mins 33.4 secs. Alas, later in that day on the way to Aosta, two women cyclists shot out of a side turning in front of GKW111. Wise evaded and rammed a lorry, disabling the Jupiter. One cyclist broke a shoulder. John Gott, close behind, felt duty bound to take the injured girl to hospital, for which action he was not penalised: the luckless Wise spent that night in police custody. Of the Jupiters therefore, only Armangaud remained for the final 450-mile run south through the French Alps to Cannes. This would take in six peaks, two almost as high as the Stelvio, and a difficult route through the Iseran Pass (the highest motor route in Europe), the Glandon, some of which was on unmade roads complicated by avalanches, the Galibier and Isoard peaks.

Hood lowered, Armangaud made a characteristically rapid ascent of the Galibier but sadly a serious boiling problem developed on the Isoard, virtually the last major peak, and he reached Cannes more than the maximum 30 minutes late.

Gott was unpenalised after an immaculate drive, winning his Coupes des Alpes: and the Javelin of Dr Smallhorn came 4th out of 5 survivors in the class and amongst the total of 28 finishers, 10 unpenalised, was Ian Appleyard winning this third Alpine cup and the best performance award in NUB120. The Jupiters, although failing to reach Cannes, encouragingly took three special awards, the fastest $1\frac{1}{2}$-litre cars in the rally.

J. Armangaud re-appeared once more with his Jupiter to win outright the AC du Savoie's all-French Rallye de l'Iseran in the French Alps, 18–19 August 1951. Second was a Peugeot 203, a car with similar engine power to a Jupiter's. Class 3rd at overall 9th was Prestail's MG.

In the two supplementary tests Armangaud had come overall 3rd in the standing km (with 42.5 secs) to two bigger-engined Citroen 11 CVs, the Peugeot recording 44.6 secs. In the 10-mile Côte de l'Iseran ascent the Jupiter clocked 4th place behind the Citroens and the 203.

Little can be said of the MCC *Daily Express* 1,200 mile National Rally, 7–10 November 1951. On a Yorkshire moor Booth drove LHR2 into a sheep, killing it and the nearside headlamp (there were penalties for damage it will be recalled); the other Jupiter was the handsome but overweight saloon KWX770, E1/SA/99R, of Edward Foulds (Jowett's Keighley agent) and K. Jones. Although undistinguished, this first rally appearance of a saloon Jupiter was a preview of what was to come.

Held from 22–29 January, the 1952 Monte Carlo Rally saw sufficient snow, ice, fog and rain as almost to ensure that victory could be secured on the road section, the French Alps becoming littered with the wrecks of cars in what drivers agreed had been the toughest motoring adventure in years for only 15 crews were unpenalised from 328 starters and 163 finishers. Last year's rule barring cars with engines not produced by the vehicle's manufacturer had been rescinded and a new one substituted, allowing only closed cars. Individually built closed variations of open cars in series production were permitted with the proviso that bodies must be completely finished for normal touring use, and not constructed for competition purposes; series production was defined as more than 50 examples before October 1951. So Sydney Allard returned in a saloon version of one of his machines and won the rally outright; Stirling Moss being second it will be remembered, in a Sunbeam Talbot. And four saloon Jupiters made their rally debut, one to record Jowett's best-ever Monte performance. It says something for the influence of this event to realise that the construction of at least five saloon Jupiters can be attributed to this rule.

The most important of these Jupiters was the Farina of Marcel Becquart. The third such vehicle to be built and his own personal car at the time, it was fully backed by the works, who rebuilt the engine to the latest specification, fitted a larger radiator, competition brake linings and fluid raised the riding height 3 inches and made many other detail improvements.

Two saloons built by Ghia Suisse of Aigle were entered by R. Thévenin, garage proprietor of Bordeaux, and Jean Latune, the long-time president of the Automobile Club of Drome, all three to start from Lisbon and entered as a team to compete for the Charles Faroux Challenge Cup. The two Ghia Jupiter saloons were not well prepared, relying as they did on Henri Zeigler, the Geneva agent, for spares and service; Ziegler's mechanics were insufficiently experienced in the complexities of the Jowett engine with regrettable consequences. Indeed, hopes for the Faroux Cup were dashed from the outset as Thévenin failed to reach the start.

Robert Ellison had returned with his saloon Jupiter MTJ300, E1/SA/81R, built for the Rally by J.E. Farr & Son of Blackburn. It too had a competition engine loaned by Jowetts, an extra fuel tank and a specially shaped luggage locker to accommodate the two spare wheels with the snow chains; the sole light-weight feature was a pair of Le Mans Seats borrowed through Horace Grimley. Walter Mason navigated. Also amongst the Glasgow starters was the Birmingham Jowett dealer Frank Grounds in a Javelin fitted with wheels, headlamps and other parts transferred from his uncompleted saloon Jupiter. Ellison had an uneventful run until soon after Bourges, by where all the rally routes had converged, and increasingly heavy snow was encountered. Ellison stopped to fit the chained wheels at Nevers, 30 miles out of Bourges. Weather conditions deteriorated so suddenly and completely that almost all competitors were faced with equal difficulties on the final road sections and from Clermont-Ferrand, through St Flour, Le Puy and on to Valence, conditions were as bad as they had ever been on the rally. Ellison, unfamiliar with driving on snow chains overslid his car on a downhill right-hander near St Flour, 130 miles from Nevers, and as there was no bank or wall went 30 feet over the edge, turning over twice. He had completed 1,640 miles and he was not alone for the road between Bourges and Valence, at the best of times a twisty and rather dangerous one, resembled in places the dead car park of a long-distance race and became lined with stationary cars. In places the drivers met a barrage of whirling snowflakes; in others there was mist with visibility 20 to 30 feet sometimes, through which it was not possible to maintian the average. The Jupiter had come to rest on a ledge about 8 feet wide and soon had the

front of a Citroen on its roof. The following day a local farmer arrived with a team of six oxen, attached them to the Jupiter with a chain, flicked the ear of the leader with a long stick, and the car was back on the road in one minute flat. After roughly straightening the roof and steering and with temporary screens fitted, Ellison drove on to Monte Carlo, arriving a day late.

At Valence only 17 cars were without penalty, including Becquart, three Simcas and a Porsche. From Valence via Gap, Digne, and Grasse it was easier only by comparison and few could have enjoyed the slippery slopes of the run down to the Riviera. On the Col des Lèques it was hardly possible to stand, let alone drive fast.

The first car to reach the finishing control was Becquart's Farina. Mud-stained, it passed through the arrival arch dropping large lumps of melting snow on to the Condamine. It was unpenalised, one of the 15, and qualified for the regularity test, held for the first time over a twisty 75-km circuit in the hills around the Col de Braus, at a required $28\frac{1}{2}$ mph, considered difficult in the wintry conditions, almost the whole length having snow. The results of this test were firstly to decide the final order of the 15 unpenalised cars, and then influence the positions of the subsequent 34; by way of

54 The saloon Jupiters of Marcel Becquart (Farina) and Latune (Ghia) at the Lisbon start of the 1952 Monte Carlo Rally. Latune second from right

55 Marcel Becquart getting away from La Turbie in the regularity run; the organisers required the white paint to be added for this test. The damage to the car's grille was caused by a large dog, which almost made Becquart late for the Paris control

example the experienced ice racer, G. Norlander (Javelin), vastly improved his position (80 points down on the road section) by being second in this test, collecting only 129 points. He was therefore placed 16th overall, class 9th although his total of 209 points was less than that of all but the best six of the unpenalised cars. Poor Norlander! The 80 points were a fine for opening the bonnet of his Javelin in the Parc Fermée at Monaco.

The Latune/Gay Jupiter lost 380 points to come class 23rd, overall 58th and so was not among the 49 qualifiers for the regularity test.

In Monaco, the heavy rain falling at the start of the regularity test became blizzards up in the mountains. At a sharp right-hand bend near the Castillon tunnel more than half the competitors spun and it was on this section that Becquart lost a disproportionate amount of points to come equal 7th in the test with 162 points (but 5th out of the unpenalised cars), whereas Dr Angelvin, in a Simca Sport (based on the 1951 production model plus many modifications 'suggested' by the ubiquitous Amédée Gordini) with 139 came 4th in the test and therefore 3rd overall to win the $1\frac{1}{2}$-litre class. Becquart's overall 5th – but class 2nd — was Jowett's best ever, alas his only prize the Coupe Cibié, awarded to 1st and 2nd in each category and the 'Rally Plaquette' awarded to the first six in the general category. Prize money for overall 5th was the same as that for 2nd place in the $1\frac{1}{2}$-litre class, 50,000 francs.

The 1,800-mile Second RAC International Rally was run from 31 March to 5 April 1952, early enough for there to be snow about. The starts were at Hastings and Scarborough, and the cars were divided into but three classes this year, class 1, all open cars, and classes 2 and 3 for closed cars of less than, and greater than, $2\frac{1}{2}$-litre engine capacity respectively. This was criticised as there was no class for the most popular size, $1\frac{1}{2}$-litre, and likely to deter overseas competitors, also, rightly as it turned out, for favouring larger engined cars in the speed tests: the RAC countered that the speed test times would be adjusted through a formula based on engine size, and, for the Mount Eppynt and Rest and Be Thankful tests, class 1 would be subdivided into less than $1\frac{1}{2}$-litre, $1\frac{1}{2}$ to $2\frac{1}{2}$-litre and above $2\frac{1}{2}$-litre groups.

Similarly, class 2 would have less than $1\frac{1}{2}$-litre and $1\frac{1}{2}$ to $2\frac{1}{2}$-litre categories. An average time would be computed for each class, with those failing to reach it being penalised.

The contentious Olivers Mount test was treated as a regularity trial of two runs, where marks lost were calculated from $3P\text{-}Q$ where P = time of slowest run, Q = time of fastest run, putting a premium on speed as well as regularity. In a 249-strong entry list containing eight Jupiters there were 26 XK120s, 21 MGs, nine Morgans – Peter Morgan in one – Nancy Mitchell and six other HRGs, 13 Javelins including that of Dr Smallhorn, at least two Porsches, Maurice Tew in a Humber and Maurice Gatsonides, the great Dutch rally man, in a Ford Consul.

The Jupiter entries were: Nancy Binns; E.B. Booth/D. Bowers (10); H. Hadley/W. Butler (GKY107); L.C. Procter/J. Randles (282); G.M. Sharp; W.J. Skelly (41); F.E. Still/Mrs Still (521); and T.C. Wise/M. Wilson (GKW111).

Jupiter MAC2 took part and may possibly be G.M. Sharp's car. This record number of Jupiters is explained by their availability on the home market from the previous November but the privately entered Jupiters would have had no works assistance of any kind. Nancy Binns failed to start and of the seven Jupiters remaining only the works/works-assisted cars of Hadley, Wise and Booth could expect to make a serious impression against the experienced and well-prepared opposition. Hadley, in the ill-fated factory car, had pre-war rally experience and was also an accomplished trials exponent (the Austin 'Grasshoppers') and his co-driver Bill Butler had been a $1\frac{1}{2}$-litre Singer trials driver. But Jowett's 'Sunday Car' was their carefully prepared rally Javelin HAK743 for Marcel Becquart.

Roy Lunn had to step in at the last moment as Becquart's co-driver but there were no navigational problems as Grandfield, with his military efficiency, had ensured that all preparations including maps on rollers, were complete. Hadley's car gave brake trouble on the way to the start but Roy Lunn, in convoy in the Javelin, was able to sort them out. Heavy snow fell in the south before the rally began and made it difficult for some Hastings entrants to reach the starting control; to the disgust of most competitors this led to the premature cancellation of the 10 lap Silverstone speed test on the first day, for the Northamptonshire snow had thawed before the test had been due to begin.

The cars moved on to Castle Coombe via Bridport for a driving test after dark by the light of the car's own lamps with best time of the evening coming equally from Ted Booth and Ken Bancroft (Morgan). These tests were of almost speed-trial distance; however the first time Hadley used reverse gear it disappeared and he was virtually out of the rally when it had hardly started – and he did not reverse again until the final scrutineering at Scarborough.

The following dawn saw a risky 2.2 mile speed test on the military roads of Mount Eppynt, narrow, and somewhat wavy in surface, over similar territory to last year; a passenger was carried and no practice was possible. In the open class up to $1\frac{1}{2}$-litre the Jupiters of Wise and Hadley were 2nd and 3rd behind the HRG of Nancy Mitchell. Hadley had really tried here but both he and Bill Butler unluckily had thought they had seen the 'Finish' board 800 yards before the actual end of the test and so slowed early. Following a breakfast halt at the Victorian spa town of Llandrindrod Wells, the cars moved on to Blackpool by way of the steep climb up Bwylch-y-Groes ascended non-stop and it was here that Merch's Porsche retired. From Blackpool,

where Hadley's gearbox was hurriedly rebuilt, the route took the cars through the Lake District familiarising the competitors with a test that lay two days ahead – and on across the Scottish border. After the night at Edinburgh, Rest and Be Thankful Hill was climbed, light rain falling after midday favouring the early cars and again Nancy Mitchell forced a Jupiter, this time Hadley's, into second place in their group. Best time of the day was Ian Appleyard's 71.6 secs in NUB120. Still it should be noted that Hadley's time of 81.6 secs was faster than all in classes 2 and 3. The cars then looped east, through Kenmore at the end of Loch Ray and, in the dark, over the pass at Amulree where locals moved boulders on to the road a little faster than the RSAC could remove them.

The following day saw the ingenious

57 RAC Rally team, 1952. Left to right: *Lunn, Wise, Bequart, Mike Wilson*

58 Booth signing in at the Scarborough finish, 1952 RAC Rally. Car now has correct windscreen with three wiper arms

Lake District trials. The three stretches through Ulpha, Hard Knott, and Kirkstone had to be taken as fast as possible. They were of unequal length but could be traversed in equal times – the aim was for consistency. Big-engined cars took the first seven places on this test (1st Ian Appleyard at 16.6 secs) equal 8th were two Jaguars, an HRG, and Bert Hadley with 17.6 secs. The 199 survivors motored into Scarborough to find that, at the end of the road section it was still anyone's rally: K. Bancroft (Morgan) headed class 1 with 60.0, Ted Booth was 8th at 64.2 and at 66.6 the 18th car in this category (the Morgan of J.H. Ray) was the lowest placed open car to qualify for the Olivers Mount regularity test. Of the remaining class 1 finishers F.E. Still came in a creditable 36th (87.4 points) well ahead of the 51st placed Nancy Mitchell (102.6). Bert Hadley was classified a lowly equal 61st (209.0) from 74 class finishers. The only Javelin in the leading 14 of class 2 to take Olivers Mount was that of M. Becquart, who at 74.6 was lying 5th, 3.4 behind his class leader.

The Olivers Mount regularity test was in two sections, to be covered in the same elapsed time. The first, slowest, section contained a hairpin followed by a steep climb, and had to be completed as fast as possible. This test saw the smaller-engined cars routed before they began as the inexperienced organisers had seen to it that the marks allotted to this test could swamp those for the previous five days of the rally.

Tommy Wise's Jupiter had engine failure about 20 miles from the finish, which had the enormous advantage of being close to his Harrogate home, while Ted Booth finished 15th, collecting 161.2, one place below the HRG of J.V.S. Brown (154.8). All cars above them were 2 litre or more with the Cadillac-engined Allard of Imhof winning the open-car class; a brilliant drive by Becquart pulled him up to class first, actually 12.8 points ahead of the winner of class 3, therefore the best closed car of either category.

Results summary:

Castle Coombe driving test, class 1

= 1st	E.B. Booth		21.6
	K. Bancroft	(Morgan)	21.6
= 2nd	J.V.S. Brown	(HRG)	22.8
	G. Rollings	(Healey)	22.8

All closed cars slower than these times.

Mount Eppynt 2.2 mile speed test, class 1, under 1.5-litre group

N. Mitchell	(HRG)	2 mins 45.2 secs
T.C. Wise		2 mins 49.0 secs
H. Hadley		2 mins 50.4 secs
J.V.S. Brown	(HRG)	2 mins 51.2 secs

Class 2, under 1.5-litre group

M. Becquart	2 mins 53.6 secs

Rest and Be Thankful hill climb, class 1 under 1.5-litre group

N. Mitchell	(HRG)	80.4 secs
H. Hadley		81.6 secs
A. Gordon	(HRG)	83.6 secs)
J. Richmond	(HRG)	83.8 secs

Class 2 under 1.5-litre group

M. Becquart	84.8 secs

The Sixth International Lisbon Rally 21–25 May 1952, was won outright by Joaquin Filipe Nogueira (Porsche) 16,850 points. Best Jowett results were: Coupe des Dames, Nancy Mitchell/Joyce Leavens (Javelin) 21,007; Joaquim Cordoso/Abreor Lopes (E1/SA/168R) class 7th, 19,423; Joaquim Nunes dos Santos (E1/SA/75R) class 9th, 20,230; Nancy Mitchell/Joyce Leavens (Javelin) class 11th. There were 24 finishers in the 1100–1500 cc class, with four Porsches above the Jupiters, and three below. There were least 132 entrants. Dos Santos was not unknown for his efforts with a BMW (1951 Monte overall 8th).

In the 1952 Volta a Portugal (a sort of Portugese Mille Miglia) the outright winner was Joaquim Filipe Nogueira (E1/SA/74R) in this national event. It was won using the engine from E1/SA/265R.

The 15th International Alpine Rally had been lengthened to 2,060 miles, for the first time with a general classification (calculated by an intricate formula that was to favour the smaller-engined cars in the early stages) and was run 11–16 July 1952 over 34 Alpine passes. The $1\frac{1}{2}$-litre cars had to maintain a general average of 35.4 mph, with 40.5 mph over the second day's 189-mile loop around the Dolomites.

The 20-strong $1\frac{1}{2}$-litre contingent contained no less than eight Porsches and a British entry of three HRGs, two MGs, a Javelin and two Jupiters: Tommy Wise, teamed with the veteran John Gott in his fifth Alpine for whom Jowetts had prepared HAK365. Wise's car had the latest oil cooler arrangement and, mindful of last year's accident, the characteristic whine of the engine could be supplemented by a pair of horns mounted on the front bumper in what was to be GKW111's last international event.

The first, and longest, day's motoring

took in five peaks in the 614 miles from Marseilles to Cortina, with a break for the standing start km test at Monza, as usual contributing only to its own special award. This year, Gott recorded 40.2 secs and Wise 40.1 secs, both about 2 secs faster than their 1951 times, but too small an improvement on the Armangaud Jupiter's class win of that year. The best HRG (42.1 secs) MG (46.2 secs) and Javelin (45.0 secs) were outclassed by the quickest Porsche at 35.1 secs and Butti's class-winning OSCA at 33.1 secs.

Nevertheless the Jupiters' first day was penalty free – only the OSCA and three of the Porsches were so distinguished – for there had already been seven retirements including both MGs. Wise and Gott were a satisfactory 6th and 7th in the general classification.

The second day saw the 189 mile flat-out drive around the Dolomites, the roads there closed for the duration. The first 30 miles constituted a special timed test which Butti class-won at 45 mins 3 secs. The best Porsche time of 45 mins 24 secs was not matched by Wise (50 mins 14 secs) or Gott (52 mins 21 secs) or the best HRG time of 51 mins 6 secs. Again the two Jupiters were unpenalised at the end of a day that had seen the retirements of the OSCA and two of the three previously unpenalised Porsches. This left Nathan's Porsche the only other 1½-litre car with a clean sheet.

If the lessons of history are not fully appreciated, they may have to be repeated: on the third day the rear Alfin brakedrums of HAK365 were found to be breaking away from their hubs, forcing Gott to retire. And a washer in the gearbox of GKW111 failed, leaving a bitterly disappointed Wise the choice of only two gears, so at the end of the third day only 32 cars remained in this the toughest of the European rally programme. Nathan and the Spanish driver de Caralt went on to take 1st and 2nd for Porsche, although both were penalised and received no Coupes des Alpes. Twenty-three crews finished out of 85 starters. The Porsches, very much faster than the Jupiters on the ascents, were, in attracting penalties, clearly not fast enough down the Alps. They suffered from as yet unsolved braking deficiencies which meant that they could not match the Jupiters on the descents until the Alfins, adequate for the lesser rigours of sports car racing, failed under Alpine hammering.

The Tour de France national rally, 9–16 September 1952, 3,438 miles, three stages, emphasised speed (no manoeuvring tests):

two hillclimbs (Col de Peyresourde and la Turbie) and four sprint tests. Of the 110 cars that started, 57 finished. First in class was Armangaud (OSCA), fourth Nogueira (Porsche), and fifth in class was the Jupiter of Latune and Thomas, presumed to be the Ghia saloon (56).

The MCC *Daily Express* National Rally, 12–15 November 1952 had an entry list of six Jupiters among a total of 431. They were N. Freedman/P. Waring (509); L.C. Procter/S.G. Dyke (282); G.M. Sharp/G.P. Jolly (MAC2?); F.E. Still/J. Carter (521); R.I.H. Sievwright/C.F. Denvey (748); and R.V. Russell/S. Eddy (HPY696). In addition the Jupiter RPF16 (539) of F. Defty took part; perhaps he was a reserve. No Jupiters distinguished themselves.

The 1952 Alpine had been the final rally for a works standard-bodied Jupiter, and following his successful drive in the RAC Becquart was to concentrate exclusively on the Javelin, with the single exception of one more Monte for his Farina Jupiter.

The touring car championship was begun in 1953 and accelerated the trend toward rallies mainly for production saloon cars, modified only slightly from standard in ways generally available to the public and recommended by the manufacturer. It was not Jowetts policy to contend, and Becquart, now their only regular rally driver, was entered just for the Monte, RAC and Tulip; rather the aim was for Jowetts to keep themselves favourably in the eye of the public and perhaps also of the financiers in Lazards, Briggs and where else who were soon to decide the fate of the struggling Yorkshire concern.

59 The badge-bar is as important as the extra lights on the Jupiter of F.Defty, 1952 MCC Daily Express Rally: Guy Griffiths

The 1953 Monte Carlo Rally, 20–27 January, run over much the same route as the previous year, was revealed for what it was, a fairly simple rally dependent on bad weather to sort out the drivers and cars. This year, apart from some fog in Belgium the weather let the organisers down and the snow that fell just before the start either thawed or was cleared from the roads by the authorities. Out of 404 starters 253 lost no marks on the road section and had to be put through the rather puerile acceleration/braking test that tended to favour the bigger-engined cars. The 100 best from this test were then sent round the 46 1/5 mile Col de Braus circuit at 40 kph, having to avoid penalty by passing a sequence of six controls at exact predetermined times. Becquart's Farina Jupiter had been prepared by Jowetts with considerable thoroughness for what they may have felt would be the last chance for a Jupiter to do well in international rallying: a Wills-ring engine, not tuned for more power as the regulations forbade this, but otherwise virtually to Le Mans specification, was installed, with new torsion bars, shock absorbers, cables, fuel lines blown through, wheels and (iron) brake drums crack-checked – could anything have been overlooked in the search for perfection?

Becquart again joined a team of three Jowetts, this time formed by Frank Grounds in his saloon Jupiter LOL1, EO/SA/29 and Javelin man Bob Foster, the TT motorcyclist (and 350 cc world champion in 1950 for Velocette). The Ghia saloon of Latune was again entered and reached Monte Carlo unpenalised, as did the Becquart team. After the usual acceleration/braking test the Jowetts, all qualifying for the 74 km Col de Braus regularity run, were placed as follows:

17	Becquart/Ziegler	23.6 secs
=50	Foster/Holdsworth	24.9 secs
=74	Grounds/Hay	25.5 secs
=79	Latune/Gay	25.6 secs

Fastest time, 21.8 secs, was put up by Sydney Allard in his saloon, thanks to its extraordinary acceleration, and von Frankenberg ($1\frac{1}{2}$-litre Porsche) recorded a second-place 22.3 secs, the more astonishing because all but four of the 30 Porches took more than 25.9 secs, therefore failing the test; similarly were the Simcas reduced in number.

Becquart was poised for a good result but it was not to be. During the regularity test, whilst on the Col de Braus itself about halfway round, his Jupiter's cooling fan disintegrated and punctured the radiator. The Jupiters final rally order was:

Grounds/Hay	Class 4th, overall 36th
Latune/Gay	Class 6th, overall 46th
Becquart/Ziegler	Class 15th, overall 78th

The class was taken by a Peugeot. Unhappily for Javelins, Ginette Sigrand and Ginette Largeot in the lavishly prepared works HAK743 failed to reach Monte Carlo; and the Foster/Holdsworth car scored a miserable 200 on the regularity run.

From 1954 the rally's ideal, a test of endurance and winter tourism, moved into closer embrace with mass production for the FIA regulation stipulating that more than 1,000 examples had to have been built was implemented. There were therefore no more Monte Carlo rallies for Jupiters.

The third RAC International Rally, 23–28 March 1953, had 195 starters. In effect a large number of special tests, diverse and ingenious, spread out over the country joined by fairly innocuous road sections,

60 Marcel Becquart (left) and Henri Zeigler after arrival in Monte Carlo, 1953 event

involving little more than everyday motoring tactics to cover the 1,600 miles in the allotted time.

The Jupiter entries were: Frank Masefield Baker/F.T. Marchant MCD28 (597); T.G. Cunane/A. Ellis NTJ930; Frank Defty/J.J. Ford RPG16 (539); Mrs Lola Grounds/Mrs Doreen Reece LOL1 (29); and A. Ross/D. Phillips YMC900.

There were two sports car classes, for under and over $1\frac{1}{2}$-litre cars, and three touring car classes, which included drophead coupés running closed, for under 1.3, 1.3 to 1.6, and over 1.6-litre cars.

Marks were based on the 'standard performance' – the average of the best 10 with all below this average being penalised. But the penalties were very heavy and a deficit once incurred could not usually be made up. The first day's test, at Silverstone, was a $\frac{1}{2}$-mile sprint from Woodcote off a standing start and stopping before a foul line 60 yards past the finish. The slightly-built Lola Grounds did badly in the braking part of this test in her hydromechanically braked Jupiter saloon.

In the Castle Coombe night-manoeuvring test by the car's own lamps (forward into a bay, reverse into another, forward and away) the expert Cunane was good early on but Mrs Grounds, her rooflight pointing skywards, was penalised for hitting a pylon. Becquart was third in this test in the works Javelin HAK743, and fifth in the Goodwood acceleration/braking test but had a partial engine seizure during the Ulpha/Hardknott regularity run and did not finish; also out was Bob Foster, who holed the sump of his Javelin on a bump on a road in Yorkshire.

The honours in the 1.3–1.6-litre touring class went well for Jowett:

1 *E. Elliott* (Javelin)
2 (a Riley)
3 *Dr D. Laing* (Javelin)

There was no Jupiter among the top 101 finishers.

In the RSAC International Coronation Scottish Rally, 25–28 May 1953, 129 competitors started the first day that included a timed climb of the 'Wee Rest'. Frank Grounds (Jupiter) came second in a saloon class (and therefore probably in LOL1) between a Riley and an MG in a day that saw thunderstorms, severe flooding and landslides across Highland roads. Before the first day was out Grounds had put his car in a ditch inflicting quite some damage – there were 17 other first day retirements.

In the 16th International Alpine Rally 10–16 July 1953, the two Jupiters among the 101 starters did not uphold the high quality of the previous year's failures. The first – 585 mile – stage led the competitors from Marseilles, over Mont Genévre into Italy to Monza for the standing km test held in bitter cold at night. After Monza the route led to Bergamo, a time-check at Male over the Mendola Pass and down into Bolzano, about 40 miles short of the end of the first stage at Cortina. At Bolzano the Jupiter of Dr A.E. Bernstein/E. Yates was seen being towed away, and shortly afterwards the Jupiter of T.G. Cunane/E. de Vadder (NTJ930) retired with a blown gasket. The 1.6-litre class was dominated by Porsches.

The 7th Lisbon International Rally, 13–18 October 1953 was the last round of the European touring car championship, and the decider this year. It was the toughest Lisbon so far, partly due to the inclusion of three winding mountain sections of unmade road and partly due to the weather which provided rain, fog, cloudbursts, mud, branches fallen, bridges swept away. At Lisbon there was an acceleration/braking test, followed by five laps of a twisty round-the-houses circuit. Nogueira (Porsche) again won. This was the last international rally to have a Jupiter participating and found Maurice Tew (620) finishing overall 25th and about 8th in the 1.3–2-litre class.

61 Mrs Lola Grounds at the Goodwood Test, 1953 RAC Rally: Autocar

The 4th MCC *Daily Express* National Rally, 11–14 November 1953, had no less than 401 starters and 321 finishers in what was primarily a navigation run, for the special tests, although searching, were not chassis-breakers. After 360 miles the routes from the seven starts had converged (at Harrogate) for the rest of the rain-soaked 1,225 mile length through the Yorkshire, Cumbriain and Northumberland moors, the Scottish Lowlands, then Wales and on down to Hastings for the finish. There was a timed downhill braking test just after Harrogate, an uphill acceleration test at Brampton, a 20-mile regularity run near Penrith, and a stop/restart test near the Bwlch-y-Groes attempted from the north, in half a gale with horizontal rain. Cars then headed south to the maneouvring tests on a hill outside Hastings for competitors dead tired after day and night driving, then on into Hastings to the sea front in sight of the finish outside the Queens Hotel for a braking and a garaging test.

The Jupiter entrants were G.A.R. Yull/Mrs G.W. Yull; B.G. Wolfson/H. Levinson; W.S. Underwood/J. Taylor; J.R. Smith; E.L. Taylor/Mrs J.A.M. Simmonds, running open, and F. Grounds/J.B. Hay (29); R. Harrison/P. Guest (929); Mr and Mrs Tew (620); A. Gordon/P. Steiner (NLX909), running closed. Grounds either failed to start or retired before reaching the first control, while Underwood reached the first control but not the second. E.L. Taylor lost 249.4 points at his third control and retired.

Bill Boddy for *Motor Sport* observed the hill test at Hastings, 'a revealing one in respect of weight distribution and awkward gear changes' and remarked that 'J.R. Smith, hood up, made a lot of noise and spin while Tew's Jupiter also gave evidence of being too light at the back . . . very excellent runs were put up by Gordon (Jupiter), Masefield-Baker (Javelin)'.

Wolfson is known to have reached the final tests at Hastings. All finishing Jupiters scored below the standard average for the class: Yull lost 46.28, Tew 38.25, Baker 30.34, Harrison 22.65 and Gordon 12.46. Gordon came 8th in the general category and third in the 1101–1500 cc closed production car class – had he run in the open class he would have been classified second. A Javelin was 20th in the general category.

On the last day the rain cleared for the Concours d'Élégance held on the Marine Parade: R. Harrison's Jupiter, suitably scrubbed, recorded a class win in the category for open cars in the price range £550–£850 before tax, excluding cars manufactured before 1947.

The 5th International Tulip Rally, 27 April–2 May 1953, contained no Jupiters but of the several Javelins the foremost was HAK743 for Becquart and Ziegler in Becquart's last drive for Jowett. He had won the 1952 RAC in that car; in the July of that year Wilkins had won the first National Fuel Economy Run in it at 67.86 mpg over 828 miles and although the 1953 Monte was not a success for HAK743, with Becquart back at the wheel it came close to a good result in the RAC a few months later. By the Tulip it was in good form but (in common with many other rally cars) bending the rules ever so slightly, in this case in that it had a Jupiter front/side exhaust pipe, and tuning options such as these had not only to be generally available but also listed in the manufacturer's catalogue.

At the conclusion of the rally the organisers swooped on eight well placed cars and disqualified two class leaders, Becquart's Javelin and Elliott's Sunbeam-Talbot. Earlier there had been disqualified the Fords of Gatsonides/Worledge, Mrs N. Mitchell/Mrs J. Leavens, T.C. Harrison/Reg Phillips, the Sunbeam-Talbot of P. Fotheringham-Parker, a Peugeot and another Ford, all over the issue of 'standard' fittings. The class was won anyway by the Javelin of Zuylen van Nijevelt/F.M.A. Eschauzier. By now, however, Grandfield had left Jowetts, few Javelins (and no Bradfords) remained to be built, the R4 was under way and clearly intended for competition if there was to be any, so Jowetts sold the Javelin and it was entered in the 1954 Monte by a Croydon garage – only to be scratched when it was clear that there would be no more production from Idle. John Bolster tested it in September 1953, still with its Jupiter pipe: 0 to 50 mph in 13.61 secs; 0 to 60 mph in 19.2 secs.

CHAPTER 4 Races and Speed Events: 1950 to 1953

Some famous drivers were gathered at the 2.89 mile Silverstone circuit on 26 August 1950 for the six races of the day and included Ascari, Fangio, Leslie Johnson, Levegh, Moss, Nuvolari, to list a few, and among the competing marques were Alfa-Romeo, Alta, Aston Martin, ERA, Ferrari, Frazer Nash, Jaguar, Lago-Talbot, Maserati, and many more. The V16 BRM made its very first race appearance (shearing a drive shaft on the start line) and on a humbler level Jowett Cars Ltd, in the person of Charles Grandfield, their engineering manager had entered their revamped Le Mans class winner GKW111 in the 1 Hour Production Sports Car Race for cars of up to 2-litres. Horace Grimley, chief experimental engineer, in his first and probably only major race, was in a 15-strong class containing John Gott (HRG) and six other HRGs, the TC of Harry Lester and the three works Stage IIC TD MGs of Dick Jacobs, Ted Lund, and George Phillips. Despite an unnerving spin at Becketts he was able to bring the Jupiter to an indicative class fifth (68.89 mph) behind the three TDs and the class-winning HRG of Gerry Ruddock (71.78 mph) but fortunately just ahead of the HRG of Peter Clark, for it rudely shook off its spare wheel on the final lap.

62 Horace Grimley waits for the off, Silverstone One-Hour Production Car Race. The car is the Le Mans class-winner GKW111: Guy Griffiths

63 Grimley earned a class 5th, after a spin at Becketts, in the 1950 Silverstone One-Hour: Motor Sport

The three-hour 18th RAC Tourist Trophy, first run in 1905 and the world's oldest established motor race, was held on 16 September 1950 at the new 7.416-mile Dundrod circuit, formed from country lanes near Belfast in Northern Ireland. Eligibility was limited to unsupercharged production cars and virtually no modifications from standard or factory-available standard tuning options were permitted. It is not clear how Jowetts circumvented the requirement for at least twenty examples to have been built for, although the Jupiter was unequivocally a true production car – and in production – only three had been completed before the race. In many ways the rules resembled those of Le Mans, with only parts carried in the car to be used during the race, and the standard jack from the car to be used for wheel changing and so forth.

The $1\frac{1}{2}$-litre class comprised the works TD II team of Lund, Jacobs and Phillips, and an HRG and a TC team, whilst among the individual entries GKW111 renewed its acquaintance with Tom Wisdom. Wisdom disheartened the MGs (their 9.3:1 compression ratio and other modifications were only admitted by the RAC after much pressure) by getting down to 6 mins 28 secs in (dry) practice compared with 6 mins 38 secs for the quickest HRG (of P. Clark) and the best MG time of 6 mins 48 secs.

Jacobs was the last away, except for Wisdom, as the Jupiter would not fire up easily in the heavy rain that was now falling. The TDs had the class lead for the first lap but on lap two, just after leaving Wheelers Corner, they were all overtaken by the very fast moving Jupiter: and although the TDs were then fully wound up it continued to pull away from them. A 'Go Faster' pit signal was continually posted for the MGs.

Alas, having built up an impregnable lead, the Jupiter's engine broke its crankshaft in the first instance of a trouble that was to cause headaches for Jowetts' best brains for some time to come. This particular crank had survived Le Mans and much further testing, but its end had come, no doubt assisted by the (probably illegally) raised compression ratio of 8.75.

Stirling Moss (XK120) won his first major production car event, a dazzling drive in the torrential rain that had descended for the entire afternoon.

The December 1950 issue of *Road and Track* alerts us to the 8-lap (52.8-mile) race for the Queen Catherine Monteur Cap, one of three races at Watkins Glen, New York State, one saturday in the fall of 1950. The straked Jupiter (1 or 5, surely 1) of L. Whiting, Jr., suffered some minor front end damage, probably haybale impact, and later retired, on the fourth or fifth lap, with sounds indicating all was not well with the engine.

The BRDC 1 hour (26 laps) Production Sports Car Race was held at Silverstone on 5 May 1951 and contesting the $1\frac{1}{2}$-litre category were five stage II TDs (Jacobs, Ted Lund, George Phillips, Dalton, Bigger), three HRGs (Ruddock, J.V.S. Brown, Keen) and GKW111, this time driven by Bert Hadley.

Hadley took the lead from the start and established himself with a second lap time of 2 mins 19 secs, a time beaten only once by Jacobs (2 mins 18 secs) and equalled by Lund. Hadley maintained a lead of between 2 and 5 secs while Jacobs and Lund swopped 2nd and 3rd places until the tenth lap, when Jacobs, the eventual winner, consolidated second place behind the flying Jupiter.

The MG's speed crept up until the energetic Jacobs was on the Jupiter's tail and getting alongside it at Club Corner. With no hope of beating the Jupiter on maximum speed he forced Hadley to use third gear for longer than he would have liked.

After 15 laps at 72.66 mph Hadley withdrew with gasket failure shortly before Lund broke a valve and ruined his engine. Fastest HRG lap was 2 mins 35 secs.

Giant's Despair Hill Climb, Philadelphia, 12 May 1951, was competed in by 63 cars, including 19 MGs, some supercharged, and therefore in a different class from the Jupiter of George C. Rand, which ascended in a best time of 1 min 32.3 secs, behind

64 Gurzeler on his way to a win at Bremgarten

five MGs and an HRG but ahead of seven more MGs and others in his class. The climb is 5280 feet, and paved all the way. There were 20,000 spectators.

Bremgarten Sports Car Race was held on the 4.52-mile forest circuit near Berne, Switzerland, in May 1951; first in the 1½-litre class was T. Gurzeler (Jupiter).

Rheineck/Walzenhauzen Hill Climb, Switzerland, was also held during May or early June. Gurzeler (Jupiter) was first in the 1½-litre class.

The BRDC International British Empire Trophy, Isle of Man, 14 June 1951. For the previous four years a Formula 1 event and originally a Brooklands outer circuit race, it was this year for catalogue sports cars, at least ten examples to have been built and sold by 1 May. Sundry engine modifications, higher compression ratio, and any fuel were permitted and the full race distance was 35 laps of the twisty Willarton circuit (3.88 miles), a street course on the outskirts of Douglas. The 1½-litre class contained three 'staged' MGs but the rest could not strictly be described as catalogue sports cars: W.H. Robinson entered his saloon Jupiter NTB603, EO/SA/37R, with at least the engine and chassis as the factory intended, whereas the two Lester-MGs and Cooper-MGs were sports-racing vehicles, made in tiny quantities for that one purpose only and were so basic as to have twice the power/weight ratio of a Jupiter. Robinson's best practice lap was 4 mins 19 secs, 53.9 mph, whereas Jacobs and Lund (MG) had practised at 4 mins 5 secs, and Griffith in the faster Lester-MG was only 8 secs slower than Moss's (Frazer Nash) 3 mins 26 secs. Goodyear persuaded Robinson to replace the Michelin S tyres he had practised on for some very stiff tyres for the race. This upset the handling and soon knocked out the front shock absorbers to further modify things to the point where spectators were scattering at his approach. The only special-bodied Jupiter to have raced in an international event was put out of its misery on the 11th lap near the top of Brae Hill when its engine seized, ending remarks by John Bolster, the race commentator, about the car's ugly bodywork having been constructed by a relation of Heath Robinson – shortly after Jacob's MG dropped out with piston trouble. It had averaged 54 mph for 40 miles.

SCCA Races at the 3-mile Studebaker Test

DOUGLAS ISLE OF MAN

3·8789 **Miles**

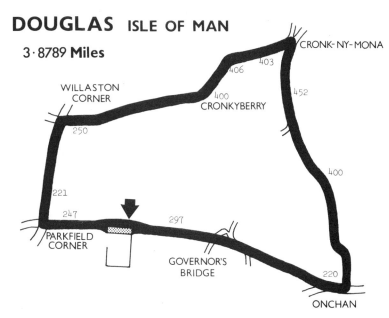

Track, South Bend, Indiana, 23 June 1951. The Jupiter of Mr Donker retired from a 10-car 1½-litre field.

SCCA Burke Mountain Hill Climb, 24 June 1951. A 1¾-mile paved climb starting at 1,900 feet and ascending to the summit at 3,267 feet, where there was an excellent view of Vermont. Its sinuosity could have been designed for Jupiters as there are five hairpins and another five sharp curves. Class 4 (1 to 1.5 litres) went to Dexter Coffin's stunning red Jupiter with 4 mins 42.2 secs from a Porsche (5 mins 04 secs) and a TD (5 mins 12.9 secs). A BMW in class 3 recorded a third place 5 mins 02 secs. secs.

Rest and Be Thankful Hill Climb, 7 July 1951. K.B. Miller (Jupiter, and by inference JGA123) was class 8th with 81.89

65 Numbers indicate spot height in feet

66 British Empire Trophy: 2 Mayers, Lester-MG; 5 R.W. Jacobs, MG; 6 Ted Lund, MG; 9 L. Leonard, Cooper-MG; 10 G.Reece, Cooper-MG; 11 B.Whitehouse, Aston Martin; 12 G. Abecassis, Aston Martin; 24 S.Hill, Healey; 26 Reg Parnell, Nash-Healey; 29 P. Scott-Russell, Allard. Robinson's saloon Jupiter is just ahead of the MG of Dick Jacobs: S.R.Keig

67 Robinson's saloon
sweeps across S.Hill's
bows, British Empire
Trophy: S.R.Keig

secs. Best 1250 MG was Ted Lund (fourth behind three specials) with 71.25 secs and another TDII recorded 75.27 secs. Best HRG was 84.27 secs.

SCCA Two-Day National Meeting, 21–22 July 1951. Races and speed trials at the $\frac{1}{2}$-mile banked track at Thompson, Connecticut. Neat cornering produced a clear win for George Weaver, driving Dexter Coffin's Jupiter in a five-lap race for $1\frac{1}{2}$-litre sports cars, against Hugh Byfield (Jupiter) and a collection of TCs, TDs, and similar cars.

Gap Hill Climb, Singapore, 3 September 1951, on the South Buona Vista road. R.E.N. Wills (HAK41, E1/SA/11OR) was timed at 58.6 secs, to be placed third in the 3-litre category behind a BMW and a TC; by inference both the Jupiter and the TC would have been supercharged. The locally-built-from-Jowett-components 'Airhen Special' recorded 56.5 secs in the same event.

The *Motor Sport* staff car, Jupiter HAK 268 (98) was in the car park for the second MCC (Motor Cycle Club) meeting, Silverstone, 8 September 1951. In the first 1 hour high-speed trial, Class 1, up to $1\frac{1}{2}$-litre, Alf Thomas (JTM100, EO/SA/38R, open Rawson-bodied Jupiter) averaged 61.10 mph, a speed higher than that of seven out of the eight HRGs taking part.

(By comparison a five lapper for $1\frac{1}{2}$-litre cars was won at 62.65 mph.)

Whilst not an actual race these high-speed trials certainly looked like them to spectators: a not too arduous target speed was set and the drivers would lap as fast as possible to see by how much the target speed could be exceeded. Alf Thomas, one of the first of the sporting Jowett agents, a fine driver and a first-class mechanic, favoured events of this type.

On the same day at Croft, in a Yorkshire Sports Car Club event, K.N. Lee (Jupiter) was 3rd in a race for saloons of up to $1\frac{1}{2}$-litre. First was G.P. Mosby (Jupiter-engined Javelin) at 58.09 mph and second was a wheel-hopping Morgan of 1267 cc. K.N. Lee was for many years a prominent member of the YSCC as were Tommy Wise and Ted Booth: the Jupiter was probably a standard car running closed, or possibly Ted Booth's car as Ted raced LHR2 (in a five-lapper dominated by MGs) at the same meeting.

The RAC Tourist Trophy took place on 15 September 1951 and was again at the Dundrod road circuit near Belfast. The date was convenient, for Jowetts wanted some publicity at this time with the UK launch of the Jupiter barely one month ahead. A change this year was that now only ten examples had to have been constructed and an ambiguity in the regula-

tions, possibly deliberate, allowed in certain non-production sports racers.

There were 37 participants in cars ranging from 747 cc to 5420 cc but the largest group was the 1101 to 1500 cc category, made up of the 1250 cc Lund/Phillips/Jacobs TD stage II trio, three more MGs and the Reece cousins' MG-engined Cooper ranged against the Lester-MGs of Lester and Mayers (MG unit bored out of 1467 cc) and four Jupiters: the three works entries, GKW111, HAK365, HAK366, for Tommy Wise, Tom Wisdom and Bert Hadley, plus the privately entered JGA123 of Bill Skelly. The three works Jupiters had the advantage of Le Mans tankage and would be able to complete the race without fuel stops.

The race was run on a handicap basis – a set distance directly proportional to engine capacity having to be covered in the shortest time, and implemented by credit laps and a staggered start. The Jupiters and Lester-MGs had one less credit lap than the 1250 cc MGs and the Cooper-MG

which were started 2 mins 45 secs after the 1467/1486 cc cars and thus received a net lead of about 60 per cent of a lap. Class positions, however, were allocated purely on an average speed basis – the race was run over nominally 43 laps, nearly 319 miles, and under the handicapping system this was the target distance for cars of over 5-litres; a sliding scale meant that the $1\frac{1}{2}$-litre group had a target of 40 laps. The race was at an end when the first car completed its target.

There was a timed kilometre stretch, following a half mile of straight after a fastish right-hander (gradient 1 in 40 down), possible as a check on how 'production' the cars really were.

The cars lined up in echelon in front of their pits for the start, drivers seated, engines stopped. The drivers pressed their starters at the fall of the flag and were sent off in bunches according to their time allowances.

The four Jupiters made a good start as

68 The Rawson-bodied Jupiter of Alf Thomas at Silverstone in 1953 :National Motor Museum

69 The Jupiter team cars ready for the 1951 TT, Dundrod

70 *1951 TT at Dun-
drod–the start. A pit
marshal holds an Allard
(No 6) at bay:* Autocar

did Mayers's Lester-MG, which swooped
around the Jupiters as they were still leaving
the pit area. Harry Lester's Lester-MG did
not start well on the button but was on
Wise's tail after one lap, having already
picked off Skelly. The three works Jupiters,
headed by Hadley, accelerated and Wise,
looking in his mirror, saw Lester recede, a
gap of $2\frac{1}{2}$ mins having opened up after ten
laps. By this time Mayers had lapped his
team mate and was a formidable 4 mins
ahead of Hadley in the leading Jupiter. One
lap later Lester's car was seen slowly misfiring its way back to its pit with a broken
rocker.

Hadley, Wisdom and Wise continued to
circulate with 45 secs between them. On
lap 14 the Mayers car retired with run
bearings and joined the MGs of Collen
(gasket) and Phillips (clutch) in the dead
car park, with nearly two-thirds of the race
still ahead.

After two hours' racing, Hadley in the
leading Jupiter was amongst the faster
MGs; Wise was trailing 40 secs behind
Hadley and a bare 2 secs behind Wisdom
who was, however, about to make a 3-
minute pit stop with a misfiring problem
and to take on oil. Skelly had been lapped
by the works Jupiters, while Reece in his
little Cooper-MG was still $3\frac{1}{2}$ mins ahead of
the leading Jupiter on handicap. Four laps
later Hadley slipped past the Sparrowe/
Loens car and within another two laps Wise

was also past what would be the highest
placed MG. Reece was by now about 1
minute ahead.

At the 3-hour point (28 laps) Hadley
and Wise were still circulating like con-
tented clockwork, 40 secs between them,
Hadley a reduced 26 secs behind the ugly
but regular Cooper-MG. Wise had opened
up a lead of $1\frac{1}{2}$ mins on Loens. The race
ended after about $3\frac{3}{4}$ hours when the
XK120C of Stirling Moss became the first
car to complete its target. Reece crossed
the finish line 14 secs ahead of Hadley and
was placed ahead of him in the general
classification, although Hadley and Wise in
averaging higher speeds were placed ahead
of Reece in the class order. The 1500 cc
cars had been required to cover 40 laps but
due to the imbalance of the handicapping
their race was over after 35; nevertheless
Hadley had the satisfaction of achieving a
higher percentage of his target speed than
Reece, meaning that had both cars continued to maintain their average speeds for
40 laps Hadley would have overhauled
Reece during lap 38.

Tom Wisdom's Jupiter, still running at
the end, had lost 9 minutes in 4 pit stops,
the engine ailment requiring both water
and oil at around the 2-hour mark: thereafter a subdued HAK365, smoking, for a
ring had picked up, lapped at the same
speed as Skelly.

Von Eberhorst was present in the Aston

Summary

DRIVER	CLASS	GENERAL CATEGORY	ACTUAL LAPS	TIME ON HANDICAP	AVERAGE SPEED (mph)	FASTEST LAP	SPEED (mph)	SPEED THROUGH TIMED km (mph)
Hadley	1	18	35	3 hrs 46 mins 40 secs	68.71	6 mins 21 secs	70.07	91.20
Wise	2	19	35	3 hrs 47 mins 03 secs	68.59	6 mins 17 secs	70.82	92.90
Reece	3	17	35	3 hrs 46 mins 26 secs	67.63	6 mins 24 secs	69.52	87.32
Loens	4	20	34	3 hrs 44 mins 25 secs	66.24	6 mins 33 secs	67.93	83.81
Jacobs	5	21	34	3 hrs 47 mins 46 secs	65.26	6 mins 37 secs	67.25	81.98
Lund	6	22	33	3 hrs 43 mins 05 secs	64.62	6 mins 38 secs	67.08	80.44
McCaldin	7	23	33	3 hrs 47 mins 29 secs	63.36	6 mins 40 secs	66.74	82.54
Skelly	8	24	32	3 hrs 48 mins 27 secs	62.33	6 mins 54 secs	64.49	–
Wisdom	–	–	30	3 hrs 44 mins 22 secs		6 mins 24 secs	69.52	90.63
Mayers	–	–	14	1 hr 27 mins 20 secs		6 mins 04 secs	73.34	86.98
Lester	–	–	11	1 hr 21 mins 09 secs		6 mins 36 secs	67.42	–

Martin pits to see his latest car, the DB3 prototype (he was responsible for its tubular chassis*) in the hands of Lance Macklin hold second place until delayed and later forced out by a cracked exhaust manifold.

The Nottingham SCC races at Gamston, 6 October 1951, demonstrated the trend in British sports car racing. At club level, where regulations were plastic, the specialist sports racing cars, typified by Hawthorne's Riley and Downing's Connaught, were supreme and it was rare for the private owner racing his own off-the-peg car to figure in the places. However, in event 3, for non-supercharged sports cars of up to $1\frac{1}{2}$-litre over five laps, K. N. Downing (Connaught), 75.46 mph, was first, P.B. Reece (Cooper-MG), 73.51 mph, second, and T.C. Wise (GWK111), 72.55 mph, was third.

Sports Car Races at Winfield, 13 October 1951. T.C. Wise entered GKW111 in two of the day's races. In the first race of the day, five laps for sports cars of up to $1\frac{1}{2}$-litres, he drove the Jupiter, hood down, to third place behind Ken Downing in his Connaught, and a Rover-engined special. Later in the afternoon, hood up, he led all the way to an easy victory in the five-lap saloon-car event to win at 64.8 mph from Ken Downing in a 2,443 cc Healey saloon, and another Healey. Skelly (JGA123) came 13th in this event and a Javelin was 17th and last.

Bill Boddy from *Motor Sport* was in attendance, having achieved a running average of 46 mph from London to Darlington in HAK268 on the way up and averaging 49 mph on the way back between those two towns. (He spent both nights at Darlington.) He reported that the total mileage of 676 miles was covered at 28 mpg.

California Sports Car Club Torrey Pines races near San Diego on 9 December 1951. The 2.7-mile circuit, situated on a gentle slope a few hundred feet from cliffs overlooking the Pacific Ocean, has two straights, one bordered by eucalyptus trees, and plenty of sharp bends. One of these was the undoing of newcomer-to-racing Newton Small (Jupiter), whose well-driven and sweetly running car spun on the last lap of the inaugural ten-lap race to lose the lead to an MG.

*Made from 4-inch and 5-inch chrome molybdenum steel tubes, the chassis showed similarities to that of the Jupiter: there was a similar triangulated structure over the rear axle while transverse torsion bars were employed front and rear.

In its review of the 1951 season *Autosport* (21 December) remarked that Britain did not produce a $1\frac{1}{2}$-litre sports racing machine capable of matching the Gordini Simcas, OSCAs, and Fiats, in short distance races and considered that the R1 Jupiter appeared to it to be the best solution to the problem. The magazine warned that the 1.1-litre Porsche, so reliable at Le Mans, would be raced in 1.5-litre form in 1952, and expressed the hope that the R1 be persevered with. Of course it was, although for just the single Le Mans event; and, with the engine's power limit quickly reached, the opportunity for streamlining the front end, presented by a change in the regulations, was allowed to pass.

For Britain the 1952 season saw the arrival of the amateur Jupiter driver, who found a proliferation of production-based specials with initially only sparse interference from the Continent, while in the USA in the production car events, where Jupiters seem most usually to have joined issue, Porsche began to take the upper hand.

71 Tommy Wise leads the field in a five-lap handicap race, Winfield, in October 1951: Motor Sport

72 Photographers rush to capture Newton's big slide, Torrey Pines, December 1951. He lost his lead to an MG: Autocar

GOODWOOD

2·4 Miles

naught, and a pair of MG specials), the rest of the pack being made up from six MGs and two HRGs. Starting positions were chosen by ballot. A series of photographs shows on lap 1 the eventual winner, Davis, pulling away from the press, while on lap 2 Robinson was holding his own with three of the MGs and the Hurgs. Later pictures show a lonely Jupiter, and partially folded front race plate suggests a brush with a straw bale, although it seems to have finished ahead of T.W. Dargue's silver MG special. The handicap affair had for the red Jupiter a more dramatic moment for when travelling at nearly 100 mph Robinson saw the car's nose dip and the oil-pressure gauge needle flip to zero – the crankshaft had broken and split the block.

Fourth Annual Palm Springs Road Race, California, 23 March 1952. The first race, for production cars of up to $1\frac{1}{2}$-litre, was won by a Siata Sports, with a TD II second and Bruce Mooney (Jupiter) taking third, there being at least 15 finishers. The other Jupiter was that of the English driver Dennis Buckley but his mount sounded poorly and retired after three laps.

Scottish Sporting Car Club Turnberry Airfield Sprint, 29 March 1952. W.A. Brearley in an unidentified Jupiter was placed class third behind a special and an MG, ahead of a Singer and two more MGs.

BARC Ludgershall Hill Climb, 6 April 1952. N. Freedman (509) was an easy first in the $1\frac{1}{2}$-litre closed car class at 36.8 secs.

Bruce Mooney (Jupiter) retired on lap 7 of the 100-mile Pebble Beach Trophy race in May 1952.

In 1952 the BRDC took over the Silverstone lease and revised the circuit in various small ways: lap length went up by 1.3 per cent, times by slightly more.

In the production touring car event, $1\frac{1}{2}$-litre class, at the BRDC *Daily Express* Production Car Races, Silverstone, 10 May 1952, the three Javelins of Hadley, Bennett, and John Marshall (GKW777) had as sole company the $1\frac{1}{4}$-litre MG saloon of MG man Dick Jacobs. Hadley's Javelin 'stepped off quite well, suggesting lightweight. It had lowered suspension and I could take most corners on full noise. One of the marshals said it looked horrifying in the corners but I liked it.' It also had a rather special engine that regrettably had seen far too many hours on a test bed; the car was very fast, indicating 105 mph on the run

The second annual Florida Handicap, on 8 March 1952, was run under SCCA rules over a 3.3-mile course laid out at the Vero Beach Municipal Airport. There were 1-hour, 6-hour, and 12-hour races, with class divisions permitting displacements from 500 cc up to an unrestricted class from which the overall winner of the 1-hour race, Paul O'Shea (Allard-Cadillac) emerged. This race had a field of 22 cars and the $1\frac{1}{2}$-litre class opposition to Richard Thierry's Jupiter included five MGs, two open Porsches (one an ex-works lightweight machine for VW and Porsche importer Max Hoffman) and an Offenhauser-engined HRG. Max Hoffman was placed overall second on handicap, winning the class from the HRG and the Jupiter.

International Race for Sports Cars and Production-Based Specials, 9 March 1952, run on ice near Helsingland, Sweden. The participating Jupiter was not among the first three finishers.

The BARC Goodwood 8th Members' Meeting, on 22 March 1952, was for sports cars only, and W.H. Robinson entered GKY256 – in its first race outing in a five-lap scratch race and a five-lap handicap. There were seven sports racers in the scratch event (Lester-MGs for Mayers and Ruddock, Davis's Cooper-MG, a Lamgia entered by Harry Lester, Ken Downing's Con-

down to Stowe and Hadley was well up in the field when with less than two laps remaining the inevitable happened and the top came off one of the pistons, making a tremendous clatter. The pistons were experimental and long past their estimated life. Jacobs, slower on the straights than the other Javelins, but quicker round the corners, went on to win, 9.4 secs ahead of Bennett.

By contrast the Production Sports Car Race, 1½-litre group, had 11 entrants: Leonard and Davis had doubled production and built another Cooper-MG, there were Lester-MGs for Mayers and Ruddock, while the true production-based contingent was made up of TDs for Lund and Line, a 1.2-litre Austin A40 sports, Sparrowe's 1.1 Morgan and three Jupiters.

The factory had loaned George Phillips HAK366; Skelly was back once more with JGA123; and John Burness had entered a Jupiter for C. Le Strange Metcalf; again no HRGs, for the TD/HRG battles were now waged elsewhere. The interest in the class lay in whether the Coopers or the Lesters were the quicker.

The start was Le Mans type, with cars lined up in order of practice times and it is worth noting that practice may have been perfunctory as there seems little difference between practice time and race average. George Phillips left the other Jupiters and the rest of the production cars far behind; Mayers in the quicker of the Lester-MGs, in the effort of keeping up with the Cooper-MGs broke a con-rod and deposited crankcase oil on the approach to Stowe. Then,

74 Goodwood, March 1952, at the start of the race in which Robinson broke his crank. Scratch car (19) was the 2,600 cc blown Alfa of Nigel Mann; in front of him is the Cooper-MG of F.C.Davis: Guy Griffiths

75 Young Bill Skelly finished ahead of another Jupiter in the Silverstone production car race, 1952: Guy Griffiths

with the retirement of Leonard's Cooper-MG, Phillips was able to bring the Jupiter in at class 3rd (70.25 mph) behind the remaining Cooper-MG (75.85 mph) and Lester-MG (72.51 mph) and one place below a Healey Silverstone in the general classification at 20th.

Moss, XK120C, was the overall winner and von Eberhorst-designed Aston Martin DB3s were close 2nd, 3rd and 4th to take the team prize. The two privately entered Jupiters, lacking works support and expertise, finished poorly behind the TDs and the Morgan.

PRODUCTION SPORTS CARS — RACE

OVERALL	CLASS	DRIVER	CAR	BEST PRACTICE LAP	AVERAGE LAP TIME	TIME	SPEED (mph)	NUMBER OF LAPS
16	1	Davis	Cooper-MG	2 mins 17 secs	2 mins 19 secs	37 mins 02 secs	75.85	16
18	2	Ruddock	Lester-MG	2 mins 28 secs	2 mins 25 secs	36 mins 09 secs	72.51	15
20	3	Phillips	HAK366	2 mins 29 secs	2 mins 30 secs	37 mins 30 secs	70.75	15
21	4	Sparrowe	Morgan	2 mins 37 secs	2 mins 37 secs	36 mins 34 secs	67.23	14
22	5	Lund	MG TD	2 mins 37 secs	2 mins 37 secs	36 mins 40 secs	67.05	14
23	6	Line	MG TD	2 mins 36 secs	2 mins 37 secs	36 mins 42 secs	66.99	14
24	7	Skelly	JGA123	2 mins 45 secs	2 mins 42 secs	37 mins 56 secs	64.82	14
25	8	Metcalf	Jupiter	2 mins 47 secs	2 mins 47 secs	36 mins 17 secs	62.92	13
26	9	Christie	Austin	2 mins 50 secs	3 mins 00 secs	36 mins 00 secs	58.53	12

(Phillips's fastest lap is estimated to have been 2 mins 25 secs approximately.)

PRODUCTION SALOONS

1	Jacobs	$1\frac{1}{4}$ MG	2 mins 45 secs	2 mins 46 secs	41 mins 32 secs	63.42	15
–	Hadley	Javelin	2 mins 45 secs	–	–	–	(13)
2	Bennett	Javelin	2 mins 46 secs	2 mins 47 secs	41 mins 43 secs	63.15	15
3	Marshall	Javelin	2 mins 48 secs	2 mins 49 secs	42 mins 08 secs	63.02	15

70

Prescott Hill Climb (880 yds), 18 May 1952. Eight hours of hill climbing in front of the largest crowd to assemble for a non-international event.

Climbs of this type are won by the cars that are quickest out of the corners and Hadley felt that his time would have been usefully lower if Jowetts had fitted the Jupiter with the lower gearing he had requested of them. Hadley had engaged the noted mechanic Harry Spears to ensure that his car was properly prepared. The first event, for the smaller capacity sports cars, had attracted 19 starters and the first good time was 53.17 secs by D.F. Ryder (Cooper-MG). Bert Hadley urged the heavier Jupiter (HAK366) up in 53.77 secs with plenty of blue tyre smoke on Pardon hairpin. Best time was 51.20 secs (Ruddock, Lester-MG) but still slower than the four-year-old HRG record. Hadley was fourth in his class.

The Fourth SCCA Annual Day of Sports Car Races at Bridgehampton, Long Island,

76 George Phillips had an enjoyable drive to class 3rd, Silverstone production car race 1952: Guy Griffiths

77 Hadley takes the TT-winning car up Prescott Hill, 18 May 1952

NY, USA, on 24 May 1952. In the 18-lap (72 mile) Sagaponack Trophy race for stock 1½-litre sports cars, Hugh Byfield (Jupiter) is believed to have participated. The trophy was won by a Porsche.

The 14th International British Empire Trophy Race on 29 May 1952 had an all-British entry of 31, of whom 27 started and only 13 finished. The race was on handicap with over 3-litre cars (all Jaguars but for a solitary Allard) on scratch, 1½- to 3-litre cars (6 Frazer Nashes, Buncombe's Healey and a DB3 for Geoff Duke) given one credit lap, and the by now familiar 1½-litre category, four credit laps.

There were three Lester-MGs for Ruddock, Mayers, and P.W.C. Griffith; Davis and Leonard had entered their Cooper-MGs whose tuning may be estimated from the capacity of their MG engines now being up to 1496 cc, against whom were ranked three TDs for M.R.G. Llewellyn/Ted Lund/J.T.K. Line, the TC of P. Jackson and an entry list of five Jupiters. Scratch race distance was 52 laps (201.76 miles) of the 3.88 mile Willarton circuit on the Isle of Man and just under three hours of driving was expected.

The Jupiter of E.W. Cuff Miller and G.A. Dudley (651) was crashed by Dudley into a stone wall at Parkfield during the previous day's practice and failed to start, as did the Jupiter of J.A. Cowap. Robinson was driving his GKY256, engine built for the race by one of his own mechanics, Leslie Armistead, and barely run in by the start of the race – therefore, mindful of last year's seizure he was to take the early part of the race carefully. The other Jupiter with a chance of finishing ahead of the MGs was E1/SA/120R of the experienced Irish Grand Prix driver Joe Kelly; and once

again Bill Skelly was behind the wheel of JGA123, starting from the back of the grid with the TC.

Fastest race lap was posted by Geoff Duke (DB3), naturally very popular with the local spectators, expecting him to repeat his motor-cycle wins. However, the handicapping favoured the 1½-litre cars, specifically the MG-engined Lesters and Coopers. Griffith immediately took the class and race lead and these cars initially filled the first five places: but after two laps (lap 7 on handicap) Kelly replaced Mayers (steering difficulties) in fifth place. After 40 minutes of racing Kelly still held class and race fifth and had averaged 57.42 mph, a speed if maintained sufficient to beat all the MGs. Five minutes later Davis retired his cooper-MG with bearing failure, permitting Kelly to occupy class 4th, although by now lapped by the three leading MG-powered cars. Duke was fifth on handicap. Kelly at his average speed would have been passed by Duke after about 1½ hours' racing but something was slowing him perceptibly, for after holding class and race fourth for 20 minutes he was passed by Duke and a temporarily recovered Mayers. Robinson, happy about his engine but unhappy about getting Kelly's dust in his eyes, realised he hadn't put his goggles on, put them on, passed Kelly and, now class fourth, set out to at least win the '1½-litre production' class.

After two hours' racing, Leonard's Cooper-MG blew its head gasket, letting Robinson into class third: on the retirement of Geoff Duke, Mike Hawthorne (Frazer Nash) moved into his final position, third on handicap and the fastest car to finish.

The race ended when Griffith, who had had a splendid race having led all the way, completed his 48th actual lap after just under three hours of driving, to be followed home by Ruddock, second in class and overall. Robinson's Jupiter came in class third four laps down at overall 7th behind the Lesters, the Frazer Nashes of Hawthorne and Savadori, and the XK120 of Sir J.S. Douglas but nearly a mile ahead of the second Jaguar, lapping the third Jaguar (Bill Black), the two remaining MGs (Llewellyn and Line) and the struggling Joe Kelly – class sixth, 1500 yards behind Line to be placed overall 10th, ahead on handicap but unlike Robinson slower in average speed than three out of the four finishing Jaguars. Skelly retired a few laps from the end (valve trouble) thus saving him from certain last place; three laps from the end Line's TC ran a big end.

78 Robinson and GKY256 before the 1952 British Empire Trophy. Only one finishing XK120 averaged a higher speed than the Jupiter: S.R. Keig

British Empire Trophy analysis

OVERALL	DRIVER	CAR	CLASS	SPEED	FASTEST LAP	SPEED
1	Griffith	Lester-MG	1	64.20 mph	3 mins 31 secs	66.18 mph
2	Ruddock	Lester-MG	2	64.07 mph	3 mins 33 secs	65.56 mph
3	Hawthorne	Frazer Nash	1	67.88 mph		
4	Salvadori	Frazer Nash	2	67.31 mph		
5	Mitchell	Frazer Nash	3	66.79 mph		
6	Douglas	Jaguar	1	65.22 mph		
7	Robinson	GKY256	3	58.12 mph	3 mins 55 secs	59.42 mph
8	Line	MG TDII	4	56.61 mph	4 mins 01 secs	57.94 mph
9	Llewellyn	MG TDII	5	56.30 mph	4 mins 02 secs	57.70 mph
10	Kelly	E1/SA/120R	6	56.30 mph	3 mins 55 secs	59.42 mph
11	Boshier	Jaguar	2	57.84 mph		
12	Black	Jaguar	3	57.07 mph		
13	Holt	Jaguar	4	51.39 mph		
	Lund	MG TDII	(10 laps)		4 mins 07 secs	56.53 mph
	Skelly	JGA123	(33 laps)		4 mins 14 secs	54.98 mph
	Jackson	MG TC	(39 laps)		4 mins 02 secs	57.70 mph

The performance of the Jupiter in tight street racing was demonstrated by an incident early in the race. Robinson was passed by the Frazer Nash of Stirling Moss and a gap of about 50 yards quickly opened up. Moss entered the chicane at the start of a very twisty part of the circuit and was slowed more than the Jupiter which closed on the Frazer Nash – Robinson actually bringing the Jupiter alongside at the apex of the corner opposite the Jolly Sailor. The temptation to pass was resisted, and Moss went on his way, to get within 1 second of Duke's best time before retiring with a variety of troubles.

Le Mans and Silverstone apart, there were in 1952 no races for the works Jupiters for reasons that are explored elsewhere, but amateur owner-drivers continued to contest the lesser events to good effect. At the Wirral MC Sprint at Rhydymwym, 30 March 1952, E.P. Scragg, the noted Alta-

Jaguar driver, in a rare appearance for him in a car not built with cycle wings, notched class third in a Jupiter.

The BARC Brunton Hill Climb, near Ludgershall, 6 April 1952. Class win for Neil Freedman (509).

The Eight-Clubs Silverstone Races 7 June 1952, opened with a one-hour high speed trial for cars of up to 1½-litre, and among the qualifiers were F.E. Still (521) and D. Crowe (Jupiter). There is photographic evidence for the presence of MXA506 (Neil Freedman) and Jupiter LRU504, which could be Crowe's car. It should be mentioned that the event's organiser, two weeks earlier, had proposed a race at this meeting for Cooper-MGs, Lester-MGs, and R1 Jupiters to determine the fastest British 1½-litre sports racer but regrettably this challenge was not taken up, partly no doubt due to the shortness of notice and

79 Silverstone club circuit–Eight-Clubs, 7 June 1952: Guy Griffiths

80 *The veteran Irish Grand Prix driver Joe Kelly at Boreham, June 1952:* Guy Griffiths

for Jowetts, the proximity of Le Mans. The MG-powered cars could lap the club circuit at around 68+ mph around this time. However, as to the R1, all one can say is that as Alf Thomas was eventually able to get the R4, of similar weight and power but poorer handling round at over 67 mph, it could have been a close contest.

The West Essex CC held their second meeting of 1952 on 20 June at the 3-mile Boreham circuit and in the first event of the day, a five-lap handicap for $1\frac{1}{2}$-litre sports cars, Joe Kelly (120) finished third behind Mayers (Lester-MG) and Davis (Cooper-MG). Kelly's speed was 71.1 mph.

The BARC/Jersey MC Jersey International Road Race, 10 July 1952, was divided into two laps and a final. G.A. Dudley (651) had practice troubles with his Jupiter and was soon left behind in his heat with the engine sounding unhappy, while in the second heat the Jupiter of A. Wake had an ignition fault and fared no better. In the Jupiter-free final, the first three places were occupied by two Lester-MGs and a Cooper-MG.

At the BARC Members' Day, Goodwood, 26 July 1952, J.D. Lewis (718) came fourth in a five-lap handicap, averaging 63.16 mph around the 2.4-mile Sussex circuit.

The 2nd 750 MC National Six-hour Relay Handicap Race held on 30 July 1952 on the Silverstone 1.608-mile club circuit. Gerald Lascelles claims to have driven the 'Rabbit Hutch' (8) for 70 laps in this event, although no confirmations from the written record has emerged; however, F.E. Still (521) drove in the Harrow CC team, overall

fifth was the St Moritz Tobogganing Club's team which contained G. Davidson (Jupiter), and fourth was the Sporting Owner Drivers' Club in which Alf Thomas (38) drove his special-bodied Jupiter JTM100.

The *Daily Mail* West Essex CC International Meeting at Boreham on 2 August 1952. In a 100-mile race for Le Mans-type sports cars, Joe Kelly (120) had a spirited scrap with Sterry Ashby (HRG Aerodynamic) behind the usual $1\frac{1}{2}$-litre sports racers until after 10 laps, 30 miles, the Jupiter retired with much emission of steam. Another Jupiter, that of C. Swain, also competed.

Aberdeen and District MC Races at Crimmond 9 August 1952. R.D. Barrack (Jupiter) finished third in an eight-lap scratch race for 1.6-litre sports cars, behind a Cooper-MG and an MG in an event that must have confused drivers and spectators alike for a race for 500 cc single-seaters and another for larger capacity sports cars was held concurrently.

Shelsley Walsh Hill Climb, 30 August 1952. A 1,000 yard ascent. Frank Grounds (29) was timed at 61.44 secs and 61.89 secs; five HRGs were faster, averaging 54.4 secs.

Yorkshire Sports Car Club Sprint Day at RAF Croft aerodrome, 6 September 1952. Distance was 7/10 mile on the old perimeter circuit. In the class for sports cars of up to $1\frac{1}{2}$-litre, W.A. Brearley (Jupiter, probably GKW111) comfortably beat Richmond's HRG (38.87 secs) with a class-winning 37.91 secs. Best MG was 39.29 secs and the best Javelin 40.86 secs.

Brighton International Speed Trial, 6 September 1952. The slower cars were allowed one run only. No timing for the Jupiter over the standing km is known, but these speeds were measured over the last 88 yards: A.O. Gosnell, HRG, 81.8 mph; N. Freedman (509), 79.3; an MG, 78.8; and a Javelin (F.M. Baker), 75.0.

BARC Brunton Hill, Climb, near Ludgershall, 7 September 1952. Another run for Neil Freedman (509).

Third MCC Silverstone Race Meeting, 13 September 1952. A chicane was added to the approach to Woodcote. First one-hour trial: first class awards to 11 cars, including N. Freedman (509), G.M. Sharp, (Jupiter), A. Thomas (JTM100). No award to R.E.C. Brookes (Jupiter).

Event 9, five-lap handicap race: C le Strange Metcalf now in a 995 Fiat Balilla was on scratch with another similar car. Limit man L.J. Spiller, in a pre-war Hillman Minx saloon, hung grimly on to his lead up to the last lap when he was passed first by Alf Thomas's fast-moving, cream-coloured Jupiter and then by Neil Freedman's very competently handled green one. Thomas's winning speed was 57.29 mph, both Jupiters having started off the same mark.

Event 10 was the *Motor Sport* Trophy, five-lap handicap, which Freedman (509) won at 55.88 mph ahead of second-placed Alf Thomas, followed by Hely's Healey, Hemsworth's Jaguar, Gibb's Riley, and Peter Morgan's Morgan.

The Bugatti Owners' Club 8th International Prescott Hill Climb, 14 September 1952. Most cars were racing cars and specials and one event saw Ken Wharton (supercharged Cooper-JAP) lower the course record to 43.70 secs, but two events attracted Jupiters. In the sports category up to 1½-litre unsupercharged, L. Townson in J.A. Cowap's Jupiter came 14th out of 14 with times of 57.64 and 58.00 secs. Comparable times were 54.33/54.55 and 56.43/58.44 by the fastest and slowest HRGs and 56.39/57.91 by a 1430 cc MG.

In the production car handicap event, three Jupiters and some comparable cars recorded these times:

	POSITION ON HANDICAP	ACTUAL TIMES (secs)	
A. Black, Javelin	14th	68.07	65.31
a 1250 MG	15th	66.40	56.77
L. Townson (Cowap's Jupiter)	16th	58.96	71.09
I. Sievwright (E2/SA/748R)	17th	59.55	59.58
a Jaguar	18th	56.51	56.39
C.F. Eminson E1/SA/494R	19th	64.55	64.69

Best HRG time was Greenwood's 54.18 secs. Eminson's Jupiter (class 3rd at the Attingham speed trial two weeks before) is known to have been entirely standard and as delivered; it had the distinction of having its photograph taken on the day and this was to represent the model in Georgano's book on sports cars. It is noteworthy that Hadley's time of 53.77 secs was not approached by any of the Jupiters on this occasion, neither was it bettered by an HRG or an MG. Jupiter JDK381 climbed the hill that day and therefore is probably Cowap's.

The Stockholm International Races, 14 September 1952 were on a 1.7 km circuit laid out on Skarpnack Airfield, and attracted entries from England, Ireland, Holland, Belgium, Germany and the Scandinavian countries. In the 1½-litre sports car race, Nathan (Porsche) was favourite, but Wahlberg's Veritas displayed surprising speed and overtook the Nurburgring class winner and another Porsche. Fourth was R. Berg in a 'Jupiter Le Mans' which can be taken to refer to the Swedish R1 replica (6). The next three places were occupied by a Peugeot, a Siata and an HRG.

Sheffield and Hallamshire Speed Trial, 14 September 1952, on a 1-mile circuit. Two Jupiters took part and that of J. Clarke was third in class.

Aston Martin Owners' Club, 20 September 1952, on the 2.7-mile Snetterton circuit. In the half-hour high speed trial which included a compulsory pit-stop to change all spark plugs, the first place in group 3 was taken by the Jupiter of G.M. Sharp, which also received the award for the best performer of the day. A 2-litre Aston Martin was second. Jupiter ECF494 (680) is known to have participated that day, but this is not believed to have been Sharp's: that is thought to be MAC2.

Bo'ness Hill Climb, 20 September 1952, W.A. Brearley (GKW111) was class 6th.

The Bristol MC Castle Coombe end of season race meeting, also on 20 September included a 10 lap race for sports cars of up to 1½-litres. It was oversubscribed and special dispensation came from the RAC, allowing it to run provided there was an echelon start; the race was noteworthy for the first appearance on a British circuit of a Porsche. Of the thirteen cars in the echelon Gillie Tyrer's white BMW held the favoured position while at the other end was the Porsche of C.C. Bannister: running on the proverbial rails the race became a procession with a German car at either end. By the eighth lap Tyrer had lapped J.D. Lewis's Jowett Jupiter (718).

SCCA Race Meeting at Turner Airforce Base, Albany, Georgia, 25 October 1952. Ashley Pace's red Jupiter was first in the under 1,500 cc production sports car race.

The California Sports Car Club's third Torrey Pines Road Races were held on 14 December 1952 around a 2.6-mile course. The first race of the day was for novice drivers over 12 laps in two classes – up to and above $1\frac{1}{2}$-litres displacement – and contained the Jupiters of Lambros, and Hunter Hackney, a student at the University of Southern California. The course allowed high speeds along the pit straight but required heavy breaking for the first corner, one of decreasing radius and reverse camber that caught out many drivers, including Lambros, who broadsided his Jupiter, smartly reversing it on to the grass to avoid a following TC which also spun. Two Singers narrowly missed the MG but a less lucky Siata put itself and the TC out. Lambros then rejoined the race while Hackney capped a successful season's rallying in his daily transport by securing the first and possibly only class victory for a Jupiter in West Coast racing with a time of 32 mins 11.59 secs, 58.15 mph. He was followed home by a Crosley Sports and a TD and was about 1/3 lap behind the XK120 that took the bigger class.

A Le Mans-start race for Production Sports Cars was held at Mount Druitt, NSW, Australia on 28 December 1952, and was probably for cars in standard production trim although state of tune would not have been strictly policed. G. Kemp (Jupiter) came third behind the TD of D. Chivas and the TC of R.W. Warnsley, both well-known names in Australian motor sport.

The Des Pinn Jupiter. Des Pinn, a young dentist from Goulburn, NSW, Australia bought a BRG Jupiter, registered AAJ555, (possibly 186) in January 1952 and proceeded to tune it to a legendary extent, as can be gauged from the need, for other than round-town use, to change spark plugs after the engine was warm. It was lightened by the removal of the usual bumpers, hub-caps, spare wheel, hood, screen, door linings and glass; oversize tyres were fitted and the compression ratio raised. Normal top speed estimated from the tachometer was 104 mph and the car was once timed at 111 mph through the flying eighth on Bathurst's Con-rod Straight (slightly downhill with an unpleasant hump about halfway along) during an unofficial practice – for the car was not actually entered for a race, such things being possible in those days. Des remembered being disappointed with lap times as the climb up the mountain caught the car between gears.

It achieved BTD at an ASCC meeting at Castlereagh (an old aerodrome circuit marked by oil drums) against XK120s and a sports Riley, when it won a scratch race; and BTD at a Mount Druitt meeting. It was a participant in the Castrol Trial of 1952 in which the Jupiter proved ideal: 'During night running the cars encountered a record snowfall on the NSW Central Highlands. At one stage the windscreen wipers froze to the screen and the dash warning light that I had always joked about came on.' One of the leading cars at the time, Des withdrew rather than risk damage as he intended to sell the Jupiter to help set up a dental practice in Rockdale and indeed before the end of the year it had been written off by its new owner, who himself died in the accident. In retrospect Des considered the Jupiter outstanding in handling but variable in reliability; he twice was let down by gasket failure.

The year 1953 saw the same sort of activity as had characterised the previous year and it is noticeable that Alf Thomas, and perhaps also his garage less than 30 miles from Silverstone, was beginning to emerge as a nucleus of competitive Jupiter activity. The season opened as usual with the BARC Members' Meeting at Goodwood on 21 March 1953. Handicap race B produced a fourth place for G.A. Dudley (651); less fortunate was J.D. Lewis (718) who badly damaged his Jupiter on some straw bales. Jupiter HKW429 (544) also raced that day.

West Cornwall MC Closed Hill Climb at Trengwainton, 6 April 1953. K.S. Crutch was timed at 33.84 secs in what the commentator referred to as a 'Jewitt Jopiter'.

Club Charterhall Races at Winfield in Scotland 12 April 1953. Five (2 mile) laps for sports cars of up to $1\frac{1}{2}$-litres. First was W.A. Brearley (GKW111, hood down) at 59.2 mph from two MGs. In a five-lap handicap for saloons of any capacity,

Brearley (GKW111, hood up), came second to a Healey, ahead of an Allard.

BARC Brunton Hill Climb, near Ludgershall, 13 April 1953. Yet another run for Neil Freedman (509).

The fifth Annual Bridgehampton (New York) Sports Car Races promoted by the SCCA on 23 May 1953. The first race, 18 laps of the 4-mile circuit for the Sagaponack Trophy, was for stock production cars of up to 1½-litres; the entry comprised six TDs, a Singer, five Porsches and the grey Jupiter of Pat Riedel. The grey car finished sixth behind the five German cars and two of the MGs retired with engine failures.

The fourth MCC Silverstone Meeting was on 20 June 1953 and in the first one-hour high speed trial, first-class awards went to G.M. Sharp (Jupiter) and Maurice Tew (620) whilst Kenneth Crutch (602) who had bought his Jupiter new from Alf Thomas, qualified second class. In the second HST Alf Thomas (38) received a first-class award, as did a total of 34 cars altogether.

Event 8, a 5-lap handicap, found Maurice Tew (620) and E.G. Walsh (Javelin) circulating whilst A. Thomas (38) had an outing in event 9, another 5-lap handicap.

US Airforce Trophy Meeting, Snetterton, 25 July 1953. T. Blackburn (Jupiter) and D.G. Dixon (Javelin) took part in the half-hour reliability run and, rather optimistically, the Jupiter was entered for a 15-lap scratch race for sports cars of up to 2-litres, which included Cooper-Bristols, Frazer Nash Le Mans, a Cooper-MG, and in all 11 cars with 2-litre engines.

The third 750 MC National Six-hour Relay Handicap Race, 29 August 1953, was this year held on a special extended version of the Silverstone club circuit, taking in the central runway to produce a lap length of 2.5 miles. A true long-distance race for the amateur driver, the aim was to convey a sash around the circuit as many times as possible in the six hours, using the cars and drivers of the team in any order and for any combination of laps. The 'Jowett' team of D.G. Dixon (Javelin), Kenneth Crutch (602) and I.A. Forbes (Jupiter Saloon, thought to be 28) came ninth out of 33 starting and 31 finishing teams. 'Jehu', a special built by John Horridge, using an unnumbered Jupiter frame, a Riley Sprite engine with Wilson gearbox, and an odd-looking body built by JH, ran in another team.

81 Madgewick Corner, Goodwood, 21 March 1953: three Jupiters in action. 14 is the Le Mans/Spa HRG, 21 is R.Gammon's MG special: Guy Griffiths

82

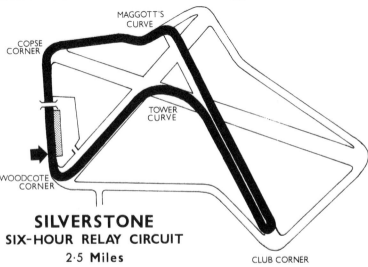

SILVERSTONE
SIX-HOUR RELAY CIRCUIT
2·5 Miles

MAGGOTT'S CURVE

COPSE CORNER

TOWER CURVE

WOODCOTE CORNER

CLUB CORNER

B & HMC Brighton International Speed Trials, 7 September 1953. F.M. Baker again aired MCD28 (597) along the one-way timed kilometre.

BARC Members' Race Meeting, 14 September 1953 at Goodwood. In event 9, a five-lap handicap, J.D. Lewis (718), his car repaired, gained a third behind an MG and a special. Another MG was fourth.

The Bugatti Owners' Club Prescott Hill Climb, 20 September 1953. The hill was ascended to no startling effect by John Horridge in a 'Jehu' that failed to live up to its biblical counterpart, and Ian Sievwright (748) also not in the results.

The Madera Road Races, October 1953, at California's Central Valley included two races for a Jupiter whose engine had been repositioned behind the front suspension. Driven by Bud Grosso in the novice race it took an immediate lead but then retired with ignition bothers; later, in the third race, Bill Behel took the wheel and supplied the spectators with some enchanting displays on the fast bends but the appalling handling forced the car to retire for more development work on its steering geometry.

Willow Springs Hill Climb, California, 13 December 1953. A class win was recorded by a Jupiter.

The 1953 Floyd Bennet Field Sheepshead Trophy Race in Florida. The Jupiter of Bill Lloyd was the winner ahead of five MG TDs. (Bill Lloyd, paired with Stirling Moss, won the 1954 Sebring 12-hour race in a $1\frac{1}{2}$-litre OSCA which possibly might explain Georgano's faux pas of attributing to a Jupiter a 12-hour win at Sebring.)

There was but a single works-supported race for a Jupiter in 1953 and that by chance, for bare survival was now the aim.
During the previous year Harry Woodhead had retired from the board of Jowett Cars in circumstances that could be interpreted as abrupt, leaving Arthur Jopling in full control as chairman and managing director. By nature a cautious man, Jopling's mind worked in terms of reducing a company for short-term advantage rather than taking the bold step for the future, an attitude undoubtedly reinforced by the financial limitations imposed from above. For Lazards were actively seeking other solutions to Jowetts problems and Coventry Climax at least is known to have been showing an interest in acquiring JCL and were thinking in terms of keeping certainly some of the cars on.

Grandfield had left in early spring and Roy Lunn was heavily involved in the R4 project; CD production was in abeyance, pending negotiations with Briggs, and the IOE twin-cylinder engine, successor to the famous SV twin that had propelled Jowetts so reliably for so long, was still not really powerful enough, save perhaps for the CD Pick-up. A three-cylinder Perkins diesel had been approved for the CD van, but it would yet have been necessary to have relied upon the expensive and touchy Javelin unit; a long-life development of this with 3-inch pistons and Wills Rings top seals, derived from the big-bore engine supplied to Jack Hepworth (of the Hepolite piston firm) for his Javelin, is believed to have been under consideration. It should be added that it was this work for Jack Hepworth that led to the engines supplied to Harry Ferguson Research for their four-wheel-drive development programme, whose eventual outcome was the brace of fwd sports cars that appeared in the mid 1960s: powered by a Claude Hill-designed flat-four engine that still retained traces of Jowett influence in its lay-out and the oval webbed crankshaft employed, these Fergusons were enigmatically christened the R5s.

Too late the decision had been taken to farm out the design of a new crankshaft – at a cost to Jowetts of only 100 guineas – resulting in the oval web shaft of Dr Ker Wilson, and even then it was not immediately put into production for not until the end of 1952 was it fully accepted that crank failure was other than purely a racing phenomenon.

Ted Lund had an entry for the RAC Nine-Hour Tourist Trophy Race at Dundrod, 5 September 1953, but for one reason or another his MG was not raceworthy. Spotting his friend Bill Robinson and daughter in GKY256 driving through Wigan on their way to Belgium for a week's holiday, he gave chase, stopped them, and proposed a Lund/Robinson entry for the Jupiter. It was instantly agreed, although Robinson had by then retired from motor sport, and the Jupiter continued on its way. In Belgium Robinson met his main agent, who immediately telephoned Idle and the upshot was a competition engine which Robinson collected from the factory on the way back from Dover, stowing it beneath his passenger's feet – another instance of the Jupiter's notable carrying capacity.

Fifty-four original entries became forty-five by the time the programme was printed, and only twenty-seven reached the starting line, mostly British. Besides the Jupiter, the class comprised a Gordini, a Cooper-MG, a Lester-MG, and two TDs, for the Porsches and the USA-entered OSCA failed to materialise. Ninety-eight laps were required of the 1½-litre cars in a race that held a chance for the red Jupiter.

In practice it was found that the engine supplied by Jowetts had Javelin jets in the carburettors and that corrected the car ran very well, Robinson doing nicely, although a couple of seconds slower than Lund, who of course knew the circuit intimately. Neither noticed anything wrong with the new shock absorbers that had been fitted for the race.

The first race retirement was the Cooper-MG but later trouble struck the Jupiter. After two hours or so the shock absorber for the nearside front wheel broke its upper fixing so Lund brought the car into the pits and, as the damper could not be replaced, rather foolishly it was removed and Lund continued. At around the three-hour point the undamped wheel movements had been sufficient to snap the track rod on that side and the wheel could then move freely, which it did with such vigour that it became virtually invisible! This happened when the car was doing 100 mph past the pits, Lund noticing that it didn't steer too well around left-handers! It was black-flagged and retired. The car was still driveable, Robinson maintaining that above 10 mph the breakage could hardly be noticed and the car was driven back to Barrow from the boat without repair. The 1488 cc Gordini went on to win the class and the 'Series Production Award' went to the George Phillips/Roy Flower TDII. There were only 14 finishers in a race that was another triumph for the DB3s (Peter Collins and Pat Griffith drove the winning one), whilst the Jupiter retired from representative racing and passed on into history.

Perhaps the review of 1953 should be completed by quoting from *Autosport* journalist and MG specialist Wilson McComb who, on 25 October, was testing cars at Goodwood at the Sixth Motor Show Test Day with the Guild of Motoring Writers.

So to the last car of the day, the R4 Jupiter, which had been besieged by eager journalists who were intrigued by its revolutionary appearance. The one at Goodwood was fitted with a hardtop and did not have the plastic body being in fact the works 'hack'. There was nothing hackish about its performance, however, and in particular McC delighted in the overdrive. Just ahead of the normal gear lever protrudes another, more slender, lever; moving this forward engages overdrive third, and backward movement engages top. The top gear overdrive was found to be so high that everything died (ideal for petrol economy this!) but overdrive third produced an extra, superclose gear, great fun to use when cornering and of course demanding no use of the clutch. Approaching a tight bend one could change from top gear to overdrive third, then with a flick of the lever normal third, when almost into the bend, and whip back into overdrive third when accelerating out of it*. Playing tunes on it made the three laps pass all too quickly and it was with great sadness that McC handed back his last, and most intriguing, motor car.

His passenger added:

The R4 Jupiter possesses well-shaped bucket seats, but the toe board was too far distant for useful bracing; at full chat round Goodwood bends in this incredibly lively vehicle, passenger's feet flailed vainly in search of a toe-hold. Its a driver's car – and we mean a *driver's* car. (*Autosport*, 13 November 1953).

*Donald Bastow explains: 'The overdrive ratio reasonably split the third–top gap. The OD switch was interlocked with the gear lever to give the quickest possible changes from third to OD third (switch), OD third to direct top (gear lever) and direct top to OD top (switch again). I believe this was Roy Lunn's idea.'

5 Minor Rallies and All Other Events: 1951 to 1966

The MCC Exeter Trial, 28 – 29 December 1951, saw Edward Foulds participating either in his saloon (99) or more probably in his standard car (472).

North Staffs MC Burnham Rally, 1 – 2 March 1952, had 45 starters and included a climb of Prescott and tests on the promenade at Burnham. The Jupiter of L.J. Roy Taylor (51) took part.

The MCC Land's End Trial, 12 – 14 April 1952, found Edward Foulds definitely in 472.

The London MC Little Rally, 19 April 1952, a pleasing day's motoring through Surrey and Hampshire countryside for the 134 competitors which included the open Abbott Jupiter (89) of Commander Milner.

The Midlands Rally, 19 – 20 April 1952, held over 200 miles. A.B.Hibbert (586) participated : the route used in 1927 was followed.

83 Hunter Hackney with his two navigators and five rally trophies: Autocar

The LAC Morecambe Rally, 16 – 18 May 1952, had 300 entrants but the class division of 1.3 to 3.0 litre did not favour the Jupiters of L.Pellowe (485), Still (521), R.W.Goodburn (618) and Ted Booth/ Derek Bowers in LHR2. Booth did better than the previous year in the final driving test at Morecambe and lost no marks – the marshals gave him a wide berth before letting him run.

The Maidstone and Mid-Kent MC Margate Rally, 27 – 29 June 1952, had 71 starters and was run over 300 miles which included two secret checks, though only a few lost marks here. The regularity test also had two secret checks and in the short final run to Margate many took the difficult route through Canterbury with its schedules that turned out to be hard to keep. There were four varied eliminating tests on the sea-front. Among the 12 MGs, an HRG and a Morgan in Class A were Neil Freedman (509) and the class winners Mr and Mrs F.E. Still in 521.

The sixth International Evian – Mont Blanc Rally for amateur drivers, 24 – 17 July 1952, was organised this year by Marcel Becquart and was restricted to 100 French and 40 non-French competitors; among the latter was the Jupiter of R.W.Austin.

The London MC's London Rally, 19 – 20 September 1952, with two starts, 690 miles, four sets of tests, 298 starters, organised by Godfrey and Nina Imhoff was of national status this year. The 2-litre class, which was won by an HRG, contained the Jupiters of G.A.Dudley/E.W.Miller (651); T.G.Cunane/ Mrs J.O.Cunane (NTJ930); Frank Masefield Baker/J. Grantham-Brown (597); the reserve, Neil Freedman (509), is thought to have run; Imhoff's HAK117 was to be seen near the start. C.A.Leavens/Joyce Leavens (Javelin) won the best mixed crew award.

Eight-Clubs Eastbourne Rally, 17 – 18 October 1952. F.E.Still/L.M.Still (521) took part.

The MG CC Moorfoot Rally, 25 October 1952. W.A. Brearley definitely in the ex-works, ex-Wise GKW111; unplaced.

The Bugatti Owners' Club Welsh Rally 6 - 7 December 1952, featured 324 miles plus a test in the Eppynt mountains and Lystep Hill climb. Ian Sievwright (748) came overall fifth; Mr and Mrs Still (521) participated.

The Four Cylinder Club of America in Southern California 1952 Economy Run class winner was Don Broderick (Jupiter).

The FCCA in SC's rally champion for 1952 was Hunter Hackney (Jupiter). With either Jim Barr or John Orlando navigating he collected five trophies in 1952, including that for winning the Lake Tahoe Rally through the High Sierras at an average speed of 45 mph.

The Cats-Eyes' Rally 31 January 1953, was a night navigation rally run by the Thames Estuary Auto Club and sponsored by a maker of spectacles alleged to improve one's night vision! Mr and Mrs F.E.Still (521) took part.

Nottingham SCC Pilkington Trophy Trial, 22 February 1953, held over a 97-mile course in the Derbyshire peaks found an unsuccessful C.F.Eminson (494) taking part.

The Ulster AC Circuit of Ireland Trial, 4 - 7 April 1953 (1200 miles and 162 competitors), found A.B.Hibbert competing this year in his Jupiter (586); last year he had done quite well on the first two days of the same event in his Javelin.

The Little Rally, 18 April 1953, organised for the LMC by Goff and Nina Imhoff, found the Jupiter of C.W.Yates, after 220 miles and some special tests, class second between two MGs.

Lancs AC Morecambe Rally, 15 - 17 May 1953. A competitor both in the rally and the Concours d'Elégance that followed was the Abbott-bodied saloon Jupiter of C.P.Swain (105).

The ECMC Felixstowe Coronation Rally, 22 - 24 May 1953, included, during its second day, high-speed touring tests at Snetterton and driving tests at Felixstowe. Alec Gordon/P.Steiner (NLX909) ran open; Neil and Mrs Freedman (509) chose to run closed.

The 7th Eastbourne Rally, 4 July 1953. Amongst the nine MGs and others in the 1200 - 2,000cc open class were J.C.Checkley (77, ex-Imhoff) and R.Holmes

in his standard-looking, special-bodied Jupiter GAP6 (242). In the equivalent closed class was to be found the hard-topped 544. This rally featured a midnight concours *after* the dance.

The Brighton and Hove MC Brighton Rally, 11 July 1953. F.M.Baker (597) won the 1.3 - 2-litre open-car class, with Alec Gordon (NLX909) coming second in an event that required some quick laps of Goodwood as one of the tests. Baker incurred fewer penalities than the winners of four out of the other six classes. Although a sometime works Javelin (and later BMC) driver his Jupiter was not

84 The Abbott-bodied saloon Jupiter of C.P. Swain, 1953 Morecambe Rally: National Motor Museum

85 The Eastbourne Rally, 1953. J.C.Checkley with the ex-Imhoff Jupiter–GAP6 is following; National Motor Museum

86 GAP6 of Mr Holmes has a replica body built in Sussex: National Motor Museum

supported; in the previous year's Brighton Concours d'Elégance Ensemble he had entered his Jupiter with actress Dolores Grey then of *Annie Get Your Gun*.

The Southsea MC Day of Driving Tests, 11 July 1953, on Southsea Common, was a triumph for B.Croucher (Jupiter), for out of 45 competitors and in front of 3,000 spectators, he won the challenge trophy for the best aggregate.

Southern Jowett CC Second Plaistow Rally, 26 July 1953, for 17 entrants. First was E.Walsh (Javelin), second Jack Bates (315), third P.Putt (Jupiter) P.Putt had won the driving tests in an SJCC event on 21 June 1953.

Gosport AC Summer Rally, 9 August 1953. 48 competitors. The three first-class awards went to a Riley special, to a Healey Silverstone, and to Alec Gordon's Jupiter NLZ909.

The London to Languedoc-Sète Touring Rally, 17 - 20 August 1953. The 29 entrants followed a route that took in Andorra, visits to wine cellars, and a 'Concours d'Elégance Ensemble which recognised the beauty of the car and the feminine accompaniment'. Dr W.E.R.Pitt's Jupiter came third in the 'car only' concours.

London MC London Rally, 11 - 12 Sept 1953 and again of national status. The entry list included 25 Jowetts, of which these are believed to have formed the Jupiter contingent: A.Gordon/P.Steiner (NLX909); F.M.Baker (597); Maurice Tew (620); Mrs Lola Grounds/Mrs Doreen Reece (29); R.B.H.Goddard/Miss L.E.G. Richardson (MXP417); and T.A.G.Wright/ P.A.Gundry-White (984). The novice award for the 1201 - 2,000 cc open car class went to Mr Wright in a nice example of a Mkla in competition.

The Southern Jowett Car Club (SJCC) Rally, 13 September 1953. Largely organised by Roy Clarkson and involving seven tests at two Essex airfields (Gosfield and Earl's Coln) with 50 road miles through narrow winding lanes between. Class B, presumably restricted to Jupiters, was completed as follows: 1   B.R.Caerns (Jupiter); 2   Alec Gordon (NLX909); 3   Jack Bates (315); 4   H.Flower (Jupiter).

Midland AC *Birmingham Post* Motor Rally, 18 - 19 September 1953, from Birmingham civic centre over 460 miles via lakeside driving tests at Llandrindod Wells to

Droitwich Spa. The 34 in the over 1301 cc class included the Jupiters of J.M.Tew/ Mrs G.M.Tew (620) and Frank Grounds/ Mrs L.E.Grounds (29).

The Lakeland Rally, 26 - 27 September 1953, but actually held in Wales this year had 130 competitors. Winner of class B1 - and therefore of the Riley Trophy - was W.S.Underwood (Jupiter).

Clacton Rally, 27 - 28 September 1953, Made interesting by the dense fog that, however, led to the cancellation of the Snetterton test. Class III was won by R.B.Goddard (MXP417).

TEAC Cats' Eyes' Rally (nicknamed on account of its size the 'Kittens Eyes' Rally), 21 November 1953, was a night navigation/map-reading run. N.Roarke/E.J. Bardell (557) ran in the closed car class as did an A40 Sports.

The year 1954 was transitional for Jowetts after the reverses of of 1952 and the first half of 1953. The decision had been taken to sell the Idle factory to International Harvesters, complete with plant and staff from management to floorsweepers, and consequently the factory commanded a very high price. Harvesters would build their new light tractor there when the sub-contract work Jowetts were doing for Blackburn & General had been completed. Jowett Cars Ltd was to become a pure spares operation in new premises at Howden Clough, Birstall near Batley on the out-skirts of Bradford (and was ultimately sold to Blackburn) and would make parts for that company: the name was changed to Jowett Engineering in 1958 and its function of supplying Jowett spares and service ceased in 1963.

Demand for Jupiters continued in 1954 and two small batches were put together, although nothing further was possible after IH moved into Idle during October except to complete the last two cars. The former works Jupiters were scattered, GKY256 went to Singapore it is believed, and possibly was raced there; an interesting move was the purchase of the prototype R4 JKW537 by Alf Thomas. In 1954 some new names were associated with Jupiters on the motor sporting scene.

Christchurch Motor Racing Club Lady Wigram Trophy Races at Wigram Air Base near Christchurch, New Zealand, 6 February 1954. In a 25-mile handicap race for sports cars on the abrasive 2-mile course 'J.L.

Holden's Jupiter was surprisingly fast but he could not make up his handicap.'

Scottish SCC Moonbeam Rally, 19 February 1954. F.D.Lang (Jupiter) came fourth in the 1.6 litre open class – and it may be recalled that he co-drove JGA123 in the 1951 Monte; further, Skelly had bought a new Jupiter in April 1953.

Nottingham SCC 80-mile Pilkington Trophy Trial, 21 February 1954. One of three competitors to receive a first-class award was Mrs H.J.Curtis (Jupiter).

The first post-war intervarsity Speed Trial, 7 March 1954 was held on a narrow and difficult 4/5 mile course laid out on Gransden Aerodrome in a succession of left-hand and right-hand 90 degree corners. One run only was allowed and the 1201 – 1500 cc closed-car class results were as follows: 1 a Javelin, 1 min 28.4 secs; 2 an MG, 1 min 29.8 secs; 3 Flight-Lt C.F. Norris (JWS187), 1 min 30.9 secs.

The fourth Bolton-le-Moors CC Rally Driving Tests, 7 March 1954, at Blackpool. Class A contained the Jupiters of L.S. Cordingley (908) and D.L.Lord (900) among the Dellows, MGs etc, while what was clearly a closed-car class included the Jowetts of T.Blackburn (Jupiter), J.W. Waddington (910), and W.S.Underwood (Jupiter).

Eastern Counties MC Race Meeting at Snetterton, 3 April 1954, in the 1½-litre handicap for sports cars, Albert C.Westwood (Jupiter) came third.

Tunbridge Wells MC High Speed Trials, 11 April 1954, required two timed laps to be performed on the new 1.24 mile Brands Hatch circuit. I.A.Forbes (28) came second in his saloon Jupiter in the 1.1 – 1.5-litre closed car class at 52.39 mph to an Aston Martin at 53.40 mph.

ECMC Autocross 28 April 1954. A 1½-litre closed class 2nd was achieved by W.T. Smith (Jupiter).

Bushmead Speed Trials, 25 Apri 1954, and a regular Bedford MC event in those days; as would be expected Alf Thomas was there and his time suggests a possible outing for the R4, although this is not confirmable. The course was over 2/3 mile with many corners:

Class 2a (1½-litre open)
1 A Bugatti	57.56 secs
2 An HRG	59.90 secs
3 Alf Thomas (Jupiter)	61.00 secs

Class 2b (1½-litre closed)
1 C.F.Norris (JWS187)	65.60 secs
2 K.Brierley (Javelin)	67.05 secs
3 Mary Chapman (Jupiter)	82.35 secs

In another class, one of the new-fangled TR2s achieved 60.95 secs.

BARC Members' Day, 1 May 1954, at Goodwood. Race 1 was a closed-car, 5-lap handicap, in which the scratch car, an XM120 coupé, reached fifth place on lap four and drove very fast to second place when the chequered flag fell, with I.A. Forbes well ahead in his nimble special bodied Jupiter (28); an Aston Martin DB2-4 was third, Forbes's speed was 63.02 mph.

The Hants/Berks Autocross was a timed trial on grass at Hill Farm, Farley Hill, Berkshire on 16 May 1954. Both D.G. Dixon and R.H. Vivian took out the same Jupiter, believed to be Dixon's 947.

The LAC National Morecambe Rally, 21 - 23 May 1954 tempted T. Blackburn (Jupiter).

Eight-Clubs Silverstone Meeting, 29 May 1954. A 40-minute high-speed trial required 21 laps to be covered at an average speed of greater than 50.65 mph and included a compulsory pit-stop to change the

87 Eight-Clubs High Speed Trial at Silverstone, 8 May 1954, required a passenger to be carried–this one appears to be asleep!: National Motor Museum

front wheels over or remove and replace four spark plugs. Participating were D.G.Dixon (947), A. Thomas (Jupiter), K. Hartridge (Jupiter), and C.F.Norris (JWS187), whose brown Jupiter went round sounding its horn to qualify as did Hartridge's. Event 10 was a five-lap scratch race in which Dixon's Jupiter was entered to be driven by A.Baker, a farmer who often raced his Land Rover at Silverstone (and was eventually killed there racing it), while event 11, a five-lap handicap, found the Jupiters of C.F. Norris (JWS187) and D.G.Dixon (947 – this time driven by R.H.Vivian) both on the limit mark.

The 26th Bol d'Or, 29 – 30 May 1954, was a miniature Le Mans for the private owner, over 24 hours at the 6.3 km Montléry circuit near Paris. 'Jehu', the Horridge Special (BEN775), was driven by John Horridge and G. Trouis to a steady second place, thanks to the reliability of the Riley engine and the retirements of several faster cars in the closing stages; the winning car went sick minutes before the end of the race but struggled across the finishing line just prior to expiring.

MMEC Silverstone Race Meeting, 5 June 1954. A. Wake (saloon Jupiter 99) started off the same mark as three Lotuses in a five-lap handicap race.

ECMC Snetterton Sprint over a ½ mile course, 5 June 1954. In class D (1.2 to 1.5 litre closed), W.T. Smith (Jupiter) first place.

Fifth MCC Silverstone Meeting, 3 July

1954. A feast for enthusiasts of the Jowett marque: in the second high-speed trial, Alf Thomas, in the earliest confirmed appearance of the R4 Jupiter, JKW537, received a first-class award as did D.G. Dixon (947) in his ivory Mk1a, C.F. Norris (JWS187) and, in spite of an alarming spin out of Woodcote due no doubt to the rainy conditions, B.T. Thomas (JTM100). Second-class awards went to J.F. Dickenson (Jupiter) and two Javelins, while 12 other cars, mainly HRGs and MGs, also received awards. Alf completed more laps in the hour – 38 – than anyone else and averaged 61.1 mph, while the next best, J. Gott (HRG) and the bespectacled C.F. Norris (JWS187), completed 36. The R4 had lapped occasionally at 65 mph, touching 100 between Becketts and Woodcote before the rain came.

Farmer Baker won the first five-lap handicap in his Land-Rover while J.R. Waller (MG) and R.H. Vivian (947) photofinished for second place, splitting a spirited scrap between the Javelins of Brierley and Tracey. With an MG Special, Alf Thomas equalled fastest lap, getting the R4 around at 61.71 mph on the wet course without reward.

The third annual Bugatti Owners' Club Prescott Hill Climb, 11 July 1954. Rather bravely Michael Beaumont entered his Richard Mead-bodied Jupiter (248).

Aston Martin OC St John Horsfall Races, 24 July 1954. Events 5 and 10a were a five-lap handicap and a five-lap scratch for 1½-litre sports cars, in which C.F. Norris pitted JWS187 against an HRG, a Cooper-MG, a Lotus-MG and similar.

Nottingham SCC Silverstone Races, 14 August 1954. Event 7 was a seven-lap scratch race which contained MGs, Lotuses, Porsche, Keift, HRGs, and C.F.Norris (JWS187) and J.M. Trimble (Jupiter).

The Sporting Owner Drivers' Club/LMC Autocross at Dunstable, 22 August 1954: C.F.Norris (JWS187) equalled first in class with an MG.

The 750 MC Silverstone Six-Hour Relay Handicap Race, 28 August 1954: of the 40 teams entered 39 started and 34 finished. Ecurie Jupiter was placed eleventh, its Jupiters being those of Alf Thomas (JKW537), Peter Waring (NTF310), D.G. Dixon (947), C.F.Norris (JWS187), and Barry Thomas (JTM100).

SJCC Tewin Driving Tests, 29 August 1954: U.K.Flemming (Jupiter) second.

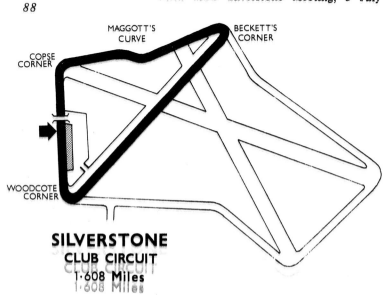

88

MAGGOTT'S CURVE

BECKETT'S CORNER

COPSE CORNER

WOODCOTE CORNER

SILVERSTONE
CLUB CIRCUIT
1·608 Miles

The 50th Anniversary LMC London Rally, 3 – 4 September 1954. Among the 13 Jowetts, D.G. Dixon and K. Brierley may have been in their Jupiters.

Peterborough MC Silverstone Races, 11 September 1954. Race 2 was a five-lap handicap race for Keift, Lotus MkVI, HRG, etc, and P. Waring (NTF310) and K.Brierley (Jowett).

In the Sunbac Silverstone Meeting, 18 September 1954, A Wake (99) was entered in a six-lap scratch race and a half-hour high-speed trial.

N Staffs MC Silverstone Meeting, 9 October 1954. Two entrants for the seven-lap handicap for production cars were A.Wake (Jowett saloon) and D.Keen (Jowett, perhaps Jupiter because he gave Wake 15 secs).

Speed Hill Climb, 17 October 1954, at Stapleford Airfield near Abridge in Essex. A.G.Davis ran the ex-works HAK366 on the $\frac{3}{4}$-mile gentle slope.

The MCC National Redex Rally, 10 – 13 November 1954. Bill Boddy spectated from a Jupiter (probably 972) at the Bwlch-y-Groes ascent and the driving test at the summit and noted in *Motor Sport* that I.Robertson's Jupiter had refused to start for this test and had to be allowed to cool off. And at the end of the rally, at Hastings, where there were four driving tests, he noted that in the uphill manoeuvring test 'I.Robertson's Jupiter was handled neatly but refused to repay such treatment, its offside back wheel spinning so furiously that from restart to finish the car only just moved. "Too much Redex" said a wag in the crowd. D.G.Dixon, in odd headgear and a Jowett Jupiter, wasted many valuable seconds.'

R.J.Hedges (Jupiter) won a third-class award.

In the TEAC National Cats Eyes' Night Rally 5 – 6 February 1955, Mr E.A.Jenner's Jupiter (994) was entered for Mr and Mrs D.E.Moore.

Cambridge University AC Intervarsity *Speed Trial* at Tempsford Airfield, near Biggleswade, 6 March 1955. The traditonal opener of the English speed season was this year held over a $\frac{3}{4}$-mile twisty course in a biting wind. Best of two runs: event 4, closed cars:

1 A Thomas (R4 Jupiter JKW537)
69.12 secs

2 W.A.Scott-Brown (Peugeot 203)
70.90 secs
3 R Dick (MG Magnette)   75.58 secs

Fourth was another Peugeot 203. The R4's time would have placed it third in the sports-car class, ahead of a Cooper-MG (69.41 secs), a TF, and an HRG but removal of the hardtop and screen would have been very unlikely to have enabled second-placed David Piper's Lotus (66.15 secs) to have been overhauled. The Jupiter was faster than all closed cars in the 1501 – 2,500 cc and over 2,500 cc classes.

Warrington and District MC Daffodil Rally, 20 March 1955. D Lunt (Jupiter) won the $1\frac{1}{2}$-litre open-car class.

Horhsam and District MC Spring Rally, 27 March 1955. Jack Bates (315) won the award for the best performance in the class opposite to the rally winner.

The MCC Easter Land's End Trial, 8 – 9 April 1955. P.Waring entered NTF 310 but the red Jupiter lost the use of all inter-mediate gears on Beggar's Roost Hill, the half-mile stone-and-boulder-strewn, observed-section climb near Lynton in Devon, and had to be driven the 180-odd miles back to London using top gear only.

BARC Race Day at Brands Hatch, 1 May 1955. Race 4, a 1500 cc sports-car race over 15 laps contained the Jupiter of R.Stably.

89 The 'KW' Saloon Jupiter raced by A.Wake at Silverstone, 5 June 1954: National Motor Museum

90 *This saloon Jupiter, here racing at Snetterton in a 10-lap handicap in August 1955 driven by J. Hall, was built by Maurice Gomm for Nigel Mann:* National Motor Museum

Eight-Clubs Silverstone, 4 June 1955. K.Brierley (564) and P. Waring (NTF310) were in event 1, a 40-minute (24 lap) high-speed trial and both received first-class awards. In a five-lap scratch race K. Brierley (564) averaged 62.4 mph to come second, and in a 5-lap handicap this same combination came third.

After this event P. Waring sold his Jupiter, which had been his daily transport for over a year in a move he later regretted, for he felt that although due to the under-column gear change and rather slow box it was not suited to the type of rally that was largely decided by 'comic' driving tests, he considered for a standard road car it had extraordinarily good handling characteristics that were very close to ideal.

Sevenoaks and District MC Brands Hatch Sprint, 3 July 1955. R.Blake and B.Bisley had runs in the same Mkla Jupiter.

750 MC Silverstone Six-Hour Relay Handicap Race, 9 July 1955. The aptly named team 'Mixed Grilles' contained a Talbot, a Darracq, an Aston Martin, a supercharged Morris Minor, and the Jupiter of Kenneth Brierley (564).

The West Essex CC International Race Meeting at Snetterton, 13 August 1955,

included a 10-lap handicap for saloons, comfortably won by a Porsche, in which the Beverley Motors-bodied saloon Jupiter of J.F.Hall took-part.

The MGCC Silver Jubilee Race Meeting and Pageant at Silverstone, 27 August 1955, had a race for cars of any capacity and any make except MG. The green Jupiter of M.G.Harrison was entered.

Brighton and Hove MC Brighton Speed Trials, 3 September 1955, and the Golden Jubilee for the event, for the Madeira Drive had been constructed in 1905 especially for speed trials. Horace Appleby (MCD28, 579) participated: the class was won by a Porsche at 33.51 secs.

London MC National London Rally, 16 – 17 September 1955; Horace Appleby drove MCD 28 with John Baker navigating.

Horsham and DMC Spring Rally, 18 March 1956. Jack Bates (315) class second.

Templestowe Hill Climb, May 1956, Victoria, Australia. E.Pearce (Jupiter) unplaced in $1\frac{1}{2}$-litre class with 74.69 secs. Mention must be made here of the single-seater, ladder-frame blown (14lb) Javelin-engined Wylie Special which had been driven up this same hill at a new record of 61.51 secs in December 1953 by Stan Jones to win him the championship, a time lowered to 58.4 secs by Bruce Polain in the same car in 1968. Besides hill climbs the Wylie-Javelin, which first ran in 1951, was raced against the best in Australia and was timed in 1954 at 132 mph.

The BARC 10th Eastbourne Rally, 16 June 1956. A Jowett ran in the 1.3 – 2-litre open-car class driven by Mrs D.E.Kenney, a class that was won – of course – by a TR2.

The 7th MCC Silverstone, 30 June 1956. One-hour blind. This opportunity for a long-distance dice was accepted by Barry Thomas (Alf's son) and JKW537 received an airing in a five-lap handicap race too.

Birmingham YCMC Midland Rally, 8 July 1956. P. Towers (Jupiter) overall third.

North Staffs MC Silverstone, 6 October 1956 and the end of the club season for Silverstone induced Alf Thomas to enter JKW537 for two handicap races, and in one of them he motored very fast into third place behind a TR2 and a Healey Silverstone. Perhaps this outing, believed to be his first at the Northamptonshire circuit for 27 months, encouraged Alf Thomas to lay plans for the forthcoming season.

The MCC National Rally, 5 – 10 November 1956. Only 1250 miles and 144 starters this year; Alan Dowsett, the third owner of MCD28 (597) drove the last Jupiter known to have participated in a national rally.

Rob Roy Hill Climb, November 1956, Victoria, Australia. 1101–1500 cc touring cars class: 2nd R.O.Robinson (Javelin) 43.66 secs. 1101 – 1500 cc sports cars: unplaced E.Pearce (Jupiter) 38.16 secs. (Best Wylie-Javelin time for this hill was set in February 1954 at 26.85 secs by Arthur Wylie, shortly after the de Dion rear end had been fitted.)

Templestowe Hill Climb, 17 November 1956 1101 – 1500 cc saloon cars class: 2nd R.O.Robinson (Javelin) 78.86 secs. 1101 – 1500 cc sports cars class : 6th E. Pearce (Jupiter) 75.65 secs. Then came the Suez Crisis with petrol rationing in Britain and consequently the suspension *Motor Sport* for the winter.

Cranleigh and District MC Versatility Trial, spring 1957. Jack Bates (315) returns with a class win.

Bugatti OC Prescott Club Practice Weekend, spring 1957. Miss E.A.Neale (R4 Jupiter) 59.74 secs.

Eight-Clubs Silverstone, 1 June 1957. The summer's first really hot day. The first

91 A view of the super-charged Javelin-engined Wylie in action in Australia. Bruce Polain at the wheel: Polain

92 *Alf Thomas plays Chase the Ace at Silverstone, 22 June 1957*

half-hour high-speed trial (Le Mans start; pit-stop for a plug change, a front-wheel swop, or to pour half a pint of oil somewhere near the oil-filler hole) saw first-class awards go to Miss E.A.Neale (564), A. Thomas (R4 Jupiter, JKW537), and K. Brierley (Javelin). A five-lap scratch race was won by K.Brierley (Javelin) at 60.25 mph with his fastest lap 61.98 mph, from a Lagonda of 3 litres, an AC tourer, and Nancy Mitchell in an MG Magnette. The Javelin then placed third in a five-lap handicap. In a five-lap scratch race A. Thomas (JKW537) posted fastest lap – 67.16 mph – to come first at 65.22 mph, ahead of Mrs Scott-Moncrief (Lotus–MG), a very potent $1\frac{1}{2}$-litre TD and a Morgan. In another five-lap handicap race Miss Neale (564) came third.

BARC Members' Day, Aintree, 15 June 1957; race 7 was a seven-lap handicap for 'closed' cars. R.F.Nanson (Jupiter) was second.

The 8th MCC Silverstone Meeting, 22 June 1957, started with a half-hour high-speed trial in which Miss Neale (564) and A. Thomas (JKW537) took part. The third event was a ten-lap handicap race with

Alf Thomas in the R4 on scratch giving 10 secs to an MGA, a minute to Miss Neale (564) and $1\frac{1}{2}$ minutes to K. Brierley's Javelin: the R4 reached fourth place ahead of Miss Neale when the chequered flag was taken. In the next event the TR3 on scratch gave the R4 Jupiter 15 secs, Miss Neale 45 secs, and Brierley the benefit of a full minute, enabling him to come in first at 60.12 mph, ahead of Peter Morgan in his Plus 4, Alf Thomas, and and MGA.

The final race was the *Motor Sport* Winners' Handicap, for which Charles Bulmer produced his best handicapping of the day with practically the whole field crossing the finish line together. By lap four it was clear that Alf Thomas (JKW537) was too fast for all except the C-Type Jaguar that stormed through the pack and caught the little R4 on the last bend to win by a length. Peter Morgan was third and an MGA fourth.

The Midlands Motoring Enthusiasts's Club Silverstone Race Meeting, 29 June 1957. Event 4 was a six lap scratch race for sports cars of up to $1\frac{1}{2}$ litres and it resolved itself into two races, one in the van for the light-weight sports cars that were now proliferating (mostly Cooper-Climaxes and

Lotus-Climaxes) and another astern for the more normal road machinery. The 'second' race was led by the redoubtable R4 of Alf Thomas, despite a strong challenge from the MGA of J.Trafford.

BRSCC National Silverstone Races, 27 July 1957. Alf Thomas entered the R4 JKW537 in a 20-lap event for series production sports cars.

750 Motor Club Six-Hour Relay Handicap Race at Silverstone, 17 August 1957. The race was run on the 2.5 mile special circuit, the normal club circuit being extended to include a hairpin known as Club Corner. The race was started at 1 pm by Colin Chapman the 750 MC president, and the 'Team Individualist' which included a Jupiter, that of K.Brierley, led from start to finish, mainly due to the big lead built up by the team's Elva Courier. A Bucker 90 did most of the rest of the driving whilst the Jupiter put in a few laps when the others were being refuelled and their drivers rested.

Lincoln DMC and LCC Lincoln Rally, 7 September 1957. J.Timms (Jupiter) overall 2nd.

High-Speed Trial and Races at Mallory Park 14 September 1957. Event 4 was a five-lap scratch race for Alf Thomas; event 6 a five-lap handicap with a Lotus on scratch, the R4 given 1 min 05 sec and Miss Neale (564) 1 min 20 secs; and event 9, a ten-lap handicap for our inseparable pair of Jupiter racers.

N Staffs MC Silverstone Race Meeting 5 October 1957. The last meeting of the year for Silverstone. Fourth race of the day was a six-lap scratch race for $1\frac{1}{2}$-litre sports cars; the R4 Jupiter of Alf Thomas (JKW537) led until the last lap when I.H.S. Smith got his homemade but very modern looking glass-fibre XPEG MG-engined wisp past him to win at 67.31 mph. Third was a 1498 cc Lester-Riley and Miss Neale (564) also ran. In a five-lap handicap Alf Thomas, given 45 secs on the scratch car, brought the R4 into third place behind an Elva and a Tojeiro.

The Lancashire and Cheshire CC end-of-season meeting at Oulton Park, 12 October 1957, was held in brilliant sunshine and 12 drivers (from 34) beat the clock in a half-hour HST that included a compulsory wheel change; one who did was Alf Thomas (JKW537) and one who did not was Miss Neale (564).

Eight-Clubs Silverstone, 8 June 1958. F.M.G.Collins (Jupiter) entered but did not run in the half-hour HST. He did, however, run in a five-lap scratch race, as did A.T. Fryer in the rear-Jupiter-engined special, the 'Scientific'; and in a five-lap handicap race a Lotus XI was on scratch. F.M.G. Collins started from the same 1 min 40 secs mark as a Lea-Francis and a Buckler V, 10 secs before the 'Scientific'.

The 9th MCC Silverstone Meeting, 18 June 1958. In the half-hour blind, Miss Neale won a first-class award. There was also a five-lap scratch race for Alf Thomas, a five-lap handicap for K.Brierley and a ten-lap scratch for Alf.

AMOC St John Horsfall Races, 12 July 1958. In a five-lap scratch race for cars of up to $1\frac{1}{2}$ litre, A. Thomas (JKW537) notched a creditable third behind an Elva-Climax (winning at 68.01 mph) and a supercharged Lotus VI. Miss Neale was entered for the half-hour blind in the R4 but a switch of drivers must have occurred for as the race commentator remarked, 'Miss Neale has a black moustache!'

N Staffs MC Silverstone Meeting, 27 July 1958. Miss Neale evidentally racing in Alf Thomas's R4 in a scratch race — it soon became clear why.

750 MC Silverstone Six-Hour Relay Handicap Race, 16 August 1958, on the extended club circuit, and for only the second time a full Jupiter team was fielded – again the catalyst was Alf Thomas. This was the climax of Alf Thomas's career as a fanatical Jupiter enthusiast for now he was able to field no less than three R4 Jupiters. The two glass-fibre models recently purchased from Jowetts (lighter than JKW537 but not quite as fast, for Alf had spent so much time with the older car) were in what was probably to be their first and only race. One car apparently lost a hub in practice but this was rectified in time to take part.

Miss E.A.Neale – Alf Thomas's secretary and the only lady driver in the race – drove the former Motor Show car SWT356, fast and without incident; Alf drove the model that had been bought 'in component form', bearing proudly the registration plates from another notable Jupiter, HAK365, and Barry would therefore have driven JKW537, a car with which he was familiar. Also in the team was the faithful K.Brierley (Jupiter) but it is not known whether he drove in the race.

Promptly at 1 pm, Holland Birkett

93 The three R4s at Kempston before the Six-Hour Relay race of 1958. Alf Thomas extreme left

dropped the flag and the 21 drivers sprinted across the track to begin their first stint. After one hour's racing, rain drenched the bakc of the circuit, narrowly leaving the pit area dry and at this point the Jupiter team found itself equal sixth with the Morgan Plus 4 team (led by Peter Morgan) and two places behind the Porsche team led by Dennis Jenkinson. Half an hour later the Jupiters were actually sharing the lead with the Chilton Car Club (TR2s) and Healeys and Friends but by 3 o'clock the Jaguar team had taken the front and the R4 team had dropped to ninth, still in touch with the race, less than $\frac{3}{4}$ of a lap behind the leaders.

At this point Alf Thomas may have allowed himself to feel pleased with the way things were going but, alas, disaster lay close at hand, for on the run down to the Club Corner hairpin the bonnet of his R4, lacking straps, snapped off and struck him on the head. The car rolled and its occupant was flung out on to the grass, wearing the bonnet around his neck like

a lavatory seat, and lucky was he to suffer only cuts and bruises.

The team sent a car out to see what had happened and to collect the sash and the race continued for the R4s, although the team was no longer able to contest the lead, until, with a few laps to go, Barry went off at Woodcote and had to abandon his car, returning to his pit on foot, bearing the sash: Miss Neale went out again to finish the race, which resulted in the team placing 14th out of twenty finishing teams. Peter Morgan's team came 2nd and the Porsches (1300, Super, 1500 Carrera, 1600 Supers) were 16th. Two of the R4s were damaged and it is believed that Thomas did not race the R4s again.

Perhaps it began with the speedboat *Pacific Spot*. Lean and hungry, the original Deep-V 'Grey Nurse' hull, she looks as fast as she turned out to be. Doug Syme, of Christchurch, New Zealand, fitted a standard replacement Jupiter engine in her in 1954 and such was the boat's success

90

that he contacted Jowetts at Birstall with a view to purchasing an R1 engine. Thanks to the personal intervention of George Green, Syme was supplied with a kit of parts to bring the engine up to R1 specification plus an oval webbed crank. With one or other form of the engine, Doug won 76 championships, bringing home an astonishing 40 trophies in the 91-cubic inch class (34 cups, 2 teapots, 2 salvers and 2 barometers) and the Australasian speed record of 53.775 mph -- indeed the world speed record for the class was once unofficially exceeded at 58.6 mph. When he retired the boat as unbeatable around 1962 the engine was removed, and after a brief sojourn in another, it was bought by Wayne Rout, and he and Vic Morrison fitted it to Wayne's Jupiter (27). The Jupiter took part in a road race in which it proved to be very fast (helped by its high back axle ratio) and from which it retired when a gearbox mainshaft washer broke. Rout did not race again, selling his Jupiter, less the engine R1/438, to Paul Illingworth. Inspired, Vic Morrison began to prepare his Jupiter (182), to become known as the 'Jaguar-Eater', for competition, and in 1964 both Paul and Vic participated in a day of races at Ruapuna. Both Jupiters had more or less standard engines and in the half-dozen or so races Paul consistently finished ahead of Vic.

For the next race day at the same circuit Vic had fitted single choke Weber carburettors, and in this form 182 was now able to finish ahead of 27. Paul then ceased racing and when Errol Blatchford raced his Jupiter (414) at Ruapuna a couple of times he too was no match for the Jaguar-Eater. Usually in these events there would be 10 to 15 cars in each race, and in most cases the cars or specials were soley used for racing, whereas Vic's Jupiter was his only car. The Benmore circuit, for example, was 220 miles from Christchurch and the car would be driven there and back in full road trim for comfort at speed: with the 14-inch wheels fitted, revs were at a constant 5500 rpm for hours on end. Screen, quarter-lights, window glass, hood assembly, spare wheel and door, headlights and bench seat (in favour of an Austin 7 bucket) were removed in the pits on arrival.

Vic obtained the R1 pistons from Doug Syme; the half-race camshaft was a standard unit reground to provide greater valve opening time. Gears were changed when the rev counter needle was at the main beam warning light, roughly 7000 rpm. Ruapuna was a one-mile oval circuit with one of the straights extended and doubled back to form a hairpin and a reverse corner: like the profile of a balled fist with pointing index finger.

South Canterbury CC Craigmore Hill Climb:
23 August 1964
    First event, engine completely standard
                                    78.2 secs
23 March 1965
    R1 pistons, half race cam, Webers
                                    71.3 secs
12 August 1965
    0.060-inch planed off heads   70.0 secs
22 August 1965
    standard cam refitted   70.5 secs

Canterbury CC Ruapuna Race Track, 20 September 1964. Race 7, for sports cars. Vic Morrison the winner, ahead of a Buckler and an MGA 1600.

SCCC Saltwater Creek grass circuit 25 October 1964. In three races Vic achieved two 3rds and a 4th.

CCC Ruapuna, November 1964. Vic 2nd behind a Morgan, ahead of a Buckler Mk 90 and an MG Midget.

Nelson CC Tahuna Beach circuit 4 – 5 January 1956. Race 2, a scratch race for cars 1201 to 2000 cc. Vic 5th out of 14 competitors. Race 10, a sports car handicap: Vic 2nd behind a Morgan, ahead of a Mistral-Consul. Race 11, open handicap, Vic the winner, Ford 10 Special 2nd. Race 6 on second day, handicap for sports/specials up to 1750 cc. Vic 3rd behind the Morgan and the Mistral-Consul.

SCCC Mayfield grass circuit, February 1965. Race 4, Vic 1st. Race 9, Vic 3rd.

CCC Raupuna, 21 March 1965. Race 7, six-lap sports car handicap: it was here that Vic earned his soubriquet by giving an XK150 saloon a 5-second start and passing it on the last lap at the hairpin to come 4th behind an XK120, an MG Midget and a Morgan Plus 4. Race 15 : sports car handicap, found Vic 2nd, half a bonnet behind the winning Buckler Mk90 but ahead of the MG Midget and the Morgan Plus 4.

CCC, 4 April 1965. Standing quarter mile. Vic 19.43 secs (full road trim).

Southland Car Club Benmore Clay circuit, April 1965. Vic 3rd and 1st in races 10 and 15.

94 *Jupiter eats Jaguar at the Ruapuna race track, New Zealand, 21 March 1965. Vic Morrison drives*

CCC Ruapuna Race Track, 9 May 1965. Vic 2nd between two Morgans in a sports car handicap race.

CCC Summit Road Hill Climb, May 1965. Vic timed at 37.54 seconds and 36.98 seconds compared with 34.49 for a super-charged TF.

CCC Ruapuna Race Track, 13 June 1965. Best lap time by Vic was 64.6 seconds, best lap by J Slater (XK150) 64.3 seconds.

CCC Ruapuna Sprint Day, 9 October 1965. Standing 1-mile lap 75.57 seconds, flying lap 67.92 seconds, the times being recorded with the Jupiter in full road trim with the standard camshaft fitted.

One-way maximum speed was measured late in 1965 with hood up, Jupiter wheels, modified engine but standard camshaft: twin SU fuel pumps were found necessary to avoid starvation at top end. Speed was read from the speedometer calibrated on a rolling road dynamometer and maximum speed, 97.5 mph, occurred at just under 5,700 rpm: speeds in the gears were 31 mph, 51 mph and 81 mph.

Five weeks outside the 1966 time limit but included here for convenience; the Castlereagh Sprints Day NSW Australia, 5 February 1967. Eddy Wolf (72) was timed at 21.25 seconds in the standing $\frac{1}{4}$-mile with 6.38 seconds along the Flying $\frac{1}{8}$ mile. Also there, was Bruce Polain with his single-seat Wylie-Javelin special, to class-win at 15.5/4.29. This, though, was down on his figures of five months previous at the same track when his standing $\frac{1}{4}$ had been 14.55 seconds and his flying $\frac{1}{8}$ had set a new Australian Racing Drivers Club record at 4.11 seconds.

CHAPTER 6 Jupiters Yesterday and Today

Although at least a couple of Jupiters are now museum exhibits, many Jupiters are still working cars and may have enthusiastic owners not only in Britain, where spares and expertise are relatively plentiful, but in many of the countries to which the cars were originally exported, the list taking in Australia, Canada, Denmark, France, Eire, Holland, New Zealand, Portugal, Republic of South Africa, and USA, where full and varied use may be made of Jupiters despite great practical difficulties. Many owners derive their satisfaction from the restoration of their car as the Jupiter's method of construction and the materials used therein lend themselves to such a pastime. It is equally the result of all these activities and the international exchange of information that ensues that the survival and use rate is at the high level it is.

The article '25,000 Miles in a Jowett Jupiter' first appeared in *Motor Sport* of November 1952, encapsulating the bittersweet impression that the model was to make on many of its owners. Mr William Boddy, editor of *Motor Sport* in those years as in 1980, occasionally garnished his magazine with references to this car (98): in June 1951 the fan incident was related (50 mph at 27 mpg on wet roads was averaged until its disintegration); not being overtaken on the run back from Darlington on 14 October that year after the races at Winfield; and, having spectated at Castle Coombe, a burn-up was alluded to in WBs instantly recognisable style: '. . . and went swiftly Londonwards in the *Motor Sport* Jupiter up with which Sydney Allard, now in a Ford Zephyr, very nearly kept!' I am greatly indebted to Mr Boddy and *Motor Sport* for permission to reproduce the article.

25,000 miles in a Jowett Jupiter
by W.J. Tee, managing director, *Motor Sport*.

Twelve months ago I made a business trip which took me as far north as Tongue and completed in all a little under 2,000 miles in nine days. I returned so enthusiastic about the Jupiter that I felt I had better let a few weeks pass before I wrote about my experiences, lest I be carried away and exaggerate in singing the praises of this wonderful little thoroughbred. When I finally wrote them they were crowded out, our editor being unable to find space.

Twelve months passed very quickly, and, with the speedometer showing 24,000 miles, we started off on the same trip. Safely home again, I am even more enthusiastic than before.

First, however, let me relate some of my experiences with the youngest member of the Jowett family.

A heavy shower of rain had fallen and the sun was just beginning to shine through as I caught sight of my red Jupiter standing in the market-place at Stamford, quietly waiting for me. My first impression was, 'You little beauty!' and as time has gone by that first impression has grown until for me it is the prettiest car on the road.

The drive back to London was taken quietly, and proved uneventful – then a period of quiet running took the speedometer along to 2,000 miles. Only then did I start to push the rev-counter beyond 3,500 rpm. It must be remembered that this Jupiter was one of the first to come from the Jowett factory, and I decided to return it to Bradford for a general overhaul at about 3,500 miles; so, at 7 o'clock one very beautiful spring morning, the editor and I left for Bradford. The speedometer seldom dropped below 80 mph and we soon realised that this little car was making really exciting headway so we pushed along a little faster but never exceeding 5,500 revs. Then, just before Stamford, the engine began to falter, and finally we came to rest by the roadside a few miles on the London side of Stamford. Obviously the engine was starved of petrol. I have no explanation as to why I did it, but I walked to the back of the car and released the filler cap at the back – a small 'pop' startled me, and I quickly realised that the quick-release cap fitted so tightly that it had

95 Mrs Tee, the Forth Bridge, and the Motor Sport *Jupiter:* Motor Sport

The large bump on the bonnet had been smoothed out and after a short run round the local roads with the tester, a quick glance at the factory and lunch, we left about 3 pm, expecting to be back in London not later than 7 o'clock – perhaps 6.30. Before we reached Doncaster, an ominous knock started and, although the oil pressure was well up, so was the oil temperature, we decided to stop at the next gagage to check oil and water. This we did, and to my amazement one quart of oil was needed to satisfy the dipstick. Out on the road again, only a further ten miles completed, a most 'sickening' knock developed in a matter of seconds to a rhythmic thud and we had no big-ends. We had to press on but, oh! what a miserable drive and it was 11 pm when Romford was reached, and anyone was welcome to the Jupiter by just taking it away.

Several months went by and at last the little red car was delivered to the office, with the remarks: 'You'll find her all right now – we know the answer to flying fans, blown gaskets and big-ends – you won't have any more trouble.' By the time 4,500 miles had been completed, the gasket blew again and the front tyres were bald, and as the back tyres showed practically no wear, it was obvious that the tracking was at fault. I was getting a little 'browned-off' for, after all, I had paid a lot of hard-earned money for this car and even the most optimistic would have to admit that I had been in trouble!

August 1951, saw the speedometer clocking 6,000 miles and the modifications that had been made looking as if they were going to be successful. The new tyres on the front were showing signs of a little unnecessary wear, but by now Jowetts had the answer to correct tracking and the necessary adjustments were made. Twelve months have quickly slipped by and the speedometer reads 25,750 miles, the last 20,000 being very nearly trouble free – 20,000 hard miles, for all of them have been completed in the service of *Motor Sport* – trials in the West country, hillclimbs in the North, large and small race meetings, and speed trials at very nearly every track in England and Scotland. Thousands of miles in torrential rain, snow and fog, and most of them in darkness. Never once has the little red Jupiter failed to get us to the meeting – never once has it failed to get us home again. The Lucas equipment has never failed to excite the engine, announce our presence, and light our way, although we favour the small Marchal spot and fog-lights. Dunlop tyres,

formed a vacuum. Drilling two small holes has since made certain that we are never caught like that again. Only a few minutes were wasted and on we sped, and at 9.50 we were five to ten miles the Bradford side of Doncaster when I thought the car had disintegrated! Several very loud bangs and violent shaking of the floor boards, and a large bump appeared on the beautiful red bonnet, and the editor shouted, 'For God's sake, stop!' In a flash, the ignition was switched off and the gears disengaged. As we were travelling at very nearly 90 mph when it happened, this easy-running little car quietly drifted a very long way before dying by the side of the road, but we were at least a little nearer Bradford. Quite honestly, I expected to see the engine in pieces and was surprised at not seeing a trail of parts in the driving-mirror. However, when the bonnet was lifted, we saw that the fan had come adrift, hit the underside of the bonnet – hence the bump – and then out of the bottom. Out luck was in, for although it had severed several wires and pipes, nothing vital was touched and the radiator was undamaged. When the fan belt was taken off, the car was cranked (the starter being quite dead), and started straight away. Driving quietly, with the water temperature well up, we proceeded to Bradford, reaching the works at about 11.30 am.

Very shortly, the car was ready for the road, and we drove to Bradford to collect it in a very lively Javelin, arriving at the works only 3 hrs 55 mins after leaving Romford.

5.50 on the front and 5.75 on the back, have never failed us, and the Girling Mintex-lined brakes have always just managed to stop us in time. Hundreds of interesting incidents rush to mind but space allows for one only, that already referred to.

One Thursday morning, at 9.50, we left for a visit to the Ferodo works at Chapel-en-le-Frith, arriving at the Palace Hotel, Buxton, at 1.10 pm. After a wash and brush-up and a very good lunch, we went to fulfil our appointment and a very enjoyable afternoon was had. The very fulfilling of this appointment reminds me of one of the strongest points that makes the Jupiter such a favourite for the businessman.

One is able to put on a cap, muffler and gloves and enjoy the exhilaration of an open sports car and, by Jove! only those who have experienced it know the thrill. Then, having reached the town, one can put up the hood, wind up the windows, and go about one's business in the town in what is virtually a closed car. A very enjoyable evening and first-class service at the Palace sent us on our way in a very good frame of mind. Up past Holme Moss television aerial, all, except a few feet of the bottom and the top (funnily enough), shrouded in thick mist. Through Huddersfield and Leeds, joining the A1 at Wetherby, leaving it just after Scotch Corner, and then into Scotland by what I think is the most impressive route, A68 over Carter Bar. We mustn't forget the old-world Wellington Hotel, Riding Mill, where the service and lunch were fit for a king. Arriving at Edinburgh about 4.30 we found that Queen Elizabeth was already there and the town full, and wherever we went we received the same answer, 'No room at the inn.' So we pushed on to Linlithgow but, before reaching it, we saw a large white house high up to our right and were admiring its position when a small board announced it as Bonsyde Hotel. We took the last room and enjoyed our stay, leaving Sunday morning after completing our business at Bo'ness. Through the Trossachs, with the sun blazing its welcome, unbelievably beautiful and peaceful – lunch was taken at Tchailoch Hotel, beside the loch – then on to spend the rest of the day and night at Killiecrankie. Mine host of the Killiecrankie Hotel has created an atmosphere of delicate charm and we were sorry to leave at 8.30 on the Monday morning, climbing to 1,500 feet through Glen Garry to Kingussie and on to Inverness. It pays handsomely here to drive back along the west shores of Loch Ness to Drumnadrochit and then west along Glen Urquhart, and finally north to Beauly. The Drumnadrochit Hotel, with its vast windows, provides one with a 'view while you chew'. Through Dingwall to Bonar Bridge, that delightful little village at the head of Dornoch Firth. Turning left in the village and running by the side of the Firth one finds oneself in Lairg – very wild and desolate countryside, most forbidding in winter, but so delightful on a sunny summer day. Tongue was reached by 5.15. The Bungalow Hotel was our home for two days; it is built of wood with little wooden chalets, overlooking the Kyle, and warmed by peat fires. Just to think of the smell of the peat, the warm welcome, the good food beautifully cooked, the delightful bays explored, gives me a glow of contentment.

The Jupiter, the first the local garage had seen, created interest, and the loving care with which it was serviced was much appreciated. Thoroughly greased (one quart of oil, one pint of water, and about 4–5 lbs in the tyres, the first attention it had received since leaving Romford 1,150 miles away), and we were ready for the wildest run to be imagined in Britain. Driving right round the Kyle, leaving Ben Loyal first on our left and then on our right, one strikes due west to Hope. Even on a glorious day one needs hope, for the boulder-strewn roads and wild, desolate scenery make one feel that without the Jupiter purring quietly and effortlessly along, all would be lost. Round Loch Eribol, divinely blue and as lovely as any Italian lake. Through Durness and following the road southwest of Cape Wrath to Scourie, across the Kylestrome Ferry, on past Loch Assynt through the wildest and roughest country in our lovely Isle, and finally dropping down into Ullapool. A memorable day's run, the Jupiter simply bounding along, it being necessary to check its onward rush up the long steep hill from Kylestrome Ferry. A most delightful evening was spent at the Grand Hotel, Ullapool, where the staff make one feel so absolutely at home. A sunset at Ullapool with the Summer Isles silhouetted against the evening sky is one of the sights one never forgets. Away next morning by 8.30 and, following Loch Broom for a short time, the road winds inland for a short way before returning to Little Loch Broom, and from there to Gairloch one passes through miles of the loveliest mountain loch and sea scenery available for man to see, Grunaird Bay with its sandy inlets forming natural windbreaks, give such marvellous opportunity to sun bathe, as we did. Miles of sand covered with thousands of beautifully coloured shells of all shapes and the sea - a translucent torquoise-blue - and ourselves alone to enjoy it. The steep hill out of Grunaird Bay was levelled by the lively Jupiter, which had to be checked before the top was reached. A very fine lunch was taken at Aultben Hotel, right by the seashore off the direct route, but worth a visit. A run by the side of Loch Maree, then through wild country with a single-track railway appearing and disappearing, past Strathcarron station and across Loch Carron by Strome Ferry. Arriving at Kyle of Lochalsh about 5 pm, with the most delightful views of Skye, which looked mysterious, the mountains appearing unreal and ethereal. Most delightful was our stay at the Lochalsh Hotel - everyone going out of their way to make us comfortable.

Leaving about 10 am, we travelled along the same road as we came in by, Skye looking quite different in the morning sun but just as mystical. The country was still quite wild but the road surface steadily improving. We reached Fort William for lunch at the Alexandra Hotel, then on to Ballachulish and so into Glencoe, bathed in brilliant sunshine. The high snow-posts, however, were a reminder of what a terrible reception a visitor can get in the winter. Through Inveraray, with views of Loch Fyne, the grandeur of which defy description, finally down Rest-and-be-Thankful to Arrochar, where we arrived about 5.30 pm. Before putting the gallant little Jupiter away, I checked tyres and water (OK), oil (a quart needed); a check-up of petrol purchased since leaving London showed that we were averaging 28 miles per gallon for the 1,600 miles completed, surely a truly wonderful performance, for about 1,000 miles of it had been run over mountain roads which are the worst I've ever driven on in Britain.

After Rest-and-be-Thankful Hill-Climb, which is held in such beautiful surroundings that the racing becomes a secondary consideration, we followed the road to Glasgow by Loch Lomond. How lucky are the Scots living around Glasgow to have such glorious scenery, as one sees by the shores of Loch Lomond, so near at hand! Through Glasgow and on to Abington to spend a most comfortable night at the Abington Hotel, where any visitor can always be assured of a warm welcome, good food and drink served under the watchful eye of the Chief. Sunday morning dawned mistily. Obviously we were in for a really hot day and, my goodness, how hot it proved to be. When travelling at 90 miles per hour in the Midlands later in the day even the wind blew

hot, but at no time did the Jupiter overheat. With no special preparation we left Abington at 8.35 and ran without a stop to within ten miles of Newark. Here we stopped for lunch, and filled up with eight gallons of petrol and one pint of oil. This took an hour and we left at 1.45 pm. At 4.45 pm we stepped out of the Jupiter at Romford, having completed the 375 miles in 7 hours 10 minutes' driving time.

Some friends said to my passenger: 'You must be dead tired,' but her reply, 'Not a bit, I should be quite happy to drive straight back,' should be noted. I myself would have been quite happy to have driven back. I was very nearly as fresh as when I started and, do not forget, the drive from Huntingdon had been through traffic which was quite heavy on this hot Sunday afternoon.

To sum up, any motor car that, after completing 1,600-odd miles over the rough roads of north and north-west Scotland, runs 375 miles with one stop of an hour at an average speed of 50 mph, with such smoothness and such airy lightness of control as to leave driver and passenger as fresh as when they started, has indeed qualified to be considered one of the finest cars in the world - and I submit that, on the evidence, the Jupiter is definitely in that class.

The Jupiter in Concours d'Elégance
by John Parker, chairman, Jupiter Owners' Auto Club

There are perhaps only some dozen or so Jupiters currently competitive in Concours events. This is a pity as the car gives you several immediate advantages over the other competitors:

1   The initial eye appeal that only a distinctive-looking sports car has.

2   Once in *true* Concours condition it is an easy car to maintain as such - my own experience after four years of inter-club contests and national concours is that with very little extra effort now it seems to get even better each year.

3   It is a delight to drive and even under the most adverse weather conditions you can still get to the events you are entered in - the mark of a serious true competitor. No organiser likes the entrant who arrives only if the weather suits him - if you have formally entered then make every effort to get there. If you have doubts then don't enter until the day - most events accept late entries and allowance is made in the programme for this.

96 Mr Parker restored his Jupiter himself

4   Finally, I consider the Jupiter is an economical car to buy, restore and maintain. It is probably the least expensive way of being really competitive up there among the XK Jaguars, Healey Silverstones, Astons, Bentleys and on occasions I have beaten top Bentleys and even a Silver Ghost RR.

For me the results speak for themselves, after buying and totally restoring my own Jupiter EHH707, I have won to date 27 awards and had a tremendous amount of pleasure in showing my car to the public as an example of my own personal standard of workmanship.

In closing I would like to offer some advice to would-be Jupiter competitors. Don't cut corners when restoring your car – nobody wants to see a 27-year-old car that looks like it has seen 27 years' service. The art of Concours is to show your car as if it had just left the factory – people want to see what they looked like when new.

In this same context get rid of those items your car has 'grown' over the years such as extra lights, non-standard hoods and windows, masses of irrelevant instruments and particularly over-size wheels and tyres. Flashing indicators are a case in point – admirable as they are at least incorporate them through the existing lights – it is not necessary to tack extra lights on to carry out this signalling function.

Try to avoid thinking of your Jupiter as a modern competitive sports car – it is not – 25 years ago it was one of the stars of the road but those 25 years have taken their toll and even the modern family car has superior performance now.

The Jupiter is a true sports car from another era and that is how it must be preserved – if you do this faithfully it will give you, and others, untold pleasure and satisfaction and perpetuate the model in its true light.

The Jupiter in historic racing
by Peter Dixon, chief registrar, the Historic Sports Car Club

By the mid 1960s, it had become apparent that the Vintage Sports Car Club were never going to accept the rarer more worthy sports cars of the early post-war era and that, unless some home for these cars could be found, they would continue to be destroyed or unsuitably modified. Thus initially, there came into being the Griffiths formula for such cars and a race and two high speed trials was held for them on 14 May 1966 at the Castle Coombe circuit, thus modestly inaugurating a new and successful arena of competition for sporting cars of the past.

Following a Jupiter (Frank Mockridge, (876) outing that day in one of the high speed trials for historic sports cars as they

96 Mr Parker restored his Jupiter himself

97

97 Peter Dixon (876) closely followd by the Porsche Speedster of D.Mallet, Silverstone 1978

came to be known, nothing else was heard regarding Jupiters, in what then became the Historic Sports Car Club, until 1972. In this year the next owner of the same car, Peter Dixon, decided that the Jupiter's inclusion in the then exclusive 'historically eligible' lists was worth celebrating. By this date the Historic Sports Car Club was featuring a regular number of races a year at meetings held under the auspices of friendly relevant clubs such as AMOC, BDC and JDC for historic 1940-60 and post historic 1960-64 cars. In sports racing, with such machines as Lotus XI, D-type and Lister-Jaguars mixing it with road sports Frazer Nashes, AC Aces, 356 Porsches and soon the Jupiter was patently one of the oldest and smallest cars racing and, not unexpectedly, one of the slowest, so much so that eventually the races were split and the sports racers went their own faster way. Following the lead of this Jupiter, which raced continuously from 1972-8 without accident or breakdown, various other owners made sporadic

appearances in these races, thus the original entrant Peter Dixon in FVG332 was joined on occasion by Pete Crosby, Geoff McAuley and Mike Smailes, all of whom had regularly competed in north of England sprints and hill climbs as well.

In fact the best Jupiter racing was undoubtedly generated by the appearance of one or more of its fellows as FVG332 normally beat either only newcomers or cars not running well or not being raced in earnest. Otherwise it came a sporting last! However, as in its heyday, people commented generally as to the excellent race handling of the Jupiter, its safety record and its noticeable reliability, including its road drives to and from all track meetings (some 36 ten-lap races). What people failed to notice was that it had no equitable competition for the 1600 cc Porsches were mostly running post-1960 American racing components giving over 100 bhp where the catalogue stated 55-75 bhp as standard for the cars of the equivalent period. The HRGs did not appear.

In 1978 the ex-Le Mans class winning R1 re-appeared to race three times in the hands of FVG332's owner, who immediately found that whilst this very historic car had considerable potential the ravages of previous restorers, engine swappers and butchers had created areas needing further restoration and chassis/suspension tuning of this 13 cwt car. However, the general feeling is that after full restoration and tuning, it should become one of the rarer showpieces of the now ever more popular and successful historic sports car racing movement. This, at the date of writing has six categories racing in different championships and now includes production sports cars of the respective eras e.g. TRs 2 & 3, MG Ts and As, Morgans etc. This movement has also gained a good foothold in Europe, Australia and America and the reappearance of a Jupiter in a Le Mans retrospective race is eagerly awaited. It is of interest ot note that the Lester- and Cooper-MG opposition is today non-existent, thus in its strict era the Jupiter has proved to be the racing survivor, and its current lap times compare favourably with the times achieved during its manufactured life.

In its first race on the Brands Hatch club circuit, 8 June 1975 its best race lap of 1 min 14 secs equalled the then 1600 cc HSCC roadsports lap record held by an MGA. Its best times to date are: Brands Hatch club circuit, 1976, 1 min 07 secs; Silverstone club circuit, 1976, 1 min 26 secs and Snetterton, 1973, 2 mins 36 secs.

A selection of performances by other Jupiters includes: Ingliston, M. Smailes (650), 1973, 75.6 secs; P. Crosby (898), 1975, 72.4 secs; Snetterton, M. Smailes (650), 1973, 2 mins 24.3 secs; and Oulton 1975 (lost its hairpin from 1975), G. MacAuley (947), 1 min 33.2 secs and P. Crosby (898) 1 min 35.2 secs.

One of Geoff MacAuley's most satisfying outings was one of his first, when on 2 September 1973 he broke the (1500) MGA record for the Topcliffe hill-climb, and at an MGCC meeting too, a record he still holds, for the hill is no longer used for motor sport. And on 19 May 1979 at the Shibden, near Halifax, $\frac{3}{4}$-mile climb, his time 32.98 secs was 1.92 secs better than a mildly tuned and well-driven MGB roadster, and 4.8 secs faster than a BGT.

Current use
by Mrs Elizabeth D. Davis

In 1966 a journey to St Ives in Huntingdon brought PZ1007 (840) into the family to join two Javelins. There were many things about it that were non-standard, but not having any previous knowledge of Jupiters we did not at first realise how much was incorrect. The seating, for one thing, had been made from the back seat of a Javelin; later, by a lucky fluke, a correct Jupiter seat was found on a scrap-heap. It had seen service as seating in a Bedford van. Whilst rebuilding another Jupiter (521) my husband was able to correct other anomalies.

I found that I really did enjoy driving PZ. Very nobly my husband agreed to my taking it over as my own vehicle, and it has been in constant use since it was purchased. The original engine was changed in 1968 for one from a Javelin, with a series III crank, just a temporary measure, while my husband prepared a Jupiter engine. The latter has never been used and the car is still running well with the so-called 'tem-

98 The Jupiters of Elizabeth Davis (left) and Ron Davis, who owns the Jupiter rallied in 1952 by F.E.Still

porary' engine at 50,000 miles plus.

Being used every day it is well-known in my area, even by the local constabulary, but not on a criminal basis! I have taken it on many visits to far-flung family and friends and have also used it for touring. One winter for over four months PZ took me nearly every day on a 40-mile journey to visit a dying relative and never once did it let me down. As my husband says, being well made in the first place it is not difficult to keep the car in good running order. He should know, as we have had only Jowett cars for the past 19 years.

Seldom a day goes by without having enquiries about the car. Once some madman took many photographs of it, even standing in the middle of a main road to get a different angle. On another occasion a man came up and introduced himself as having frequently seen and admired the car way back when it was new in Northern Ireland. He was a student at the time at Bangor University and he remembers vowing to have such a car when he was older. It seems that Bob McKee of the Belfast Jowett agency (who was to lose his life in PZ) lived in Belfast but had a girl friend in Bangor to whom frequent visits were made with the car.

May I just finish by extolling the car's virtues as far as I am concerned. First it is so easy to park, having an excellent lock and good visibility. Secondly with a well-fitting hood and wind-up windows I find it a warm car even in the coldest weather. In summer with the hood down it is the only sports car I have ever driven where you do not get an uncomfortable back-draught. I also find I can pack an amazing amount into it: I take stalls at many auto-jumbles and antique fairs, and the quantity of cases and boxes that I can stow away in it never ceases to surprise me. It is my ideal car.

The year 1953 began sadly for Jowetts, for in January the last few Javelin and Bradford bodies were received from the Briggs Doncaster factory. A lathering of snow coated the Javelin bodies stored to the side of the Jowett plant: would Briggs ever restart the flow when more were needed? As British Ford tightened its grip on the British arm of the American bodybuilding firm, the Experimental Department were informed that a new sports car, if ready in time for the Motor Show the following October, might save the company. It would have to be cheap, easy to make, and not require the service of Briggs. So, much midnight oil was burned and by March it had been styled by Phil Stephenson, the inspiration probably being the Ferrari America of Carozzeria Touring; by no means a plagiarism, rather it was an original and well-developed variation. The intention was to attack the MG Midget market.

As chief engineer, Donald Bastow had overall responsibility but with the departure of Grandfield and Korner the biggest contribution came from Roy Lunn. Bastow had joined in September 1952 with the prime requirement of getting over the many engineering problems which had been hanging about for some time, and others which were beginning to show up. (Frank Salter had rejoined as technical director at the same time and had a similar brief regarding production problems.) Roy Lunn was proving to be a natural engineer, good at getting things done in a hurry, a very forceful character, impulsive; he provided a lot of ideas but still at this time needed a guiding hand. Work began on a car in April and the highly skilled Experimental staff showed their worth, often having to make parts before they were drawn. In full spate Phil Stephenson once completed no less than 47 separate drawings in a single 24-hour period. Elements were incorporated from the CDs whenever possible as they were fully developed and tooled and it was still hoped that CD production might yet take place.

The chassis was formed from box-section fabrications of quite exceptional depth, further reinforced by a welded-on scuttle and complete tail panel, the complete assembly having considerably greater stiffness than the Mk1 design, yet being lighter. It was one Friday in early spring that the Experimental Department monthly staff paycheques bounced and, although the matter was quickly settled, Stephenson took the hint and during June he left Jowetts. George Green, the sales manager, visiting the USA that same month on another matter, took photographs of the new car and reported that many could be sold there.

99 Underside view of JKW537 after the fitting of the overdrive. Part of the 1950 Le Mans pit sign, bottom right: C.H.Wood

*100 Cockpit of the
R4 after the fitting of
the overdrive. Switch to
the right of the tacho-
meter sounds horn when
tilted in any direction:
C.H.Wood*

The first R4, chassis 100/1 was registered JKW547 in July 1953 and on the 10th of the month was photographed with 148 miles on its odometer and with only aero-screens for weather protection. It was being prepared for a continental proving run, to be driven by Roy Lunn and riding mechanic Teddy Fannon.

Six weeks later it was again photographed, having returned from France and Italy:its bonnet, straight again after an incident in the latter country, was now louvred, the gearbox had an overdrive unit attached, and 4,766 miles were now showing on the odometer.

JKW547 had its bonnet assembly and boot-lid made of metal, but Lunn had other ambitions. When it had become clear that Briggs were looking for ways to shed their commitment to Jowetts the Experimental Department began looking into the use of fabric reinforced plastic for Javelin door and boot panels (an all-FRP Javelin was not, however, contemplated) and some disadvantages of the new wonder material became evident: the vapours were highly inflammable, the resins were not self-colourable and, taking days to cure, could and did self-ignite during the curing process. The finished product did not take paint readily and paint caused crazing only minimised by selecting white or near-white. The end product itself was inflammable and, being brittle, could fragment and splinter on impact. Undaunted, the decision was taken to use this material for the fronts of two pre-production cars and all-night sessions laying up the FRP for these bore fruit. Panels from JKW were used for the moulds and since they had not been designed as such it sometimes took many men to pull the mouldings out.

Just in time, a glass-fibre hardtop was finished and fitted to JKW as was a newly designed bonnet emblem – an RAC badge had up to then sufficed. The day the show opened, photographs of the prototype appeared in the *Manchester Guardian, Daily Mail, Daily Mirror,* and the *Evening News*; Bastow and Lunn drove it south and Phil Green gave demonstration runs in it through London's streets. On the Jowett stand, attracting a lot of comment, stood one of the newer cars, ivory with blue upholstery. Its electric cooling fan was noted, as was the change from rack-and-pinion to cam-and-lever steering. The car was awarded second place in a sports coachwork competition (below £800 division) to the TR2 with the TF third, and was the lowest priced 100+ mph car present at £773 4s 2d after tax.

The third R4, dove grey with red interior went to the Albermarle Street showroom and one report has it that whilst there its coverings were never removed.

On 25 October JKW was tested by journalists at the Goodwood Test Day, wearing its hardtop and full front screen. On 13 November the Scottish Motor Show began; only a pre-production car made the journey and it was neither listed in the catalogue nor accompanied by any explanatory literature.

Jowetts were now virtually car-makers no longer so Ford (through the Briggs connection) 'headhunted' Roy Lunn and his illustrious career took its new turn when he joined Ford in January 1954 to design the 105E Anglia. He had regrets, for he was sure his R4 was potentially a winner.

There was still some unfinished business. There was a soft top to be fitted to the show car and this was carried out and it had a photographic session in this form on Christmas Eve. A little development work continued after Roy Lunn left and this included a speed check on JKW at MIRA by John Brace: a 0 – 60 mph time of 12.6 secs was obtained but there was some difficulty on the high-speed banked track when the 100 mph was attempted. The screen had to be removed and the magic figure was then just achieved.

JKW was then loaned to Frank Masefield Baker of Ovingdean near Brighton for evaluation. Frank had driven a works Javelin (1953 Monte) and he was instructed to use the car and report – he remembers it was a bit rough with odd wiring everywhere, but thought it a 'cracking little motor car' and took it up to its maximum speed, indicated 114 mph, every time he used it.

102

Jowetts meanwhile temporarily forgot that Masefield Baker had JKW537, later in 1954 writing and asking for it back! They had a buyer for it in the person of Alf Thomas of the Central Garage, Kempston, Bedford and his plans for the car centred on the club racing scene at Silverstone nearby. Alf had crashed his first Jupiter, the Rawson-bodied JTM100 (38) within a week or two of collecting it in 1951, when he spun it into a ditch * and brushed with death, a broken rib puncturing his lung. Alf drove JTM at Silverstone from the latter part of 1951 to 1953 but with the acquisition of the R4 his son would drive the light, fast but rather tail-happy earlier car; on occasion he would take out the R4 too.

Eric Turner was the chairman of the Blackburn and General Aircraft Co and he became the chairman of Jowett Cars Ltd after Blackburn took over Jowetts (now at Birstall) in September 1955. He took a liking for the R4 and consequently the show car (chassis R4/1) was registered for him in July 1956 – SWT356 – and in November the car became Turner's. After the Motor Show in 1953 the Albermarle Street R4 disappeared and like its sister it does not seem to have been held at Birstall, although it might have gone to Brough where Turner lived, possibly dismantled to avoid the necessity of a purchase tax payment. It is believed that Turner did not cover a great mileage in his

*JTM100 required a new chassis and the car was then driven to Lionel Rawson to straighten out the bodywork (the bonnet travelling separately by Bradford van); thus Rawson made some profit from the repairing that he had failed to do from the building.

R4 and in July 1958 the car appeared at Birstall for a minor Isopon job to the front, for a check-over, and for sale.

Again the buyer was Alf Thomas and he also purchased enough parts to build a third one, it must be assumed the dismantled Albermarle Street car. One of his mechanics, D.Whitworth, and Alf himself assembled the hitherto unused collection of bits, making up a new exhaust system, and having the three cars ready for the Six-Hour Relay Handicap Race of 16 August 1958.

The newly assembled R4 was never registered by Alf Thomas (purchase tax again probably) but for the race wore the registration HAK365 – it is not known why the 1951 Le Mans class-winner's number was used.

The competition history of the R4s in the hands of the Thomases has been recorded elsewhere: of the way they performed it is known that Alf was initially critical of JKW, claiming its handling was unpredictable although by 1955 he was already trying to buy another one. Barry has reported that the 'R4's handling was good but you had to get to know them – then you could chop them round corners very fast.' The R4 would slide easily and once Alf was black-flagged for taking his hands off the wheel on a corner.

An inspection of race results shows that JKW was quite a competitive $1\frac{1}{2}$-litre production car at that time, normally quicker round the Silverstone club circuit than the $1\frac{1}{2}$-litre MGA and where Alf had managed the occasional lap at 65 mph in 1954 this had risen to 68 mph, sustainable for a five-lapper (faster than TR2s when they first appeared) in 1956/7. By 1958 the R4 is believed to have been able to

101 Glass-fibre-fronted R4 Jupiter at the preview for the 38th International London Motor Show, Earl's Court: Popperfoto

put up the occasional race lap at about 1 min 24 secs, around 69 mph; by comparison, in 1956 a Lotus-MG winning speed might be 67.3 mph (though a year later Lotus Climaxes were a full 10 mph faster). In 1956 a 1½-litre TF might lap Silverstone in 1 min 32.4 secs (62.65 mph), a 1½-litre MGA might return a best of 1 min 26.6 secs and a Healey Silverstone might manage 1 min 29 secs around the circuit whose name it bears. By 1958 the MGAs were putting up typically a 69.6 mph fastest, with a 67.7 mph race average.

One race is known for Alf Thomas and JKW at Crystal Palace; it is believed to have been the BRSCC meeting on 10 June 1957, probably the production sports car event won by a Lotus-Ford. An eyewitness has it that it 'saw off TR3'.

R4 engines differ in certain respects from the standard Jupiter's unit. Externally the highest point, the top of the water pump, has been lowered to the minimum by flanging the pump/timing cover joint, and engine oil is replenished through a capacity tube incorporating the pcv breather valve, located over the right-hand push-rod cover. Internally the compression ratio was raised to the 1951 Le Mans figure of 8.5:1 and the standard camshaft was re-timed, the overall effect being a slightly reduced torque with increased bhp appearing at higher rpm (84 lb-ft at 3000 rpm down to 81 lb-ft at 3,500; 62.5 bhp at 4,500 up to 64 bhp at 5,000). An interesting advance in the matter of cylinder-head seals was contributed by Donald Bastow. Hitherto only Wills rings had proved completely reliable at a compression ratio of 9.25:1, the 1952 Le Mans figure, and these were fiddly, expensive, and not really suited to production. The invention utilised standard head gaskets: it received a lot of testing at 9.25:1 and was found to be as reliable as the earlier method. Finned aluminium cuffs were pressed or shrunk on to the cylinder liners, making them incidentally dry liners. A disadvantage of the standard production arrangement had always been the short cylinder-head studs, all but one being threaded into the head faces of the crankcase. Since the liners are seated low down in the case, differential expansion between liner and case actually reduces the liner top/cylinder head squeeze on the gasket as the temperature rises. Alternate heating and cooling causes corresponding fluctuations in force and the shrunk-on aluminium cuff on a machined-down liner neatly eliminates this effect, and may more efficiently cool the liner too. The

Albermarle Street car, though, at least when sold by Peter Michael, did not have this type of liner but rather had a Le Mans-type Wills ring set.

One of Alf Thomas's modifications was to the con-rods: the 'top half long side' of the big-end eye would be built up with weld in an attempt to prevent high-rpm breakage which can occur at this point.

The gearbox casing is quite different from the Javelin and Jupiter and is of the form developed for the Javelin-engined CD Bradfords, that is to say a gearbox casting that is a unit casting with its bellhousing, and it mates to a short intermediate housing positioned between it and the normal crankcase. Inside were to be found the conventional late Javelin components – wide ratio according to the brochure – and the final drive is by 4.44:1 rear axle to 15 inch wheel rims carrying 5.90 x 15 tyres. Theoretical speed at peak power in the optional overdrive top gear is 102 – 105 mph. Gearing in normal top $16\frac{3}{4}$ mph per 1,000 rpm.

An unconcluded development of 1957 was the dohc hemispherical-combustion-chambered cylinder heads of Paul Emery. At that time well-known for his ingenious and successful front-wheel-drive Emeryson 500 cc single-seaters, Emery conceived the idea of a 1½-litre formula 1 engine based on the Javelin/Jupiter block with dohc aluminium heads, the patterns being made by Louis Giron. An immediate 100 hp was seen at the flywheel with four Amals (fuel injection was to follow) but blocks cracked across the push-rod wells, leading to the project's abandonment. A year later these heads were in Alf Thomas's hands but as has been noted elsewhere on the report on the 1958 Six-Hour Relay, a second close encounter with the Reaper, when the 9 Dzus fasteners holding the R4's front end let go, leaving Alf in the cornfield badly bruised, led him ultimately, and with much reluctance, to give up racing.

In February 1960 Alf Thomas advertised the three R4s for sale as 'The only three made before the sad end of production of Jowett Cars.' His Jowett days were over and he was to die of cancer six years later.

Jowett owner and enthusiast Peter Michael, a student at the time preparing for what would be a brilliant career in electronics, sold his mother's car without her knowledge to raise the £1500 or so Alf would accept for the trio. One car was immediately prepared for Mrs Michael and she took over the all-metal prototype JKW537, with detuned engine and minus its overdrive, the car being re-registered 4488BY, but not before its front end had once again served as a mould for the new bonnet set that was required for the Albermarle Street car, soon to be sold bearing JKW537 plates. Peter Michael fitted the overdrive unit into the show car SWT356 and registered it in his own name in March 1961. In addition to a new front end, a pattern for the finned sump was made and magnesium sumps cast.

For the superstitious bad luck runs in threes and so it would seem as within three years all three R4s were destined for what to normal cars would have been terminal accidents, and in the first instance was. The Albermarle Street car, wearing JKW537, was sold on a nebulous sale-or-return basis to a Glaswegian named Ian MacCaskill. On his return to Glasgow, MacCaskill lost it in a big way on a straight but irregular street in Glasgow frequently used for burn-ups, wrapping the car round a lamp-post and bending the chassis into a U. MacCaskill's insurance company argued that the car was not his and therefore not their responsibility, and likewise Michael's maintained that the car was de facto sold. - such are the methods of insurance companies. Naturally the car was stripped of anything saleable, the cast sump going on Ian's sister's boy friend's saloon Jupiter (35), the gearbox to SWT356's new owner as a spare, and so forth. Fortunately George Mitchell saw the log book and observed therein the registration, JKW537, and the chassis number, 100/1. Mrs Michael disposed of the true JKW537, wearing 4488BY (its logbook endorsed 'made up from spare parts' and alleging the chassis number to be R4/2) and it went to the Watford area around 1962 (where its tachometer failed - the makers AC were then contacted and reported that it was a prototype instrument, one of only three made) and the car seems to have been in London NW9 in 1963, although soon to disappear from there. In the mid-1960s it appeared in Owens of Oakengate, near Telford, having been written off and probably rolled, and was resuscitated by a scrap-metal dealer named R.G.Kurswell, who ran the R4 untaxed and uninsured (there was no logbook) until the law caught up with him. He sold it to some college youths from south Wales who evidently revived the 4488BY registration, for it bore this when in 1971 R.N.Thomas of Bristol bought the car, found the chassis marking of 100/1 and was able to re-establish the car's correct registration. At the time of writing a thorough restoration is under way in the hands of its present owner, George Bird.

Peter Michael sold SWT356 to Alan George, who registered the car in his name on January 1964. But by February of that year it had been heavily crashed into a railway bridge near Ray Browne's village – Ray Browne was the librarian of the old Southern Jowett Car Club (SJCC) and the car was being joy-ridden it not being certain whether Alan George or Ray Browne was driving. Browne at least required a hospital stay and the wreck went under a tarpaulin in Ken Braddock's yard, Leighton Buzzard, its glass-fibre front end in fragments. It was purchased by Arthur Rutland around March 1967, its odometer reading 43,437 miles and many years would elapse before it again travelled under its own power. Mr Rutland did not enjoy good health but he gave the car his devoted attention, gradually and meticulously restoring it to the point at which it could be trailered to the 1979 Classic Car Show at Alexandra Palace virtually completed; and its photograph, taken at Ferrers Mere, Higham Ferrers, appeared on the front cover of the magazine *Thoroughbred and Classic Car* in September 1979. After Mr Rutland's death in 1979, the car was taken over by his step-son Len Jones. In the same way that JKW537 must always be associated with Alf Thomas and Silverstone, so SWT356 will be with Arthur Rutland, who took on the car when no one else would consider it and who was finally cheated of driving the car to which he had applied himself for so long.

CHAPTER 8 Special~Bodied Jupiters: The Coachbuilders

About 48 fully equipped rolling chassis were delivered to British coachbuilders and it is a fair bet that virtually all were built up, the majority within a year of delivery. Something is known about almost all of them and a survival rate higher than for the standard product says something for the regard in which even the least attractive examples have been held by their owners over the years. They vary from the elegant Abbotts, Meads, Rawsons, Coachcrafts and the like through some very good tries to some odd individual designs; though noses should not be turned up at bodywork that in its way is representative of the types that were being fitted to many other chassis at that time and at bottom expresses the feel of the immediate post-war era - times long gone. For that was a time when in the motor industry at large, chassis-building capacity outstripped body-building capacity and there were for a while, opportunities for many small concerns to survive, just, at the few-off level, on such as Healey, Alvis and Lea Francis, as well as Bristol and Bentley.

Jowetts, too, initially had hoped that outside coachbuilders could collectively take over the construction of Jupiter body-work but it emerged that the bespoke market was rather marginal for a 2/3 seater with only 1½ litres of engine. During the

first 12 months of the Jupiter's production life, however, no less than 35 per cent were rolling chassis. These were mechanically complete, some at least actually being road-tested, bodyless, over a 100 mile test course before being shipped. With the chassis went the instruments, grilles, bumpers, and electrical equipment, including the wiring harness. If Jowetts approved the bodywork, the car when completed would be covered by the usual six months' warranty.

Aesthetically the newer continental ideas varied in influence from the whole-sale lift (725) through more or less direct or indirect (37,48) to second or third hand or none at all (12,253). And two (10, 242) at least are a reminder that for 15 months complete Jupiters were for export only and the construction of near replicas could overcome this local difficulty.

For some, the need for a sports saloon was met by working back from a standard Jupiter bonnet (29 and 97), a solution only possible from 1952 when body parts were more freely available.

At least three out of the four Swiss coachbuilders most active after the war built Jupiters, in fact they built bodies, mostly dropheads on the majority of British cars with separate chassis, and of course Fiat. As Switzerland was perhaps the healthiest European market after the war there was enough custom to keep a handful of coachbuilders busy, though much of their bread and butter work was probably commercials: few of them survived into the 1960s.

Of the fourteen chassis sent to European coachbuilders all but three have been identified and as unwanted chassis were returnable, it is again likely that all were constructed.

Abbott

E.D.Abbott, of Farnham, Surrey, are well-known for their Rolls and Bentley bodies and the Abbott Healey, of which come hundred were built in 1950. Some of their

102   Three Jupiter saloons. left to right: *Adams & Robinson (725), Flewitt (97), Maurice Gomm (30)*

106

lesser-known cars are the Lammas-Graham of 1936 – 8, the Atalanta, Lagonda Rapier, Connaught L35R sports car of 1951 (12 laid down, possibly not all completed) and the open version of the glass-fibre Bristol 404/5. Shooting-brakes were produced. An XK120 four-seater tourer was made for a New Zealander, and in 1951 two open Jupiters (32,89) were completed, resembling the type-57 Bugatti from some angles; two fixed-head versions (105,247) otherwise identical, followed in 1952, the first for C.H.Swain of H.R.Owen Ltd. The fixed-head coupés retailed at £2,210 10s – including extras and tax.

Adams & Robinson

In 1951 Philip Fotheringham-Parker, a racing driver who had in his time competed in a wide variety of events (prewar in Frazer Nashes and Alvis, including one of the works Silver Eagles, and post-war in ERA, Maserati, XK120, Connaught), decided to have a saloon Jupiter built, possibly with a view to the Monte Carlo Rally, and he took delivery of chassis 725 in February 1952. It so happened that around the same time Roy Clarkson, one of the best of the rally specialists of the day, rallied (1951 Tulip, Scottish, MCC) and raced (a poor 23rd at the Silverstone production car race) a beautiful blue type-212 Inter Ferrari with an intricate saloon body, by Carozzeria Touring of Milan; and suitably fortified, arranged with Peter Morgan to have a saloon body fitted to a Morgan chassis to evaluate its suitability for rallying. Both chassis went to the yard of Adams & Robinson Ltd, Sunbury-on-Thames, and on these Charlie Robinson built a pair of saloon bodies very closely replicating the sculptured curves of the aforementioned Ferrari, Robinson having already acquired an envied reputation for skill in multidirectional aluminium panelwork, typifying the highest standards of craftsmanship learned or developed in the wartime aircraft industry.

Both cars, it seems were intended for the 1953 Monte Carlo Rally. Work on the Jupiter stagnated for the firm was in financial difficulties, and funds for the Jupiter were diverted to the Morgan. Maurice Gomm helped complete the Morgan, perhaps explaining why it has a very similar windscreen to the saloon Jupiters Gomm was building for Beverley Motors. Clarkson registered it VNO600 in time to hurry to the Munich start, only to retire in the early stages. Although the Jupiter's panelling was formed and the tail section hung on tubing welded to the frame, Fotheringham-Parker saw little progress and lost interest. Ultimately, Robinson was taken over by John Willment of Willment Bros and Willment Racing, possibly so that Willment could get hold of the Jupiter. With difficulty, Robinson was persuaded to complete it and the car was eventually put on the road near the end of 1957; unlike the Morgan, though, it had a forward opening bonnet *au* Rawson. Other cars built by Adams & Robinson include Emerysons for Paul Emery, a Cooper-Triumph, Austin and MG specials, and a Pycroft Jaguar is claimed.

Armstrong

The *Carlisle Journal* of 13 June 1952 reported that the firm of J.J.Armstrong of Carlisle had just completed a closed Jupiter (12) at their Thomas Street garage, and that though the firm had been building commercial bodies for 20 years this was their first private car. Their rather home-made-looking Jupiter was apparently to the design of Mr Armstrong.

Barnaby

Cliff Golan of Barnaby Bodybuilders of Hull constructed a Jupiter (10) for Ted Booth to enter as a team car in the 1951 RAC Rally; as it had to resemble standard, body drawings were supplied by Jowetts.

Barton

Barton's Transport built, of all things, a camper body on chassis 107 for the firm's managing director, Mr C. Barton, to the design of his foreman Tommy Shirley. Mr Barton toured Switzerland in it during 1953.

Bendall

Under the heading 'Carlise Firm Improves Car' the *Cumberland News* of 15 March 1952 announced the completion of a neat and original open Jupiter (253) by James Bendall & Sons Ltd of Carlisle. Jim Bendall designed the body and thought of using the Riley front wings, while Douglas Workman and Jack Dodds of Armstrong & Fleming, Penrith, carried out the mechanical work. Reg Sheppard drove it down to London for auction when the original customer withdrew. Peter Ustinov once owned the car and it went to Hollywood with him for a couple of years.

Beutler

Gebruder Beutler of Thun in Switzerland completed the last Swiss Jupiter (291) around July 1951. A very eye-catching car, it was entered in the International Automobile im Festklied in Lucerne (a

103 *Award-winning cabriolet by Gebruder Beutler, Switzerland*

'beauty contest for cars') in the first week of that month, where it was awarded second in class to a 1400 Fiat of Ghia Turin.

Beverley

Nigel Mann of Beverley Motors, New Malden, Surrey, besides supplying individual coachwork on Alfa Romeo chassis, collected no less than six Jupiter rolling chassis together in 1952; two saloons were built by Maurice Gomm (builder of the first, aluminium, Lolas) for Beverley Motors and they were put on the market at £1,100 + tax, late in 1952. One year later Beverley Motors went into liquidation and the saloons are believed to have been unsold at that time. J.F.Hall raced one at Snetterton on 13 August 1955, and, judging from its unperforated front bumper, it had not been road-registered at that time. One of these saloons (40) was first registered 53CPA on 1 December 1956 and some exaggerated claims were made for it about fuel injection, 120 mph and connections with Mike Hawthorne before it disappeared in 1964, possibly abroad. Though one cannot be sure, 53CPA is not thought to be the Snetterton car. Nigel Mann, a relative of the brewery family that bears his name, was a well-known and consistent competitor at Le Mans, Goodwood and other venues in his DB2 and 2.6 litre Monza Alfa.

In 1954 there remained the four unbuilt chassis but by 1957 two had disappeared and their fate is a matter for conjecture. The remaining pair (30,246) were bought in 1957 for £200 apiece then resold to two airline pilots, who each had Maurice Gomm build saloon bodies on them to their own specifications.

Coachcraft

Coachcraft of Egham, Surrey, certainly built two saloons (28,48). Although not replicas, believably 48 was advertised in 1958 as 'Farina-copied' and in this context 28 has no bonnet scoop (see Farina) but 48 has one. The first car was on the road in March 1951, whereas 48 was delayed by financial difficulties at Coachcraft, the car being completed in November elsewhere, the delay allowing time for the bonnet scoop to become known about and incorporated. Also incorporated on 48 from new was a neat Wade supercharger installation, put in by Pat Whittet & Co. The pleasant open Jupiter (47) is probably another product of coachcraft. What is believed to be 28 was comprehensively reworked from about 1958 until its re-registration as CPG63B in 1964.

Colinsons

See Rawson.

Crouch

The Australian sporting driver John Crouch of John Crouch Motors, Sydney, the major specialist dealer there in the 1950s (Bristol, Cooper, Dellow as well as Jupiter) ordered four Jupiter rolling chassis and subsequently obtained a further two from Tasmania, with the intention of having ash-framed but otherwise replica Jupiter bodies built on them and S.O.Hodge, a local body-maker, constructed this coachwork on five out of the six frames. There may have been a system of rationing imposed by Jowetts, allowing an importer a maximum of three and obliging Crouch to obtain one through the Adelaide agent. Although this, one, 13, is the only one known for sure to have had a Hodge body there is little doubt that 11, 15, 16 and 22 also have – or had. 24 is known to have been left over, having at some stage an unidentified Vauxhall body fitted: it was sold by John Crouch to Bill

Webb for £600 and it covered some 70,000 miles before exchanging coachwork with a by now damaged 13. This wore Vauxhall for a short while only, before being sold bodyless to Eddy Wolf whereas Bill Webb had second thoughts about repairing and refitting the Hodge panelling to 24, scrapped it and set about fitting proprietary kit-car coachwork in the form of the glass-fibre Milano. This work has since halted incomplete.

Farina

Stabilimenti Farina began around the turn of the century repairing then building horse-drawn and later horseless carriages and by 1910 Giuseppe (Pinin) Farina, younger brother of the founder, was designing for his brother's firm. In 1930, however, he left to found his own coach-building concern, Pininfarina, although always maintaining friendly relations with Stabilimenti, just around the corner on Via Tortona, Turin.

The 'Italian Look' can be traced to Pinin's 1936 – 9 designs on Alfa Romeo, Lancia Astura, and other chassis, and post-war was refined with the Cistilia of 1946 and several other designs of which the best-known are probably Lancia's Aprilia of 1948 and the Aurelia that followed. Confusingly, at times Stabilimenti designs were built by what became a much larger Pininfarina and vice versa when the cars often carried the emblem of their builders rather than designers. It is probable that by 1951 Stabilimenti was separate only in name, for around 1953 the older was absorbed by the younger company.

Harry Ainsworth, longtime general manager of Hotchkiss (until the 1950 Peugeot takeover) and friend of Marcel Becquart was in 1950 retained by Jowetts

104 Coachcraft of Egham: The faired-in reversing lamp came later

as consultant for the British New York Motor Show of April 1950, later becoming Jowett's European sales manager and, not liking the shape of the standard car, he seems to have been behind Jowett's move to have Farina body a Jupiter (7). The New York importer Max Hoffman had a Chicago office and perhaps it was not pure co-incidence that the second of the first pair of Farina Jupiters (33) appeared many years later in Chicago, titled 1951.

It is known that four chassis were bodied by Stabilimenti Farina (7,33,59, 109) but as they so closely follow the Aprilia/Aurelia line they may be assumed to be Pinin designs and it is worth noting that, around the time in question, Pinin invented the bonnet airscoop: whereas the 1950 cars 7 and 33 have plain bonnets, the later two were scooped.

Other cars being built by Stabilimenti around the time in question include Fiat

105 The production of replica Jupiter bodies in Sydney, Australia

106 Good accessibility to luggage in the Farina Jupiter. Doors are pillarless: C.H.Wood

1400 saloons, Ferraris, and a Mercury for Henry Ford II.

Jowett's Farina, after its two shows in late 1950, spent some time in the London showroom before moving north to Bradford where it was transferred to the Experimental Department and registered for the road on 30 March 1951. Its photographic session near the factory's weighbridge 1 October that year was presumeably just prior to its sale. Its last British licence was drawn on 15 July 1952, after which it went abroad, turning up in Malaya in 1958 before being brought to New Zealand by a NZ airman; by then it may already have acquired its Jaguar grille and its bonnet airscoop.

Farr
J.E.Farr & Son Ltd of Blackburn, Lancashire, built four saloons (81,245,252, 583), the first for Robert Ellison to use in the 1952 Monte Carlo Rally. The *Blackburn Times* reported (4 January 1952) that 'the two directors J.E. Farr and his son J.S.Farr have incorporated ideas which have come to them during the course of many years' experience in this type of work . . . they outlined their ideas to Mr Tom Edwards who transferred them to the drawing board.' The weight was 18 cwt, a disappointment to Ellison, and the price was 'more than £1,750'. The last car built (583) was first used by one of the Farr family and is the only one to have been dismantled.

Flewitt
Flewitt of Vicarage Road, Birmingham built a saloon (chassis 97, body 2248-3) in

1953 but it was not until 1958 that it was first put into use. Two of the years 1953 – 8 were spent in a dealer's showroom. Flewitts are believed to have built on Rolls-Royce chassis at one time, and in 1952 they offered an XK120.

Ghia
Ghia Suisse of Aigle, a much smaller concern than its Italian namesake now owned by Ford, built a nice three-seater cabriolet (31) that was seen at the 1951 Geneva Show: Michelotti was the chief designer at Aigle at that time. A pair of saloons (56, 93) were built for the two French rallyists Latune and Thévenin. Other British chassis built on by this firm at the time were MG TD and Singer $1\frac{1}{2}$ litre.

Gomm
See Beverley Motors.

Grounds
Frank Grounds the Birmingham agent had a saloon (29) constructed in his own coachworks, cunningly matching a Jupiter bonnet to Morris Minor doors.

Hartwell
George Hartwell Ltd, Bournemouth, Hants, built an interesting open car (250) for Mr Vincent Louis Smith, a local hotelier. It incorporated a V-screen with split halves, the top halves opening, and two sets of seats for either rallying or touring. Although heavy it apparently was noted for its good cornering at 90 mph but it is doubtful if it was ever rallied. There were similarities between it and the Hartwell Alpine, (the car that led to the Sunbeam Alpine) that Hartwell was building on the Sunbeam 90 chassis.

Hodge
See John Crouch.

Kanrell
The first production chassis (6) was imported into their country by the Swedish agent AB Motortillbehor of Stockholm, displayed at a motor show and bought by Rune Berg (owner of a fast TC with replica aluminium bodywork, and, later, a standard Jupiter as well as No.6); it was then clothed in near-replica R1 bodywork by Karl-Gustaf Kanrell. Factory drawings of the R1 were slow in arriving, forcing Kanrell to work from photographs and it is evident that front views only were available to him. An R1 power unit was purchased from the works for £50 and

used as a model for what were at times fruitless engine experiments.

The car's first outing was in an international race at Skarpnacks airfield in 1951, when Berg brought it to fifth place behind the factory Porsche team of four cars headed by Max Nathan; however at least the Jupiter was the only car not lapped by the German cars. In the 1952 event, as has been noted elsewhere, Berg managed fourth.

Kanrell himself never raced the car but has recalled 'the roadholding was fantastic for its time, top speed as well. Many times I drove at 170 and 180 kph (106 – 112 mph) on normal roads.'

Berg parted with the car in 1954; its third owners were Olsson and Bohman of Stockholm, who used it in ice races and perhaps it was around this time that the front-end bodywork was changed slightly and for the worse. Kanrell became one of Sweden's leading racing mechanics and worked for Joakim Bonnier up to 1957.

KW

Mr Kitchener joined Lansdowne Bodies of Blackpool from his native London during the Depression, rising through the firm to become the 'K' of KW Bodies Ltd; at one time employing 73 men, mostly busy with Rolls-Royce bodies and shooting-brake conversions, they are now a much smaller concern. Three saloon Jupiters were attempted and the first two are recorded photographically and were not similar. Bill Robinson's car (37) was raced by him just the once (1951 British Empire Trophy) before a friend of Bill Skelly's took it in exchange for a TD. The 99 we have also met in competition but nothing is known of 113 beyond its first owner having been a Mr Green of Leeds, a businessman in fancy goods who had a holiday home in Blackpool.

Leacroft

In January 1955 Chilton Cars of Leighton Buzzard offered a one-owner open 1950 Jupiter for sale for £455, claiming that its special body had been built by *Leacroft*. If truly a 1950 chassis, as the price seems to indicate, it would have to be chassis 50.

Mead

Richard Mead of Dorridge, Warwickshire (34, 87, 117, 248, 249, 251, perhaps one more) may be better known as the designer and builder of the Rover-based Marauder, but actually less Marauders were built by him than Jupiters. Richard Mead's father designed and built the Rhode car (1921 – 9) then moved to Morris Commercial at Adderley Park and it was here that the young Richard started coachbuilding, mainly on shooting-brakes and ambulances. He next joined Meredith Coachraft – started by his father – leaving that firm in 1934 to work for people like Marendaz Special Cars, John Charles Ltd on Railtons, Corsica at Cricklewood on a variety of Bentleys and Mecedes, and Newnes at Thames Ditton on the pillarless Lagonda Rapiers. He spent the war years in the aircraft industry, and began his coachbuilding concern in 1946 with a design of his own on TA14 Alvis chassis for a customer of Ted Lloyd-Jones the speed-trials man. About six of these were made and he then bought a dozen 1939 Tickford 18/80 MG bodies that had been stored in a pub in Newport Pagnell throughout the war, and they were mainly fitted on Alvis, although a few went on Rolls and Bentley, one on a 8 litre. He then used AC, Austin Princess, Bristol, Marauder, Talbot 10 and the Jupiters, besides carrying out repairs, renovations, building new bodies on old chassis and the like. He was once saved from extinction by an order for milk floats on Ford 10 hp chassis.

Having seen a Jupiter chassis, he made a

107 Preliminary sketch of the Richard Mead Jupiter

sketch of a proposed design and circulated it around the Jowett agents, who took orders and sent him the chassis. Although considering himself a drophead coupé specialist, only one Richard Mead Jupiter (251) is a true drophead: it was offered at £1265 pre-tax, while the unlined hood/celluloid sidescreen version was £170 cheaper. One of his Jupiters (34) has its luggage locker externally accessible and a one-piece curved screen in place of the V but this is probably a modification. Richard Mead sold his business in 1958.

New Moston

The New Moston Sheet Metalwork Co whoever they were, may sound like the wrong people to be let loose on a Jupiter frame (9) but not so. They have produced an unexpected and charming open Jupiter with something of the Crosley Hotshot about it and its charm is enhanced by being in unspoilt early condition. The body is supported on the chassis by a sturdy steel tubular superstructure.

Motor Panels of Epsom

Motor Panels of Epsom (or Epsom Motor Panels) of East Street, Epsom, Surrey, took more than a year to build their saloon body, Superleggera-style, on chassis 49. To the design of its first owner, Yorkshireman John Watkinson, its finely shaped tail suggests the Zagato Fiat 8V, while the idea of fitting the all-enveloping and forward-hinging bonnet came from the ex Lance Macklin Aston Martin that Watkinson owned at the time. The car was first registered 12 January 1952.

Park

W.M.Park (Coachbuilders) Ltd of Kew, London, built rather nice aluminium-on-ash hard tops for Mk1 Jupiters, one of which was modelled by and used in competition on HKW429. The firm is not known to have built any special-bodied Jupiters.

Radford

The coachbuilders Harold Radford & Co. Ltd, South Kensington, London, may have a relevance beyond their two odd, dissimilar open Jupiters (8, 14), a relevance that reaches back into the pre-JCL penumbra of the Jupiter's gestatory period in the summer and autumn of 1949. It is therefore worth setting down what is known.

The bodybuilders Searcy & McCready of Chase Road, Southgate, London N14 built the first few Harold Radford Bentleys in 1948 – 9 and it was this wooded type of 'rich man's utility', whose seats could fold to make two comfortable beds, that became the Radford speciality through the 1950s. However, in 1949 Radford dispensed with the services of Searcy & McCready (and their body-contructing activities may have ceased not long after), opening his own coachworks in addition to his Bentley and Hotchkiss dealerships. Later, unwooded, posh utilities appeared on Silver Dawn, Armstrong-Siddeley, Humber and the like including Citroen, indeed the Citroen Safari owes a direct debt to the original dozen or so that came out of Melton Court.

Now Searcy & McCready are reliably reported to have built some sort of prototype on a Jupiter chassis, feasible as Leslie

108 Even the radiator can be topped up in comfort with the Richard Mead Jupiter. Body framing was steel and wood. Front half of wheel arches removable (15 minutes) for full access to the engine: Autocar

Johnson lived in their general area of London; but, further, Radford himself remembered building a Jupiter body for Jowetts and that *subsequently they did not want it*. There is little doubt that this refers to the ERA-Javelin bodywork of October 1949, corroborated by visual similarities (doors, rear wheel spats) on Jupiter 8.

At ERA, chassis and suspension work was by Eberhorst, David Hodkin, and a draughtsman named Alderton. Eberhorst, Leslie Johnson, but mostly Hodkin, carried out the development driving, using an extraordinary wooden-framed body, roughly a park bench across the chassis, a box on the back with weights to get the centre of gravity right, and an aluminium and plywood bonnet held onto the front cross-tube by Jubilee clips. This 'body' was transferred from chassis to chassis. David Hodkin, wearing a flying suit, drove it in all weathers, often covering 400 miles a day, and often, too, being stopped by the police as the vehicle would obviously be illegal today. It is noteworthy that when Jowetts got hold of their first chassis, in subjecting it to rather more vigorous testing, found it sagged in the middle and the temporary measure of welding angle-iron along the undersides of the main chassis sidemembers was to remain throughout the production life of the frame.

Two of these ERA chassis seem to have had saloon bodies fitted, a green one to the order of Jowetts and a black one, Porsche-like, for ERA and used by Mr Hodkin for about 18 months. The fate of these is unknown, but in his book on the history of the London Metropolitan Traffic Department, Chief Inspector K.Rivers lists a 'Jowett ERA $1\frac{1}{2}$-litre 13 hp saloon' as being used for various duties including use by superintendents and instructors from 1950 to 1955, before being transferred to the Metropolitan Police Driving School at Hendon for two years. A Javelin bought in 1947 is also listed.

Both Radford's 'Jowett' Jupiters were on the first (August 1950) batch of production chassis. The Queen's cousin Gerald Lascelles ordered the first example (8), notable for its short doors and high sills giving a stiff and draught-free ride. However 14 had less straightforward origins. Elongated front and rear, as a two-seater it gives the appearance of immense length, not in itself an insuperable problem, and though by the look of it it must surely be of 1950 – 1 construction, yet it was not registered for the road until 1956. Ten years later, its then owner advertised the car as having been built by Graber and having been in the 1952 Geneva Motor Show – and all the while the car was carrying Harold Radford's sill plate. Performance Cars advertised in 1955 a 'special coachbuilt Jupiter roadster, new, unregistered, cream . . .' and it is likely that this was the car in question.

113

110 *Jupiter 14 by Harold Radford. It was not registered until 1956*

Rawson

Lionel Rawson restarted building cars immediately after World War II. A name was created using the two first names of the sons of Rawson and his partner, hence the exact spelling, John Colinsons – neither son had any further connection with the business. Rawson pioneered the fully opening bonnet on an SS100 he built for

111 *Lionel Rawson working on one of his Jupiters:* Rawson

Paul Pycroft in 1946, this type of front later appearing on the DB2, E-type Jaguar and many other cars, although not on the Jupiters he made (25, 35?, 38, 39).

A deal was set up, probably by Alf Thomas (38), for three open Jupiters to Rawson's design and constructed by him and Arthur Jennings at their works at Slough, Bucks, the cars being built side by side and virtually identically, in style suggesting something of the DB1 of Claude Hill. A fourth car (35), looking identical except for being in fixed-head form, existed but its derivation remains a mystery as Lionel was later unable to recall its construction. Mr Rawson may be better known as the builder of the 18 Healey Sportsmobile cars of 1949, and the Austin-Healey record breaker (192.6 mph) of 1954.

Searcy & McCready
See Radford.

Sommer

Erik Sommer was a Danish engineer who had begun importing cars into his country soon after the war and who handled Jaguar as well as Jowett. He built experimentally various vehicles using a variety of imported components, notably the Bradford-based saloon, the S1, and a front-wheel-drive van powered by an opposed-piston two-stroke engine designed by von Eberhorst. None of his ideas, however, resulted in series production, probably due to the small size of the Danish home market. In 1951 he felt an urge to take on the Italians with special coachwork on sports chassis, beginning modestly enough with a standard Jupiter (170), received in the early summer of that year and on which he fixed a suave hard top, the car, it was said, being sold to a Swedish customer.

Next, the only two left-hand drive rolling chassis were ordered from Jowetts, the first (500) arriving at the end of 1951, with standard bonnet, and an elegant fixed-head coupé body, resembling the Bentley Continental, was built behind this bonnet, the shape being perfected by constructing a lattice of steel rods, bent to shape by Sommer until he was happy with the result. Thus experiments were made at full size instead of with the small models usually employed, with the disadvantages not only of the difficulty of building replicas but even of getting the body truly symmetrical. Another problem stemmed from Sommer's apparent desire to raise the top speed of the car by 10 per cent by superior aerodynamics; like some other saloon Jupiters, there is insufficient headroom for the tall driver.

Although the body shape had been determined by the end of January 1952 the complete car was not registered for the road, it is believed, until the following October. As for the second chassis (746), shipped in April, for this Sommer is thought to have had ambitions for his own design of front end: regrettably his plans came to nought and the chassis had to be returned to Jowetts where it was built into a right-

hand drive car, ironically as previously a returned right-hand drive chassis had become a left-hand drive car.

Warblaufen
This Swiss coachbuilding firm constructed a rather Teutonic cabriolet on chassis 23 which, together with their open tourer Javelin was shown at the 1951 Geneva Motor Show. Other work included Siata, Ford Vedette, and Austin A70.

Whittet
Jowetts shipped chassis 46 to a 'Mr Graham, Ceylon'. The BARC *Gazette* for March 1951 tells us that a Mr B.Gordon

112 Jupiter 39, body by Rawson

113 The Sommer saloon Jupiter (500) built by Erik and Ole Sommer, showing method of design: A.Whyte

114 Profile of the Sommer saloon

Graham had ordered a four-seater open sports body for his Jupiter chassis from Pat Whittet & Co of Lightwater, Surrey, while the *Gazette* for January 1952 says that Mr Graham had by then sailed for Ceylon and his four-seater open sports Javelin-Jupiter was to follow: 'He is very pleased with its performance and hopes to take part in competition motoring in his new surroundings.' It certainly arrived, for 20 years later the engine was known to be powering a Javelin in Sri Lanka.

This review is regrettably incomplete, for one can only speculate on the dozen or so chassis not accounted for. A saloon Jupiter, white with a red top, a split screen, non-winding windows and with instruments grouped in the centre of its wooded instrument panel, was reported some few years ago in New Zealand.

Gordon Gilliver, way back, owned a saloon Jupiter with a standard bonnet and rear wings, bowed single front screen and possibly a Javelin rear screen. It was first registered in 1955 for a dental mechanic in Clay Cross but was said to have been London-built.

A photo exists of an unidentifiable open Jupiter about which nothing whatsoever is known: there is a report from Scotland of a special bodied Jupiter there, possibly 101 as that car was new there; there may be a seventh Richard Mead Jupiter; and whatever became of chassis 986, the only Mkla sold in rolling chassis form? Did it really go to Beirut? The list of reported special-bodied Jupiters probably exceeds the list of available chassis.

In time there may be seen special bodywork built onto chassis formerly housed in standard coachwork, the bodies having decayed and been discarded – this was pioneered a long time ago by Louis Paladini (855).

116

CHAPTER 9 Jupiter Register

Factory Jupiters

—	E0/SA2/R	—	exhibition chassis 1950 onwards
GKW111	E0/SA/4R	April 1950	Le Mans 1950 etc.
GKY106	E0/SA/19R	24 Nov 1950	demonstrator, then 1951 Monte
GKY107	E0/SA/21R	24 Nov 1950	demonstrator, then 1951 Monte
GKY256	E0/SA/18R	28 Sep 1950	1951 Monte, etc.
GKY804	E0/SA/20R	26 Jan 1951	show room car
HAK317	E0/SA/7R	30 Mar 1951	Stabilimenti Farina body
HAK364	E1/R1/1	7 Jun 1951	1951 Le Mans etc.
HAK365	E1/SA/132R	7 Jun 1951	1951 Le Mans etc.
HAK366	E1/SA/131R	7 Jun 1951	1951 Le Mans etc.
HKU 56	E1/SA/76R	16 Oct 1951	JC Ltd Bradford
HKU 92	E1/SA/255R	6 Jul 1951	JC Ltd Service Department
HKU639	E1/SA/339R	16 Oct 1951	show room car
HKW 48	E2/R1/56	20 May 1952	1952 Le Mans
HKW 49	E2/R1/62	20 May 1952	1952 Le Mans
HKW197	E1/SB/560R	11 Feb 1952	prototype Mk1a
JAK 74	E2/SC/942R	21 Oct 1952	Mk1a demonstrator
JKW537	100/1	July 1953	prototype R4

Approximate introduction of Bradford registration marks*

FAK October 1947
FKU May 1948
FKW October 1948
FKY March 1949

GAK August 1949
GKU December 1949
GKW April 1950
GKY September 1950

HAK February 1951
HKU June 1951
HKW December 1951
HKY April 1952

JAK September 1952
JKU January 1953
JKW May 1953
JKY August 1953

KAK December 1953
KKU March 1954
KKW May 1954
KKY September 1954

LAK December 1954

*From *Car Numbers* by Noel Woodall (Garnstone Press, 1969).

Numbering systems

Jowetts stamped four series of numbers on Jupiters, two on the car and two on the engine. These were the chassis, body, engine, and crankcase numbers.

Chassis number

Post-war Jowetts were allocated a chassis number arranged into a three-part code. The first part indicates the year of manufacture, EO = 1950, E1 = 1951 and so on; for the Jupiter the second part consists of S for Sports (P would indicate Passenger car or Javelin, C for Commercial or Bradford van), followed by A or C for Mk1 or Mkla followed by L if the car is left-hand drive, and the third part is pure serial number starting from 1 (note some numbers were not issued, others withdrawn) suffixed by an R which serves no known function.

On very early cars, before about 41 it was stamped on both sides of the front structure top plate (radiator-surround top face), all others were stamped on the left-hand bonnet catch bracket close to the front cross-tube welding line, often totally obscured by paint.

Complete cars were also provided with a brass plate mounted in the underbonnet area, right-hand side, on the internal mudwing for cars where this component was chassis mounted, or on the firewall for all others, usually 1953 – 4 cars. The 'Model No' of the brass plate is the car's chassis number.

All Jupiters up to 939 are Mk1, that is SA, types; E2/SC/940R on are all Mk1a (SC). Only the Mk1a prototype, HKW197, was designated an SB. Although Jowetts became quite adept at welding the extensively triangulated chassis frames, welds would break unless the entire assembly, still on its jig, was stress-relieved in a special furnace built for that purpose.

Body number

The body panels were hand-made, being only roughly shaped on 'Rubber Press' tools by Western Manufacturing at Woodley Aerodrome, these machines being normally used for low-production-run aluminium pressing, so typical of the aircraft industry of the time. Jowett craftsmen had to iron out the ripples (a two-man job requiring rollers), form the flanges, pierce them and carry out the final shaping on the car by which time the panels were in sets and not necessarily interchangeable. Consequently they were given their own serial number, which was stamped on a flange of all the panels of a set, and also on the steel strap in the doors beneath the door trim. Trim panels themselves may still carry the number as it was chalked on, and it can sometimes be found pencilled under wooden door tops and so forth. The firewall was also stamped. Panels supplied new, separately, often carried a single letter.

The 'Chassis-Body' number of the brass plate is the car's body number and it should be noted that at the start of Jupiter production Jowetts evidently tried to build Jupiters in a certain 'Body number order' and in this they did not entirely succeed. This means that some of the early cars have a different body set to that shown on the car's brass plate.

Engine number

This is stamped on the raised plinth forward of no 1 cylinder and *as original to a car* was identical to the full chassis number ('Model No' of the brass plate). This of course also applied to Javelin engines and it is worth pointing out that in 1952 the assembly of Javelins was undertaken in Australia and New Zealand and for these cars a new series, beginning again from 1, was allotted with 101 to 120, 201 to 220, and 281 to 300 assembled in Australia and the rest in New Zealand. Some in the series had letters JKD or KD in indication of the assembly

of the Javelins from knocked-down components: examples are E2/PD/14 and KD/E3/PE/340. No more than 400 were so constructed.

Reconditioned engines

These had their plinths ground clean and restamped with numbers from one of two series, the first starting in 1949 at R1; Javelin and possibly Bradford engines were intermingled in the same series and it is also possible that some numbers were not taken out. This was known as the 'Low Level' series and it continued up to the cessation of activities by Jowett Engineering Ltd in 1963, using series I and series II crankcases destined for Javelins: at 10 000, some time after the advent of the oval webbed crank in 1955 the prefix 'R' was changed to 'RO'. When the Laystall nitriding crank was introduced around 1956 the *suffix* 'N' was added. The last engine in this series was RO 17736 N completed 13-11-63: rarely an all-new engine might be required when the prefix was 'N'.

In 1954 the 'high-level' sequence began, for all new crankcases and all returned series III cases. All Jupiter-specification reconditioned engines were in the high-level sequence, which began at 25,000 and was prefixed 'R' or 'N' as before, the two sequences running in parallel. There was initially no distinguishing code for Jupiter reconditioned engines but internally O-ring liners were grooved for and fitted in addition to other Jupiter-specification parts.

About the time that the 'low-level' sequence began 'RO' prefixes, the 'high-level' series acquired the prefixes 'RO' or 'NO' for Javelin units and 'JUR' or 'JUN' for Jupiter units; still later the suffix 'N' was added as for the 'low-level' series to indicate nitriding. Some JUR engines were ordered by Javelin owners. JUR26381N delivered in July 1963 was one such.

The not inconsiderable number of reconditioned engines built by JCL and JEL is a comment on the development and reliability of the Javelin/Jupiter unit. A score or more of midifications to bearings and their lubrication was introduced during the engine's commercial life: first the big ends were changed to copper/lead/indium, the front and centre main following. Curiously, the rear main stayed white metal except in competition engines which, from early on, had trimetal mains throughout with separate thrust bearings.

Some of the modifications helped oil to

appear where it was most needed after the least start-up delay. Others increased total flow. The last one in this series was the long-reach oil pump of early 1953.

The journal and crankpin hardening found essential for the harder bearing material was at one stage thought to be responsible for crankshaft failure, leading to abortive experiments with more careful hardening and greater radii in the bearing corners. Finally the metal-to-metal liner seat (from around 1953 on Jupiter reconditioned engines) and the oval webbed crank (1955-6) were introduced to the unit that was to propel Jupiters pretty reliably from the mid-1950s to the present day.

Bulletin 149 engines
Service Bulletin 149, dated August 1953, listed 63 crankcase numbers of engines built with O-ring liners (see below). The new design of liner seated metal-to-metal in the crankcase, which was chamfered to take the O-ring. These engines are believed to have been delivered from the autumn of 1952 to the Californian agent and they, on fitting them to Jupiters, seem to have mischievously stamped the plinths (left blank by Jowetts) with the numerical part of the chassis serial number preceded by E3 SCL. These are easily detected as the Jupiters concerned are SA types. It is clear that these engines were the immediate precursors of the true JUR engines.

Additional codes
If Glacier big-end bearings were used the recon plate at the rear of the engine was stamped with an 'X' before or after the engine number. Some very late engines carried the suffix 'S' and these were either the 'odd-half' crankcase engines carrying the double letter single or double digit crankcase numbers, or very rarely a new matched-pair crankcase. The main bearing housings were bored oversize and machined for a separate thrust rear main – no replacement main bearing shells were ever available for these engines. This 'S' suffix series should not be confused with the 'S' prefix numbers which could apply to reconditioned engines of any age; the 'S' appearing on the recon plate only would indicate that a customer's own unit had been serviced, whereas if the 'S' appeared on the plinth it indicated that the plinth had not been previously stamped, that is, it was not initially a factory-built unit. If the service Department did not service the customer's unit but provided an exchange engine this would be an ordinary reconditioned unit and the Jupiter's chassis

number would be stamped above the plinth.

Finally a small run of probably not more than five engines was produced for Harry Ferguson Research, HFX1 on, having 3-inch pistons (1645 cc), strengthened liners and Wills rings head seals.

Non-Jowett stampings include a series of highly modified and powerful reconditioned engines produced in Christchurch, New Zealand, during 1967 and 1968 by the gifted motor engineer Leao Padman, which he called the 'PL' series. Although the final versions, type PL90, produced a whisker under 90 bhp with water pump and generator self-driven, these were true roadgoing engines, smooth and sweet, with a normal life expectancy. This in spite of a 9.25 CR, special camshaft, larger valves, reshaped combustion chambers, and around 1700 cc: by comparison, Javelin engines in standard from would not reach their rated 52 bhp on Mr Padman's dynamometer with their accessories attached. His engines were numbered F7 PL 1 to F8 PL 14 N or higher.

The RGM1 series, suffixed 'J' for Jupiter units, are engines reconditioned by George Mitchell.

Crankcases held by agents as spares had crankcase numbers but unstamped plinths. When built up, the plinths were sometimes left blank, sometimes stamped with the car's chassis number or whatever came to mind, and of course there would be no recon plate.

Crankcase number
This number is found stamped on both sides of the crankcase at the front. From the start of production in 1947 the crankcase numbers roughly followed Javelin engine numbers (less date and model codes) more or less in parallel up to the introduction of the Jupiter: Jupiter number seven had crankcase 10546. The series continued up to about the last quarter of 1952 when the ribbed series III casting was introduced at around 19,000. Initially the ribbed castings were given numbers prefixed by an 'X', but before 20,000 the 'X' was discontinued. With the introduction of the full series III engine, Jupiter units were stamped with a 'G' on both sides below the crankcase number (similar to the 'PE' on Javelin) thus Javelin reconditioned engines with the 'G' were new on Jupiters. By the last quarter of 1953 crankcase numbers had passed the 25,000, Javelin production had ceased, and the 'G' stamping was dropped: no E4 SCs are known to carry this letter.

When case numbers reached about

26,000, crankcase numbering started again from 1, but the 26,000 series continued in parallel with the new series, stamped a larger size just above the plinth. At about 1000 it acquired the prefix '9'.

At the end of Jupiter production the 'Big' series ceased and the upper ('low') series – by now in the 1,000s – continued still prefixed '9'. Series II and III crank-cases had been gravity die-cast externally, with sand cores, but when new crankcase castings of this type became unavailable from 1956, sand castings were reintroduced and were numbered A1 to A100 or there-abouts; B, D and H series crankcases are recorded, all with numbers less than 100. It is believed that not more 500 such engines were produced, and constituted the end of new crankcase production.

The 'odd-half' crankcases
Old halves were then used, as good returned halves of any age had not been thrown away: a punch was used to attempt the obliteration of existing identifying codes. New numbers, usually comprising two letters and one or two digits were employed DD . . , HC . . , CC . . , OS . . , are known, stamped on both sides, some-times on the rear. Sometimes the right-hand (old series) crankcases number was transferred to the left-hand side above the plinth.

All the 'odd half' engines had over-bored main-bearing housings and cam-shaft housings, the camshaft having over-size journals while the main-bearings, employing identical copper-lead shells on all three journals, were especially made from thicker backing steel; end-thrust was carried on a separate thrust washer.

The gearbox
The gearbox, too, had its share of attention from the Experimental Department. For the first three years of its production life, the Javelin had been fitted with a gearbox brought in, complete, from Henry Meadows Ltd. At the point of introduction of the Jupiter, however, in the autumn of 1950, Jowetts began producing their own, in-tended for both models. The new unit was serial numbered from 1 but prefixed 'J' and its (close) ratios were 1, 1.37, 2.17 and 3.56 compared with the old (wide) ratios which had been 1, 1.5, 2.38 and 3.88. There were sufficient other detail modifications for the mechanisms and casings not to be interchangeable. The factory seriously underestimated several crucial manufactur-ing processes and as a consequence there took place a major interruption in Javelin

production, with the emergence of the Jupiter also possibly affected. Between Experimental and the factory there then raged many heated arguments about production and processes, and it may even be that Meadows had to be persuaded to recommence the manufacture of their wide ratio box for the Javelin for a time; but even if that was so, then at the latest the J-box must have been in production by mid-1951. There followed a train of irritating service problems. Written sources agree however that Jowetts intended the Jupiter to begin its production life with the (Jowett-built) close ratio box. By the summer of 1952 only one service problem remained, that of jumping out of third gear. This was eventually cured by the incorporation of a simple interlock, although it seems not to have been imple-mented until after the reversion in Javelins to the old ratios at box J8153 in the early part of 1953 – the 'J' prefix continued as the boxes were Jowett-made throughout. These Jowett wide ratio parts were fitted to the R4 Jupiters and at least some late standard Jupiters as well. The Meadows unit is recogniseable externally by its pure number serial code, prefixed usually by a 5 or a 6, and internally by the practice of etching part numbers on the gears for which a higher grade of steel was employed; hence laygear tooth stripping, all too common on 'J' boxes, is a rare ocurrence indeed for the Wolverhampton-made com-ponents. A fault confined to the Meadows box however was the weakness of the three mainshaft 2nd and 3rd gear locating washers. Dependent upon which one failed one could be left with 3rd and top only, jumping out of 2nd and 3rd, etc.

Fairly rare is the Jowett reconditioned box which has an R-prefixed serial number stamped near the original, unaltered, serial number.

Jupiters in California and the Bulletin 149 engines

Little is known with precision of the import of Jupiters into California except that it cannot have been an altogether happy experience for the owners of many of them. The West Coast distributor, Angell Motors of Pasadena, imported more Jupiters by far than any other agent anywhere and the 34 brought in during 1951 rose to about 24 per month for the first five months of 1952; they had around 39 western outlets, mostly in California, but covering ten states in all. They eventually went bank-rupt. Jupiter crankshafts seemed to have

had particularly short lives under Californian conditions, although the Jupiter's reliability and serviceability may have been no worse than that of some other specialist foreign makes at that time – to what extent it contributed to the downfall of Angell Motors is unlikely ever to be known. In his report on the testing of a pair of Jupiters (*Road and Track*, March 1953) the editor, Robert Dearborn, had this to say:

> In glancing over the figures recorded during the tests, one wonders whether the Jupiter distributor in the West Coast region hasn't been guilty of awkward blundering in the presentation of the car to the public. Needing little more than 15 seconds to attain the 60 mph mark, and having the ability to record gratifyingly high figures on the Tapley meter, it would seem that the car could have done other than trail ignominiously behind all 1500 cc competition in the past two years of West Coast racing. Had he chosen good drivers and backed them with efficient mechanics, the distributor would unquestionably have brought home some winning cups – and of course would be enjoying a greater number of Jupiter sales than is now the case.

In mid-May 1952 the flow of Jupiters to Pasadena ceased, although all must have been sold in the normal way for another 14 were dispatched from Bradford at the end of August. It is believed that these Jupiters

115 The original American caption read: 'Ginny Baxter (left) and Jaqueline DuBief, 1952 Olympic world's free skating and figure skating champions . . . in a Jowett Jupiter sports car loaned the stars by British Austin Ltd, Hollywood'

116 Cal Marks (left) and Hunter Hackney display their Jupiter stock cars which won five out of a possible nine trophies awarded in three races during 1953 Phoenix sports car racing meet. These two cars accounted for second and third places in the 20-mile, 1500 cc run; a second in the 50-mile, 1500 cc stock novice and swept both first and second in the Governor's Cup race, 100-miles for 1500 cc stock cars. The two also won the team prize for the day's racing against all comers in their class

remained in bond until George Green's visit in the June following.

It is not known when the so-called 'Bulletin 149' engines were ordered or by whom but two surviving ones are date-stamped September 1952, and by crankcase number comparison there is agreement that certainly early deliveries were being made around November 1952, and most if not all seem to have gone to California. They would have had the then new series III machine-sided crank and the inclusion of O-ring liners suggests that gasket blowing was another frequent cause of trouble in the USA. What is believed to be Angell's last advertisement for Jupiters, referring as it does to the Torry Pines race of 14 December 1952, went to press in January 1953 and World Wide Import Inc's first is probably the one in *Motor Trend* of the next May, suggesting that Angell placed the order for the engines but also that World Wide may have taken delivery of them and were responsible for stamping their plinths E3 SCL . . . R, causing confusion in later times as most went into E2 SAL Jupiters. They were to series III specification and the SCL or 'series III' Jupiter had been announced by Jowetts the previous October so perhaps syllogistically they were inferred to be 'SCL' engines. The next step might be the loss of the brass plate, a frequent occurrence in low-rainfall areas like California for the chassis mounted mudshields carried the brass plate and these mudshields would be eventually left off after an 'engine out'. The car would change hands and be retitled with the E3 SCL number off the plinth, possible not even the E3 SCL engine it first received: in this way spuriously numbered Jupiters made their appearance in the USA. If the brass plate is missing the chassis tube must be checked and, if that has been renewed following crash damage, then the number of the body set must be determined by checking as many body panels as possible (and from at least

122

one other than the bonnet set), referring these findings to the Jupiter Owners' Auto Club.

George Green went to California in June 1953 to sort out the cars that remained in bond – he remembers they numbered fewer than 20 and were probably the last batch of 14 dispatched the previous August.

No engine changes were needed, merely rectifying body and upholstery damage sustained during storeage. The better ones were prepared and sold first, paying for a few more to be readied: in this way they were cleared in about six weeks.

World Wide Import Inc, frustrated in their desire to sell R4 Jupiters, continued to act as agents for Jowetts through the 1950s and up to it is believed 1962. Thereafter what was left of their spares passed into private hands – Milton C. Green owned them in the mid 1960s and was able to provide a service to Jupiter owners with the assistance of George Mitchell in Scotland. When he dropped out his stock was bought by an actor and Jupiter owner Walker Edmiston, who in 1978 sold them to Ted Miller. At the time of writing (1980) Ted could be contacted for spares at 250 S. Griffith Park Drive, Burbank, Ca 91506.

The 'Bulletin 149' engines

The identification of more is sought.

Crankcase number	Engine number
25394	
25475	E3 SCL 808R
25479	
25486	
25578	
25597	E3 SCL 787R
25624	
25632	
25479	E3 SCL 782R
25884	E3 SCL 987R
25888	
25894	
25898	E3 SCL 789R
25904	E2 SAL 703R, Sept 1952
25911	
25912	
25916	
25918	E3 SCL 771R
25920	
25955	E3 SCL 519R
25982	
25988	
25989	E3 SCL 772R
26004	E3 SCL 770R, Sept 1952
26007	
26011	
26017	
26039	
26049	
26053	
26055	
26060	
26063	E3 SCL 754R
26070	
26072	E3 SCL 817R
26087	
26088	
26111	
26120	
26129	
26157	
26436	
26500	E2 SCL 773R
26501	
26502	E2 SAL 781R
26503	
26504	
26505	
26506	
26507	
26508	
26509	
26520	
26521	
26526	
26541	
26545	
26546	
26547	
26549	
26550	
26551	
26573	

Bulletin 149 was issued by the factory in August 1953 and merely listed the above crankcase numbers with the comment that the liner bottom seal was a synthetic rubber sealing ring, trapped in a chamfer machined in the crankcase, the liner making metal-to-metal contact with the case. The liner penetrated fractionally deeper into the case and the consequent elimination of the composition Hallite seal made liner sinkage impossible. This lower liner seal was standardised on Jupiter engines from c-26574. These engines also have deeper counterbores for the longer studs, which are increased by 3/16 inch.

The register

The chassis number, shipment date and destination (the first three items) are taken from the Jowett factory records. If the car has not been heard of since leaving the works, the above will be the only data, unless the factory registered the car, in which case the registration no will be the fourth entry (e.g. personal export cars). Chassis numbers suffixed + indicates car shipped in rolling chassis form. (Any additional data indicates that the car has been heard of since leaving the works; if since 1970 the owner's name will be given if known. If this is not known or pre-dates 1970, the relevant year is given in parentheses.)

After the country of destination will be found, in this order if the information is known: Present country (only given if different from the country of destination), colour; body no; engine no; crankcase no; registration no; owner's name or date of most recent sighting; history, if applicable. Jupiters in the USA have the State indicated where known.

Body, engine, and crankcase numbers are preceded by b-, e-, or c- respectively. An engine with no stamping on its plinth is shown thus: e-(ns).

Abbreviations used
Countries

						American States			
A	Austria	NL	Holland		Al	Alabama		Nv	Nevada
AUS	Australia	NZ	New Zealand		Ak	Alaska		NH	New Hampshire
					Az	Arizona		NJ	New Jersey
B	Belgium	P	Portugal		Ar	Arkansas		NM	New Mexico
BR	Brazil	P/Ex	Personal		Ca	California		NY	New York
			Export		Co	Colarado		NC	North Carolina
CAN	Canada		(country		Ct	Connecticutt		SD	South Carolina
CH	Switzerland		usually not		De	Delaware		ND	North Dakota
CO	Colombia		known		Fl	Florida		SD	South Dakota
CY	Sri Lanka				Ga	Georgia		Oh	Ohio
		RCH	Chile		Hi	Hawaii		Ok	Oklahoma
D	W.Germany	RL	Lebanon		Id	Idaho		Or	Oregon
DK	Denmark	RSR	Zimbabwe		Il	Illinois		Pa	Pennsylvania
DZ	Algeria				In	Indiana		La	Louisiana
E	Spain	S	Sweden		Ia	Iowa		RI	Rhode Island
		SF	Finland		Ks	Kansas		Tn	Tennessee
F	France	SGP	Singapore		Ky	Kentucky		Tx	Texas
GB	Great Britain	U	Uruguay		Me	Maine		Ut	Utah
GBZ	Gibraltar	USA	United States		Md	Maryland		Vt	Vermont
			of America		Ma	Massachusetts		Va	Virginia
					Mi	Michigan		Wa	Washington
HK	Hong Kong				Mn	Minnesota		WV	West Vigrinia
		WAL	Sierra Leone		Ms	Mississippi		Wi	Wisconsin
I	Italy	WAN	Nigeria		Mo	Missouri		Wy	Wyoming
IRL	Eire	YV	Venezuela		Mt	Montana		DC	District of
					Ne	Nebraska			Columbia
JA	Jamaica	ZA	Republic of						
JAP	Japan		South Africa						
MA	Morocco								
MEX	Mexico								

The register

E0SA 1/29Mar50/USA: First prototype. Shown at British Motor and Engineering Show, New York, April 1950; raced the following autumn.

E0SA 2+/Jan50/GB: The exhibition chassis: Brussels, Geneva, 1951. London, 1951, 1952, perhaps 1953; continuously updated and probably built into 1033.

E0SA 3+/29Mar50: Exhibition chassis at British Motor and Engineering Show, New York, April 1950. Records say loaned to Angell Motors, Pasadena. Fate unknown but may have been returned to England and rebuilt into another Jupiter.

E0SA 4/Apr50/GB: Class win Le Mans 1950; RAC TT 1950; practice and recce car 1951 Monte Carlo Rally; RAC TT 1951 class 2nd (T.C. Wise); other events included Alpine Rally 1951; private owners were 1st, T.C. Wise, 2nd, W.A. Brearley. After its Le Mans victory the car was rebuilt to resemble the first production cars 17–21. Was in London area late 1950s and is believed to have been abandoned on a London street around 1962.

E0SA 5/29Mar50/GB/CAN: Prototype test car, British reg. GKU764. Toured British Isles, France, early spring 1950, driven by H. Grimley/C. Grandfield. Appeared in Silverstone paddock before export to Canada 19Jul50. Rescued in poor state in 1958, restored and converted to LHD with floor gea-shift. Red. R. Hirst.

E0SA 6+/11Aug50/S: The first production chassis. Semi-replica R1 body by Karl-Gustaf Kanrell. Raced when new including at least two inter-nationals; at Skarpnack, 14Sep52, driven by R. Berg to 4th. (1978).

E0SA 7+/14Aug50/GB/Malaya/NZ: FHC body by Stabilimenti Farina. In Paris and London Shows 1950; briefly Jowetts' London showroom then north to Idle. Reg HAK317 on 31Mar51, probably sold autumn 1951, last UK licence taken 15Jul52 when it was still maroon. In 1958 owned by Eric Ooi a Chinese schoolteacher in Malaya, who sold it to a NZ airman who took it to NZ. Colour now white. e-F7 EX3. W. Fletcher.

E0SA 8+/16Aug50/GB: Black; DHC by Harold Radford, London for Hon. Gerald Lascelles, who raced and rallied it with little success. Toured Dolomites on owner's honeymoon. Known as 'Rabbit Hutch' after front grille, since modified. e-R2671; c-21294; MGP999; G.M. Mitchell.

E0SA 9+/18Aug50/GB: Red; open tourer by Moston Sheet Metal Co Ltd. e-SA EO 9R; c-10686; AJM470; J. Truelove.

E0SA 10+/17Aug50/GB: Black; DHC by Barnaby Body-builders of Hull, in near replica of standard, for Ted Booth. Jowett team car, 1951 RAC Rally. Best result 15th in 1952 RAC Rally. LRH 2; P. Guneratne.

E0SA 11+/12Sep50/AUS: Believed to have received a replica standard body from S.O. Hodge for John Crouch Motors, Sydney.

E0SA 12+/21Aug50/GB: White; FHC body by J.J. Armstrong of Carlisle. e-D8 1831; c-2629; EHH897; F. Mitchell.

E0SA 13+/31Aug50/AUS: Originally received a replica standard body from S.O. Hodge for John Crouch Motors, Sydney. In early 1960s received an unidentified Vauxhall body ex 24. Soon removed and scrapped. e-SA EO 13R; c-10930; E. Wolf.

E0SA 14+/28Aug50/GB: Blue; open tourer by Harold Radford, London. Supposed to have been built 1951 but not reg or used until Jan56 when reg WAR182 (1981).

E0SA 15+/30Aug50/AUS: Believed to have received a replica standard body from S.O. Hodge for John Crouch Motors, Sydney.

E0SA 16+/12Sep50/AUS: Believed to have received a replica standard body from S.O. Hodge for John Crouch Motors, Sydney.

E0SA 17/4Dec50/F: New to M. Thévenin of Bordeaux. Believed to have been seen in a Paris suburb unused, still blue, around 1970. This was the 1st production standard car.

E0SA 18/28Sep50/GB: Red; Jowett team car 1951 Monte Carlo Rally driven by Robinson/Ellison to class win, overall 6th. Works car 1951 RAC Rally (M. Becquart) and 1951 Tulip Rally (W. Robinson). 1st private owner W. Robinson: 1951 Alpine Rally, 1952 Br. Empire Trophy race (class 3rd), 1953 RAC TT Dundrod, with Ted Lund. Sold at end 1953 when it went abroad, possibly to Malaya. GKY256.

E0SA 19/24Nov50/GB: Red; Jowett team car 1951 Monte Carlo Rally driven by T.C. Wise/H. Grimley. Road tested by *Motor*. Probably sold in 1951. GKY106.

E0SA 20/26Jan51/GB: GKY804; thought to have been the 1950 Motor Show car and then in London showroom.

E0SA 21/24Nov50/GB: BRG; Jowett team car 1951 Monte Carlo Rally driven by G. Wilkins/R. Baxter to class 2nd. Driven by H. Hadley in 1952 RAC Rally. Experimental Department 'hack' used to test R1 engines prior to Le Mans. Once covered 16 miles in 10 mins dead on York-Scarborough dual carriageway (96 mph). Around Nov51 Phil Green drove it to Bridgewater and back in 1 day (6 pm to 11 pm) to return a faulty Krypton gas analyser. Mileage was 543 across country. The car was used as a tender at such races as the TT thanks to its ex-Monte substantial tail rack, and also for such tasks as evaluating new designs of head gasket. GKY107. Chassis frame, tail, and possibly bonnet survive. Cars 17–21 carried the fore and aft strakes but were otherwise normal production cars initially.

E0SA 22+/12Sep50/AUS: Believed to have received a replica standard body from S.O. Hodge for John Crouch Motors, Sydney.

E0SA 23+/15Sep50/CH: Probably the Warblaufen DHC. Ph *Motor*, 14Mar51, at Geneva Show.

E0SA 24+/11Oct50/AUS: Sold by John Crouch Motors with unidentified Vauxhall body. After c.70,000 miles and a crash the bodywork was replaced by glass-fibre Milano, not completed. e-E0 SA 24R; c-11058. W. Webb.

E0SA 25+/10Oct50/GB: Black; open body by Lionel Rawson for Sir Hugh Bell; e-JUR25703N; GPY859; G. Tozer.

E0SA 26+/27Nov50/JAP:

E0SA 27+/27Nov50/JAP/NZ: Brought to NZ by a NZ airman. Chassis bought from VW Motors, Christchurch 1955 by Ian Baird and bodied by him, using major parts imported from Jowetts in England. He made what he could not import. First car to be powered by the ex-Pacific Spot R1-specification engine in 1962/3. In 1968 a Ford Falcon engine was fitted, a failure. Body removed and 100E Ford body fitted for stock-car racing. Now dismantled: bonnet on ch221, doors and tail on ch 189. C Tarrant, chassis only.

E0SA 28+/8Nov50/GB: This chassis is thought to be that of the Coachcraft of Egham saloon, reg PPF746 in Mar51. What is believed to be the identical car was bought at the time PPF was sold in Nov55, in the same area, by Bob Graves who spent several years thoroughly rebuilding it; he obliterated the chassis mark so that it could be re-registered CDG63B in 1964. For a time it was run with a supercharger when Wills ring seals (ex-Alf Thomas) were fitted. It is believed that PPF746 was raced in 1954 by I.A. Forbes. Now owned by Roger Gambell.

E0SA 29+/6Nov50/GB: Green; saloon body with standard bonnet built by Frank Grounds for him to rally. Best result class 4th in 1953 Monte Carlo Rally. First reg LOL 1; re-reg on sale SON142; A. Raybould.

E0SA 30+/8Nov50/GB: Purple; saloon body by Maurice Gomm, reg 6504MH in 1960; prior to that, chassis stored by Nigel Mann and then Gomm.e- E0 SA 30R; c-91466; G. Duce.

E0SA 31+/9Nov50/CH: Brown, cabriolet body by Ghia Suisse; (1955).

E0SA 32+/10Nov50/GB: Blue; DHC body by Abbott of Farnham, Surrey. Ph *Motor* 12Sep51. e-R026377NS; c-CD18G; K. Patchett.

E0SA 33+/17Nov50/USA/Il: FHC body by Stabilimenti Farina. Has Ford 7-litre V8 engine poorly fitted. C. Schwab.

E0SA 34+/13Nov50/GB: Red; open tourer by Richard Mead; single bowed screen and externally accessible boot. e-(ns); c-23677; XRE550; E.J. Powter.

E0SA 35+/17Nov50/GB: Grey; saloon Jupiter possibly by Lionel Rawson; SNU866; disappeared after crash in 1966.

E0SA 36+/23Nov50/AUS: This chassis has never been used. e-E0 SA 36R c-22769; sold 1979.

E0SA 37+/17Nov50/GB: Saloon body by KW Bodies of Blackpool for Bill Robinson; entered 1951 British Empire Trophy. Exchanged for a TD by a friend of Bill Skelly. Possibly scrapped in 1964.

E0SA 38+/17Nov50/GB: White; open body by Lionel Rawson for Alf Thomas; extensively raced on the Silverstone Club circuit by A. and B. Thomas.

JTM100. e-JUR25277; c-92366; J. Stetson.

E0SA 39+/20Nov50/GB: Blue; open body by Lionel Rawson. e-E0 SA 39R; c-11656; EPR900; J. Riley.

E0SA 40+/20Nov50/GB: Saloon body by Maurice Gomm, built 1952 but reg 53CPA in 1956. May have gone abroad in 1965.

E0SA 41/19Dec50/GB: White; b-6; e-R5629; c-23468/2; used in competition by first owner Bill Skelly of Motherwell with singular lack of success in 1951-2. JGA123. Last sighting 1969.

E0SA 42/19Dec50/NL/GB/AUS: Green; b-8A; e-R016652N; returned unsold to GB in 1952, sold new 1953 reg JKW294; taken to AUS in 1968 (with overdrive fitted by owner). AUS reg KCW706; M. Allfrey.

E0SA 43/29Dec50/B

E0SA 44/4Jan51/P/ex: GKY644.

E0SA45/5Jan51/B

E0SA 46+/31Jan51/P/ex: To Ceylon by Mr Graham, with 4-seater open coachwork by Pat Whittett & Co of Surrey.

E0SA 47+/27Nov50/GB: Black; open tourer body, possibly by Coachcraft of Egham; e-E0 SA 47R; c-12260; RPB882; D. Day

E0SA 48+/27Nov50/GB: Bronze; FHC by Coachcraft of Egham; Wade-Ventor supercharger from new; e-R5234; c-22317; G.M. Mitchell. Apparently ERA's contract with Jowett called for six chassis and Jowett's initial programme absorbed five. Like the ERA show chassis of 1949, this one never had an ignition coil bracket welded to the frame. Further, it carries the stamping 'J/6', suggesting it could be ERA's sixth.

E0SA 49+/29Nov50/GB: Blue; saloon body by Motor Panels of Epsom. RPD934; (1981)..

E0SA 50+/29Dec50/GB

E0SA 51/15Jan51/GB: New to Major L.J. Roy Taylor, who bought it in primer so that he could have car sprayed his own colour. Had 4.1 rear axle fitted, externally accessible boot mod. Used in N. Staffs Club rally in 1952. Sold to Rex Catell, a Prescott timekeeper, in 1952, who kept it several years. Possibly scrapped. Reg NMA507

E0SA 52/5Jan51/P/ex

E0SA 53/22Jan51/USA

E0SA 54/16Jan51/USA

E0SA 55/16Jan51/USA/Ma: Red; b-15A; e-N25133; c-91702 and 27504; E.A. Steiman.

E0SA 56+/5Jan51/CH: Thought to be the FHC Ghia Suisse of Jean Latune, driven in the 1952 Monte Carlo Rally, Tour de France, and probably other events.

E1SA 57/24Jan51/USA

E1SAL58/USA/Ca: The prototype LHD car. e-E1 SAL 58R; c-12096; No body number, indicating construction in the Experimental Department. The only LHD car with door lock on the drivers side, otherwise has all the typical early car features. Unlicensed since 1962. (1978).

E1SA 59+/16Mar51/F/NL: Stabilimenti Farina FHC body built for Marcel Becquart and used by him with considerable works support in the 1952 and

1953 Monte Carlo Rallies. Best result in the 1952 event: class 2nd, overall 5th 1st Fr reg DT-90-77; 2nd Fr reg 7007-AL69; Dutch reg DT-90-77. J. Compter.

E1SA60/24Jan51/USA

E1SA 61/29Jan51/CAN: Red; b-21 (panels); e-E1 SA 61R; c-12821; R. Gilbert.

E1SA 62/31Jan51/USA/Al: Red; e-E1 SA 62R; c-13187; E.J. Renner.

E1SA 63/31Jan51/USA/Oh: b-21 (plate); (1963).

E1SA 64/31Jan51/USA

E1SA 65/7Feb51/USA/NY: b-23; e-E1 SA 65R; c-13153; R.W. Hess.

E1SA 66/20Feb51/CH:

E1SA 67/7Feb51/USA/NY: b-18; (1963).

E1SA 68/31May51/S: Originally to CH, 1Feb51 but Swiss plates TI 642 not collected.

E1SA 69+/5Mar51/AUS: Open body; rear chopped 8 inches behind rear axle; TF petrol tank. Lightweight aluminium panelling on steel tubing: cylinder heads project outside bonnet. 2673 miles from new (in 1979).

E1SA 70/7Feb51/USA/Ca: b-27; e-JUR26319N; A. Montrand.

E1SA 71/14Feb51/CAN

E1SA 72/15Feb51/AUS: Bronze; b-32 (panels); e-E2 PE JKD 102; c-24396; (owner has orig engine in a Jowett-engined special called 'The Spad') Jupiter reg ESW006. E.S. Wolf.

E1SA 73/15Feb51/CH

E1SA 74/6Mar51/P: Orig P. reg BF-17-18, new to Joaquim Nogueira who won the 1951 Lisbon Rally outright in it, the car being sponsored by the importers Leacock Ltda. Also outright win claimed for it in the 1952 Volta a Portugal. Jose Martins.

E1SA 75/6Mar51/P: Orig P. reg BF-17-17; driven to class 9th in 1952 Lisbon Rally by first owner Joaquim Nunes dos Santos. It is believed that this is the Jupiter in North Oporto (1980).

E1SA 76/16Oct51/GB: Blue; b-30; e-E3 PE 24656; c-1124 & 27281; HKU56. Jowett works car 1951/2. Possibly London Motor Show 1951. Road tested by John Bolster for *Autosport* Jan 1952. Used for publicity photos 1952 (*Sport and Country, Scottish Field,* etc). In November 1952, whilst being test driven at Motor Industry Research Association (MIRA) test track, the car collided with one of the concrete-filled oil drums used to mark out part of the course. It turned over on to the driver, whose life was saved by the softness of the ploughed field upon which car and occupant came to rest. Car was rebuilt by a Jowett employee. For sale in 1980.

E1SA 77/6Mar51/GB: First owner Godfrey Imhoff; Jowett team car 1951 RAC Rally; Morecambe Rally 1951 2nd in class B, 11th in production car category. HAK117. Possibly scrapped.

E1SA 78/8Mar51/USA/Az: Red; b-35 (plate), 34 (doors); unusual pattern of louvres in the bonnet. P. Teske and B. Hessemer.

E1SA 79/10Mar51/S

E1SA 80/8Mar51/USA

E1SA 81+/19Feb51/GB: Orange; FHC by J.E. Farr & Son. Designed for 1st owner Robert Ellison to use in the 1952 Monte Carlo Rally (retd near St Flour). MTJ300. C.E. Porter.

E1SA 82/28Feb51/CH

E1SA 83+/9Mar51/CH

E1SA 84/28Feb51/CH

E1SA 85+/20Mar51/NL

E1SA 86/10Mar51/I

E1SA 87+/13Mar51/GB: DBC by Richard Mead, believed the first. Reg MBJ519 and cost '£1400 in November 1951'. Went to Coventry in 1960.

E1SA 88/20Mar51/NL/NZ: Reg EH15 in NZ and had covered 60,000 km in 1974. S. Heighway.

E1SA 89+/7Mar51/GB: DHC built by Abbott of Farnham for Cdr Milner, who rallied it – 1952 'Little' rally. Originally registered RPA7, it was rereg WPC121. P. Whitehead.

E1SA 90/13Mar51/P/ex: HAK183

E1SA 91+/16Mar51/GB: Standard body fitted later but not quite finished. Car never used but stored, and has since deteriorated. Sherriff.

E1SA 92/19Mar51/USA

E1SA 93+/24May51/F: Presumed to be the Ghia Suisse FHC built for M. Thévenin to use in the 1952 Monte Carlo Rally.

E1SA 94/19Mar51/USA/Il: This Jupiter still existed around 1970 but in a poor state of repair.

E1SA95+/18Jun51/CH

E1SA 96/19Mar51/USA/NJ: b-45A; E.H. Jessup.

E1SA 97+/13Jul51/GB: Black; FHC body by Flewitt of Birmingham; built 1953 but reg HCW83 in 1956. Car has standard bonnet. e-JUR26065N; c-92609; J. Casey.

E1SA 98/28Mar51/GB: Red; first owner W.J. Tee, managing director of *Motor Sport*. HAK268. Last sighted 1968, in poor condition.

E1SA 99+/12Jun51/GB: FHC Built by KW Bodies of Blackpool for Edward Foulds, golf and rally enthusiast and Jowett agent; reg KWX770. Later raced by A. Wake at Silverstone.

E1SA 100/19Mar51/USA/DC: Red; b-47A; e-E1 SA 100R; c-14658; H. Perry.

E1SA 101+/19Jun51/GB:

E1SA 102/21Mar51/S: b-48A; once had foreign engine fitted. N. Jonassen.

E1SA 103+/15Jun51/GB

E1SA 104/21Mar51/S

E1SA 105+/15Jun51/GB: FHC Bodywork fitted by E.D. Abbott of Farnham, CCP966; selling price £2,210 including heater, radio, and screenwashers. Entrant in 1953 Morecambe Rally. Commenting on the car the *Autocar* remarked 'this is a much more elegant car than the standard coupé.' It was driven over a cliff in Wales in 1965, finishing off the car and its occupants.

E1SA 106/2Apr51/MA

E1SA 107+/18Jun51/GB: Camper-type body fitted by Tommy Shirley of Barton's Transport, Calverton, Notts. Owner toured Europe in it in 1953. NAL323. (1955).

E1SA 108/2Apr51/USA

E1SA 109+/6Jul51: There is little doubt that this is the fourth FHC by Stabilimenti Farina; exhibited at the 1951 Paris Salon, finished in dove grey, unlike the earlier three which were all maroon. Another unique feature was the provision of semaphone arms rather than turn indicator lamps, a clue to its destination.

E1SA 110/3Sep51/SGP: New to F.E.N. Wills who drove a Jupiter in Singapore's Gap Hill climb in Nov51 (class 3rd). Its UK reg HAK41 indicates it was a p/ex car whose sale must have fallen through or been prolonged.

E1SA 111/20Dec51/GB: Clearly intended to have been a special-bodied Jupiter, and by its body number bodied in December. Car has seen daily use with present owner since 1963 as sole year-round transport: its oval web crank has now completed, untouched, in the region of 180,000 miles. The rest of the engine has Dennis Sparrow 'HSCC' modifications, giving car a top speed of 94+ mph and the ability to cruise at 90. Purple; b-270A; e-(ns); NYD273; J. Cheetham.

E1SA 112/11Apr51/USA

E1SA 113+/5Oct51/GB

E1SA 114/2Apr51/USA

E1SA 115+/7Jul51/NZ:Never used, although its engine went into a Javelin some years ago. S. Wickens.

E1SA 116/10Apr51/CH: b-55; e-E1 PCL 16121D; R. Renfer.

E1SA 117+/28Jun51/GB: Blue; open tourer by Richard Mead. e-(ns). TVW999. P.R. Stevens.

E1SA 118/10Apr51/USA

E1SA119+/25Jun51/GB

E1SA 120/11Apr51/IRL/GB: Yellow; b-57A; e-R017104; c-3837; Irish reg ZL6262; raced by Joe Kelly, with best result the 1952 British Empire Trophy when it was placed class 6th, overall 10th. Joe Kelly was its second owner; the first was Victor Ross who tried hill-climbing it. It survived a bad crash in Donegal in the hands of its third owner. Acquired its UK reg AIJ1824 in 1967.

E1SA 121/6Apr51/CH

E1SAL122/24Apr51/USA: Possibly scrapped by M.C. Green.

E1SAL123/24Apr51/USA: Red; b-60A; e-(ns); c-753G; J.H. Caldwell

E1SAL124/22Jun51/USA

E1SAL125/24Apr51/USA

E1SAL126/22Jun51/USA/Ca: b-64 (bonnet); F. Coscia.

E1SAL127/23Jun51/USA

E1SA 128/30Apr51/USA

E1SA 129/30Apr51/USA/Tx:? D. Cleveland's b-68 may be this one.

E1SA 130/29May51/USA

E1SA 131/7Jun51/GB: Jowett team car Le Mans 1951, driven by Hadley/Goodacre. Original colour green, reg HAK366. Team car in 1951 RAC TT driven by Bert Hadley to class win. Lightened bodywork and many special features that survive to this day including its unstamped body panels indicate construction in the experimental department. Green; e-(ns); c-26137G.

E1SA 132/7Jun51/GB: Jowett team car Le Mans 1951, driven to class win by Becquart/Wilkins. Original colour blue, reg HAK365; John Gott identified his Alpine Rally car (1952) as the Le Mans class-winner. Wisdom drove it in the 1951 RAC TT. Twin car to HAK366. In 1966 it was sold to an American who took it to Spain with him; it was apparently seen there in 1969.

E1SA 133/23May51/USA/Al: G. Kemp.

E1SA 134/30Apr51/USA: There is some evidence to connect this chassis number to the Chevrolet-Va-powered Jupiter raced under an SCCA formula by Jon Clifton in the late 1950s. Last known owner C.B. Tabron.

E1SA 135/1May51/USA

E1SA 136/4May51/AUS: Red; b-73A; e-E1 SA 136R; D.L. Anderson.

E1SA 137/23May51/USA/Ct: Dark green; b-72A; e-E1 SA 137R; c-14867; less than 20,000 miles from new; C.A. Schneider.

E!SA 138/11May51/F

E1SA 139/23May51/USA

E1SA 140/23May51/USA/Al: Green; b-75; E.J. Renner.

E1SA 141/23May51/USA

E1SA 142/23May51/USA

E1SA 143/30May51/USA

E1SA 144/29May51/USA/NY: Red; b-79A; e-E1 SA 144R; c-15232; 9,000 miles from new; R.J. Gormley.

E1SA 145/29May51/USA

E1SA 146/23May51/USA

E1SA 147/29May51/USA/Ca: b-82A; van Buren.

E1SA 148/29May51/USA

E1SA 149/29May51/USA/Ca: b-84; (1962).

E1SA 150/29May51/USA

E1SA 151/29May51/NL: b-86A; e-R25021; c-742 G 26833 but plinth restamped E1 SA 151R. UX-70-15. W. Nievwerf.

E1SA 152/5Jun51/USA

E1SA 153/13Jun51/F: Red; b-88; e-E1 SA 153R; c-15482; H. Louis.

E1SA 154/6Jun51/A

E1SA 155/19Jun51/U

E1SA 156/4Jun51/USA/Pa: b-95 (plate), 85 (panels); no engine. G. Pfisterer.

E1SA 157/5Jun51/USA

E1SA 158/4Jun51/USA

E1SA 159/5Jun51/USA/Ma: Red; b-95A (plate); e-E1 SA 159R; c-15166; E.A. Steiman.

E1SA 160/26Jun51/NL: Red; b-100; e-R014439; c-2025; once had 1300 cc Porsche engine fitted; was reg ST-18-16.E.de Bruyn.

E1SA 161/18Jun51/NZ: Blue; e-E1 SA 161R; CT6895; D. Youren.

E1SA 162/19Jul51/AUS: b-99; D.L. Anderson.

E1SA 163/26Jun51/AUS: This may be B. Houston's other Jupiter.

E1SA 164/26Jun51/CY: e-B630; Prastitis, Famagusta, 1973. Had owned the car from new.

E1SA 165/26Jun51/AUS

E1SA 166/12Jul51/AUS: L. Buchanon.

E1SA 167/19Oct51/NZ: Blue; e-E1 SA 167R; AW25; E. Greenway.

E1SA 168/31Aug51/P/GB: b-104A; Rallied by 2nd
owner, Silva Cardoso, in 1952 Lisbon (class 7th).
Came to England about 1956, UK reg OS12. Sold
in 1964 to an owner who failed to register the
transaction.

E1SA 169/13Jul51/USA

E1SA 170/28Jun51/DK

E1SAL171/24Aug51/BR

E1SAL172/3Sep51/USA

E1SAL173/29Aug51/USA

E1SAL174/6Nov51/P/ex to CAN: UK reg HAK731.

E1SAL175/27Aug51/BR

E1SAL176/29Aug51/USA

E1SAL177/27Sep51/NL

E1SAL178/29Aug51/USA

E1SAL179/27Aug51/BR

E1SAL180/3Sep51/USA

E1SA 181/5Jun51/HK: (The Richard Mead Jupiter in
NZ (249) has for many years been spuriously
registered under this number.)

E1SA 182/20Jul51/NZ: White; b-107A; e-E3 PE 400:
DW7458; raced by Vic Morrison 1964-5, when it
became known as the 'Jaguar-eater'. S. Wickens.

E1SA 183/24Jul51/P/ex HKU43

E1SA 184/8Nov51

E1SA 185/19Jul51/AUS: Red; b-110A; Mr White.

E1SA 186/12Jul51/AUS

E1SA 187/11Jul51/P/ex: HKU90

E1SA 188/20Jul51/NZ: White; b-113A; e-E1 SA 188R;
CY2305; A. Grudnoff.

E1SA 189/20Jul51/NZ: (dismantled: b-122A), Chassis
with N. Dawber.

E1SA 190/26Jul51/CH

E1SA 191/26Jul51/CH

E1SAL192/29Aug51/USA

E1SAL193/3Sep51/USA

E1SAL194/28Sep51/USA

E1SAL195/2Sep51/USA

E1SAL196/30Aug51/USA

E1SAL197/28Aug51/USA/Ca: Met. bronze; b-143
(plate), 137 (panels); e-E1 SA 197R; c-16877; car
in family since March 1952.

E1SAL198/28Aug51/USA

E1SAL199/28Aug51/USA/Az: Yellow; C. Deitrich.

E1SAL200/29Aug51/USA

E1SAL201/29Aug51/USA/Az: 1962.

E1SA 202/9Aug51/AUS: R. Maddocks.

E1SA 203/20Jul51/NZ: White; engine, front part of
chassis including front suspension is from a
Standard Vanguard. J. Triplady.

E1SA 204/13Aug51/P/Ex: HKU37.

E1SA 205/7Sep51/AUS: b-133(panels); e-E1 SA 205R;
c-16616; B. Polain.

E1SA 206/27Jul61/P/ex: To Mr & Mrs Gene Fowler,
Beverley Hills, Ca, the gift of Red Skelton. b-126
(plate), 138 (panels); e-E1 SA 206R; c-21747.
UK reg HKU284. J. Kenna.

E1SAL207/28Sep51/USA

E1SAL208/3Sep51/USA

E1SAL209/28Sep51/USA

E1SAL210/24Mar52/Tripoli, Libya or Lebabon:
Originally delivered to the Paris agent (1Sep51)
as RHD.

E3SA 211/GB: Delivered to the Paris Agent 12Sep51,
ret Mar52, reissued 8Sep53, registered 18Sep53
KAM941; Green; b-146A; e-R014392; c-19081;
tail (from 924) 685; C. Skipp.

E1SAL212/6Feb52/B/GB: e-E1 SAL212R; E. Trimble.

E1SAL213/1Sep51/USA/NJ: Red; b-205;
e-E1 SAL213R; raced by first two owners, 1951,
1952. Present owner bought car in 1953, raced it
twice: Okmulgee, Ok, and in the Aspen Road
Race, Co. Did not finish either event. Present mileage 53,000 . R.L. Barns.

E1SAL214/28Sep51/USA

E1SAL215/11Oct51/USA

– 216: not built.

E1SA 217/20Jul51/NZ: b-117A; e-E1 SA 217R;
CF5320; W. Fletcher.

E1SA 218/20Jul51/YV

E1SA 219/20Jul51/NZ: Red; b-119A; e-EO PB 8477;
BB6217; I. Clegg.

E1SA 220/20Jul51/NZ: Yellow; b-93A; e-E3 PE 327;
DA7058; A. Moffatt.

E1SA 221/20Jul51/NZ: Red; b-128A; e-EOPB 10191;
CS2260; I. Birdling.

E1SAL222/28Sep51/USA

E1SAL223/24Sep51/BR

E1SAL224/27Sep51/USA

E1SAL225/2Sep51/D

E1SAL226/1Oct51/USA

E1SA 227/9Sep51/P/ex: HKU93

E1SA 228/27Jul51/P/ex: To Mr & Mrs David Rose,
Beverley Hills, Ca, the gift of Red Skelton. b-162.
In a Sun Valley wrecker's yard, Nov77, lacking
engine, gearbox, bonnet, trim. HKU286

E1SA 229/19Sep/51/P/ex: To Accra, Nigeria: Returned
to UK in 1953, when registered PTT243; Green;
b-139A; e-D9 PB 6766; J.H. Preston.

E1SA 230/20Aug51/P/ex: HKU22?

E1SA 231/14Sep51/CH

E1SAL232/26Oct51/MEX

E1SAL233/12Oct51/USA/NH: White; b-261A;
e-RGM28J; c-91578; D. Chambers.

– 234 to 241 inclusive were not built.

E1SA 242+/13Jul51/GB: Red; DHC resembles standard,
built for R. Holmes of Burges Hill, Sussex. GAP6;
D. Marshall.

E1SA 243+/4Jul51: Returned to the factory and built
up as car 886.

E1SA 244+/4Jul51: Returned to the factory and built
up as car 939.

E1SA 245+/27Jul51/GB: Red; Saloon body by J.E. Farr
& Son; OTB559; C. Porter.

E1SA 246+/26Jul51/GB: Green; originally a blue saloon
body by Maurice Gomm, completed and registered
538KOR in 1964. Crashed a few years later, and
rebuilt using standard body parts throughout in
1972. D. Cox.

E1SA 247+/10Jul51/GB: Blue; FHC by Abbott of
Farnham; e-R11132; c-6176; KOU605; M.J.
Edgington.

E1SA 248+/18Jul51/GB: Open tourer body by Richard
Mead, built for Michael Beaumont, later Seigneurie
de Sark, who said 'Its roadholding was excellent
particularly in snow and the wet when one could

guarantee to outperform MGs, TR2s, and their like in local club events'. Once broke crank at Brands Hatch. Body has latterly been removed and destroyed but chassis and mechanicals remain.

E1SA 249+/25Jul51/GB/NZ: Red; open tourer body by Richard Mead; e-E1 PC 18854; inexplicably this car has for many years been believed to be E1SA181, a standard car. CY3377; J. Bayly.

E1SA 250+/17Jul51/GB: BRG metallic; DHC by Geo. Hartwell Ltd. LRU888 (1960).

E1SA 251+/5Jul51/GB: Red; drophead body by Richard Mead; e-E3 PE 23214; MBM305; sold 1975.

E1SA 252+/13Jul51/GB: Saloon body by J.E. Farr; FRJ351; D.G. Day.

E1SA 253+/19Jul51/GB: Red; DHC body by James Bendall & Sons Ltd, Carlisle. Owned by Peter Ustinov for about two years in the mid 1950s and went with him to Hollywood once. LRM577. D. Sparrow.

E1SA 254/9Aug51/AUS: R. Maddocks.

E1SA 255/1May52/GB: Originally intended for a p/ex customer but taken over by JC Ltd Service Department, hence reg HKU92. b-128 (plate), 129 (panels); e-R2254; L. Hills.

E1SA 256/27Jul61/P/ex: To Mr & Mrs Bo Christian Ross, Sr, Beverley Hills, Ca, the gift of Red Skelton. HKU285.

E1SA 257/27Jul51/MA

E1SA 258/27Jul51/D

– 259 to 263 inclusive were not built.

E1SA 264/28Aug51/GBZ/GB: Returned to UK 8Oct55. Gold; b-147; e-E1 SA 264R; c-16827; RYR89; A. Beeden.

E1SA 265/19Sep51/P: b-135A; original engine transferred to Nogueira's Jupiter for the Volta a Portugal. Replacement engine did not arrive until late 1953, therefore car not sold to J. Touzet, still its owner, until 18Mar54. Reg CL-17-82.

E1SA 266/27Sep51/P/ex: To Mr & Mrs Red Skelton, Beverley Hills, Ca.; b-136; e-E3 SCL 754R; c-26063; UK reg HKU283; P. Cooper.

E1SA 267/18Sep51/AUS: Green; b-154. Chassis number assessed from body number. T. Hocking.

E1SA 268/4Oct51/SGP

– 269 to 274 inclusive were not built.

E1SA 275/24Oct51/HK

– 276 to 280 inclusive were not built.

E1SA 281/19Sep51/P: b-167A; CL-17-83 (1952).

E1SA 282/18Sep51/GB: Rallied by 1st owner L.C. Procter in 1952; PEH796.

E1SA 283/4Oct51/SGP

E1SA 284/4Oft51/SGP/GB: b-170 (plate), 190 (panels). Reg in UK TKC240 in July 1955; N. Reeves.

E1SA 285/24Oct51/HK

E1SA 286/2Nov51/NZ: b-171; e-E1 SA 286R; fixed hard top well fitted. AZ56670; D. Gorrie.

E1SA 287/25Sep51/D

E1SA 288/26Sep51/GB

E1SA 289/5Oct51/P/ex: HKU537.

E1SA 290/5Oct51/NZ: Copper; b-177A; e-F7 PL 14N built into original crankcase; over-

drive; one owner from new; BZ4941; H.W. Youren.

E1SA 291+/21Sep51/CH: Carbriolet body by Beutler. L. Oberholzer.

– 292 to 314 inclusive were not built.

E1SA 315/23Nov51/GB: First owner Sir John Hodge. Rallied by second owner Jack Bates 1953–8. Written off by third owner in 1960. HKU607.

– 316 to 335 inclusive were not built.

E2SAL336/24Nov52/CO

E2SAL337/18Jun52/F

E1SA 338/7Nov51/AUS

E1SA 339/16Oct51/GB: b-174; factory car (JC Ltd) Possibly demonstrator at 1951 Earls Court Show. HKU639. P. Quirk.

– 340 to 399 inclusive were not built.

E1SAL400/12Oct51/USA/Tx: White; b-184A; D. Cleveland.

E1SAL401/11Oct51/USA

E1SAL402/11Oct51/USA

E1SAL403/8Oct51/B

E1SAL404/11Oct51/USA

E1SAL405/12Oct51/USA

E1SAL406/11Oct51/USA

E1SAL407/17Oct51/P/ex: HKU756

E1SAL408/9Nov51/USA

E1SAL409/20Nov51/USA

E1SAL410/20Mar52/USA

E1SAL411/8Nov51/USA

E1SAL412/8Nov51/USA/Mi: b-355; C.L. Sample.

E1SA 413/1Nov51/P/ex: HKU538

E1SA 414/19Oct51/NZ: e-E1 SA 414R; E. Blatchford.

E1SA 415/17Oct51/NZ/GB: Red; b-198 (panels); e-E1 SA 415R; c-18220; returned to UK in 1976. Given the 1948 registration LUG347 in 1980. P. Riley.

E1SA 416/19Oct51/Bermuda

E1SA 417/19Oct51/NZ: M. blue; b-203; e-E3 PE 23775; BG7371. M. Bergin.

E1SA 418/24Oct51/AUS: b-201; M. Stone.

E1SAL419/9Oct51/NL

E1SAL420/6Nov51/P: b-210; HH-18-02; (1953).

E1SA 421/22Oct51/AUS: B. Kelsall.

E1SA 422/18Oct51/NZ: M. blue; b-202A; e-F8 PL 13; overdrive; DE3644; M. Wickens.

E2SAL423/20Mar52/USA

E1SAL424/12Nov51/P: b-216A; AE-18-17; (1952).

E1SAL425/8Nov51/USA/Ca: b-217; e-E1 SA 425R; c-18232; V. Collins.

E1SAL426/8Nov51/USA

E1SA 427/20Oct51/AUS

E1SA 428/7Nov51/AUS: b-220 (panels); for sale in 1980.

E1SAL429/12Nov51/P: b-219A; HH-18-01; (1952).

E SAL430/25Mar52/Portugese W. Africa.

E1SA 431/7Nov51/AUS: D. Rath.

E2SAL432/20Mar52/USA

E1SA 433/31Oct51/AUS: Simpson.

E2SAL434/20Mar52/USA/NJ: H.Y. Jackson.

E1SAL435/7Mar52/RCH

E1SAL436/8Feb52/B

E1SAL437/12Nov51/P: b-226A; HH-18-00; (1952).

E1SA 438/31Oct51/AUS

E2SAL439/20Oct52/USA/Ca: Said to have been raced by 2nd owner Bill Rush. (1963).

E1SA 440/7Nov51/AUS

E1SAL441/8Nov51/USA

E1SAL442/21Mar52/USA/Ca: Orange; b-321 (plate), 376 (panels) e-E1 SAL 432R; c-18417; J. Bunten.

E1SA 443/29Oct51/AUS: White; b-234A; R. McGown.

E1SA 444/30)ct51/AUS; B. Houston.

E1SA 445/8Nov51/NZ: Red; A40 engine; 'one heluva mess', thanks to front end smash; Ray Larsen.

E1SAL446/8Nov51/USA/Mo: Sold around 1969 for use as a planter for flowers!

E1SA 447/8Nov51/NZ: e-E1 SA 447; CQ6665; D.H. Davies.

E1SA 448/8Nov51/NZ: b-238A; CN7925; L. Gourdie.

E1SA 449/9Nov51/GB: b-249A; HKW360; G.M. Mitchell.

E1SA 450/14Dec51/GB:

E1SA 451/31Oct51/AUS: Scarlet; b-233A; e-E1 SA 451R (repl); c-21940; C.B. Shute.

E1SA 452/28Dec51/GB: Red; HFY845; P. Quirk. The 'Ineson Special' – Jupiter frame, homemade body, was registered NWU1 in May 1954, with chassis E1SA 452, e-E1SA 59R. In 1960 it lost this engine and its bodywork. In 1980 it existed as a rolling chassis less some tubes front and rear; cycle wings are attached to front-brake backplates. Owner A. Lockey.

E1SA 453/8Nov51/NZ: Green; e-25202; BG502; D. Youren.

E1SA 454/9Nov51/NZ: b-243A; e-E1 SA 454R; c-18687; once had Ford 10 hp engine, original engine salvaged from a Javelin. Body set 505 from chassis 681 fitted. AV7817. R. Winder.

E1SA 455/9Nov51/NZ: Red; e-F7 PL 15; AR2096; A.A. Stanley.

E1SA 456/31Oct51/AUS: D. Rath.

E1SA 457/3Dec51/GB

E1SA 458/16Nov51/WAN/GB: Green; b-246A; e-JUR25502; c-92296; returned to UK, 28Dec55, reg SGX64. B. Shaw.

E1SA 459/23Nov51/GB

E1SA 460/19Nov51/CL

E1SA 461/22Nov51/GB

E1SA 462/16Nov51/GB

E1SA 463/19Nov51/GB: b-253 (panels); BCW140; G. Ricketts.

E1SA 464/27Nov51/GB

E1SA 465/11Dec51/GB: (1967)

E1SA 466/23Nov51/GB: Blue; b-258A; e-R025457; c-23295; OWB179; R.A. Ward.

E1SA 467/9Nov51/GB: Black; b-262A; e-R026295; c-24051; HKU888; G. van Jennians.

E1SA 468/3Dec51/GB/NL: Yellow; b-263A; e-E1 SA 468R; c-2439; UK reg JSF282; taken to Holland in 1964; 99-DU-82. S. de Bruyn.

E1SA 469/23Nov51/GB

E1SA 470/19Nov51/GB

E1SA 471/12Dec51/GB: KBC444. Possibly scrapped.

E1SA 472/23Nov51/GB: KWY821; rallied in 1952 by 1st owner, E. Foulds.

E1SA 473/12Dec51/GB:

E1SA 474/7Dec51/GB

E1SA 475/12Dec51/GB: LUF420. Body scrapped, rolling chassis survives. A.R. Lynton.

E1SA 476/4Dec51/GB

E1SA 477/29Nov51/GB: MND444. Possibly scrapped.

E1SA 478/26Nov51/GB: FBA368. (1971).

E1SA 479/26Nov51/GB:

E1SA 480/4Dec51/GB

E1SA 481/23Nov51/GB: Green; b-340A; e-E1 SA 481R; c-19092; OWA845; E.F. Newbold.

E1SA 482/12Dec51/RSR

E1SA 483/12Dec51/SGP/MAL: Green; b-342A; e-R025070; c-91485; (1979).

E1SA 484/28Nov51/GB: Green; e-E1 SA 484R; c-19107; KBT702. C.W. Ellicot.

E1SA 485/31Dec51/GB: Rallied by 1st owner L. Pellowe in 1952 Morecambe.

E1SA 486/19Dec51/GB: e-R6112; OTJ428; L Richardson.

E1SA 487/20Dec51/GB

E2SA 488/23Jan52/P/ex: HKU878

E1SA 489/31Dec51/GB

E1SA 490/14Dec51/GB: b-268; sold 1979.

E1SA 491/17Dec51/GB: e-JUR25142; JTR777; D. Thom.

E1SA 492/12Dec51/SGP

E1SA 493/10Dec51/GB: b-367A; e-E3 PE 24000; AFA875; P. Young.

E1SA 494/12Dec51/GB: LDT3; used by first owner C.F. Eminson at Prescott and in Pilkington trial in 1952. (1952).

E1SA 495/11Dec51/GB: White; b-368 (plate); e-E1 PD 19317; c-18993; Withdrawn from Christie's auction, 1977, at £1200. KBT696. D. Walton.

E1SA 496/15Jan52/GB: Green; b-271A; e-R5551; c-25635; XME740. P. Bennett.

E1SA 497/22Jan52/N. Ireland/England: Red; b-267A; e-R012326; NZ3395; (1968).

E1SA 498/29Feb52/GB: Red; b-273A; e-R6918; RPF981; C.W. Battersby.

E1SA 499/19Feb52/GB:

E1SAL500+/29Nov51/DK: Green; FHC by Sommers using standard bonnet, spare-wheel door. Car resembles Bentley Continental in miniature from rear. e-R025891N; c-361 & 91882; DW58-921. A. Clausager.

E1SA 501/16Jan52/GB: b-274A; GB0888; possibly scrapped.

E1SA 502/26Feb52/GB: KTM250; (1970).

E1SA 503/15Jan52/GB: Green; e-26193; JEB 4; D.J. Copsey.

E1SAL504/20Dec51/USA

E1SA 505/31Jan52/GB: Red; b-278; e-D9 PB 6637; EHH707; J. Parker.

E1SAL506/20Dec51/USA

E1SAL507/20Dec51/USA

E1SAL508/21Dec51/USA/Ca: b-372A; J. Casburn.

E1SA 509/5Feb52/GB: Green; b-374A; raced and rallied for 1st 18 months by 1st owner N. Freedman, with engine tuned by Ramponi; MXA506; C. Le-Bas.

E1SAL510/20Dec61/USA/Ca: Possibly scrapped around
1967.

E1SAL511/20Dec51/USA

E1SAL512/20Dec51/USA

E1SA 513/21Dec52/GB/NZ: b-279; exported to NZ
Oct56. e-(ns); c-92208; was reg BH7166; but when
meticulous restoration has been completed should
have new reg JJ1951; R.L. Bolter.

E1SAL514/21Dec51/USA

E1SAL515/21Dec51/USA/Mi: b-355; e-EO PBL 10577;
J. Spalding.

E1SAL516/21Dec51/USA

E1SAL517/21Dec51/USA

E1SAL518/21Dec51/USA

E1SAL519/21Dec51/USA/Ca: b-377; e-E3 SCL 519R;
c-25955; T.J. Glynn.

E1SA 520/30Jan52/GB

E1SA 521/14Jan52/GB: Blue; b-260A; e-N7970; rallied
by 1st owner F.E. Still:1952 RAC (36th); 1952
Margate class win; in six-hour relay race team, etc.
NNK560. R. Davis.

E1SA 522/12Mar52/GB

E1SAL523/7Jan52/USA/Ca: Blue; b-396 (panels);
e-X19533; W. Tandberg.

E1SAL524/8Jan52/USA

E1SAL525/8Jan52/USA/Ca: b-362; e-E1 SAL 406R;
T. Stranahan.

E1SAL526/8Jan52/USA

E1SAL527/8Jan52/USA/Mn: b-294; e-E2 SAL 812R;
O. Sutton.

E1SAL528/29Jan52/HK

E1SAL529/8Jan52/USA/Ca: (1969)

E1SAL530/7Jan52/USA/Ca: b-323 (panels); e-E2 SAL
SAL 634R; P. Ekstrom.

E1SAL531/8Jan52/USA

E1SAL532/8Jan52/USA

E1SAL533/8Jan52/USA

E1SAL534/8Jan52/USA

E1SAL535/8Jan52/USA/Or: Red; b-359A; MGA engine
and transmission; E.A. Bussey.

E1SA 536/4Feb52/GB: b-410A; original reg KSP 1; now
81HYN; M. Chevers.

E1SAL537/7Feb52/USA

E1SA 538/30Jan52/GB: Grey; b-288A; e-E2 PD 23359;
c-25724; MUW599; L. Proudlock.

E1SA 539/7Feb52/GB: Turquoise; b-289A; RPF 16;
Rodwell.

E1SA 540/21Jan52/GB

E1SA541/16Jan52/GB: Bronze; b-289A; HJF602; A.
Wright.

E1SA 542/15Feb52/GB: b-299A; R. Flowers.

E1SA 543/20Feb52/GB: Green; b-295A; SW8760;
A.A. Cleaveley.

E1SA 544/31Jan52/GB: Red; e-E2 PE 22627; c-24198;
HKW429. (1971).

E1SA 545/15Feb52/GB: White; b-308A; FNL300.

E1SA 546 21Jan52/GB/Jersey: Red; e-JUR26305;
992LMD; G. Richman.

E1SA 547/22Feb52/GB

E1SA 548/29Jan52/HK/GB: Grey; b-391A; e-E1 SA
548R; c-19963; returned to UK in Nov 1959,
reg XXT59; W.G.F. Scott.

E1SA 549/29Jan52/HK

E1SAL550/6Feb52/USA

E1SAL551/6Feb52/USA

E1SAL552/7Feb52/USA

E1SA 553/23Jan52/GB

E1SA 554/17Mar52/GB: Green; b-388 (plate); UEV555;
P. Boothroyd

E1SA 555/23Jan52/GB: b-298A; XME508; possibly
scrapped.

E1SA 556/22Feb52/GB

E1SA 557/13Feb52/GB: Blue; b-395A; e-R013201;
c-1862R; JKY832 (must be a re-reg); M. Sleep.

E2SA 558/11Feb52/GB/NL: Red; b-305; UK reg
OKP822 but car seen in Heeze, Holland, 1978.

E1SA 559/1Feb52/GB: Beige; e-EO PB 10045;
c-10863; OAU861; G. Butterwick.

E1SB 560/11Feb52/GB: HKW197. The protoype Mk1a;
road tested by *Autocar, Motor*; and in France by
Milestones for the Motorist magazine, in what
amounted to a recce of the 1953 Languedoc-Sète
Touring Rally. The only 'SB' Jupiter. Believed
scrapped but its bonnet survives.

E2SA 561/15Feb52/GB:

E2SA 562/24Jan52/GB: Green; e-E2 SA 562; c-25640;
JYS603; C.S. Cale.

E2SA 563/23Jan52/GB: KYG606; C.J.W. Guerrier.

E2SA 564/23Jan52/GB: HKW386; used by Kenneth
Brierley at Silverstone during 1955–6, and by
Miss Neale during 1957–8. Possibly scrapped.

E2SA 565/6Feb52/GB: Red; OMB522; F. Livesey.

E2SA 566/23Jan52/GB: b-303; MLV797; probably
scrapped.

E1SA 567/1Feb52/GB

E2SA 568 22Feb52/GB: OHY423; (1967). First owner
broke crank 3 times.

E2SAL569/11Jan52/B

E2SA 570/4Feb52/GB: WHite; b-300A; originally a
present by Lord Nunburnholme to his daughter.
From 1965 to 1972 it was falsly registered as
GKW111; correct registration has not been
determined.

E2SA 571/29Jan52/GB: b-302; NOD759; possibly
scrapped.

E2SA 572/22Jan52/WAN/GB: b-307A; e-JUR26375N;
c-91337; returned from Kenya in 1955 on
temporary plates QE612, which seem to have
become permanent. The second owner of this car,
who worked in Nigeria for a shipping company,
frequently brought the car back to England with
him usually to take in a visit to Batley.

E2SA 573/4Feb52/GB: b-328A; e-JUR26206N; c-987
& 27209; ORL812; E.G. Baker.

E2SA 574/1Feb/52/GB

E2SA 575/4Feb52/GB: Red; b-312A; e-R25136;
XME857; V. Smithson.

E2SA 576/14Feb52/GB

E2/SA 577/7Feb52/GB: HKW482; frame, body, sold
separately from engine, gearbox, in 1967.

E2SAL578/6Feb52/USA/Ca: J.C. Pawtrey.

E2SA 579/1Feb52/USA/Ca: Blue; b-319; e-R015138N;
c-6912; KGA548; G.W.P. Edwards.

E2SAL580/6Feb52/USA/Ca: BRG; b-351; e-(ns);
c-22002; John Petrey.

E2SAL581/7Feb52/USA

E2SA 582/18Feb52/GB: Red; b-327A; e-E2 SA 582R;
c-20284; HBL 11; T. Ramussen.

E1SA 583+/4Feb52/GB: FHC by J.E. Farr & Son.
EBV429; believed scrapped.

E2SA 584/7Feb52/GB

E2SA 585/12Feb52/GB: b-326A; CKS334; R. Howard.

E2SA 586/8Feb52/GB: Participant in Circuit of Ireland
Trial, April 1953 driven by A.B. Hibbert; b-330;
M. Bertram.

E2SAL587/7Feb52/USA

E2SA 588/15Feb52/GB

E2SA 589/6Feb52/GB: HKW480; M. Leah.

E2SAL590/11Feb52/USA

E2SAL591/6Feb52/USA

E2SAL592/6Feb52/USA

E2/SAL593/6Feb52/USA/Co: b-385; V. Collins.

E2SAL594/6Feb52/USA/Ca: b-425A; e-E2 SAL 594R;
c-20387; W. Johnson.

E2SAL595/6Feb52/USA

E2SAL596/11Feb52/USA

E2SA 597/11Feb52/GB: Green; b-412; e-JUR25178;
used in rallies by first three owners. Best result:
class win of Brighton & Hove MC Rally 11Jul53
driven by F.M. Baker. MCD28; N.A. Seale.

E2SA 598/13Feb52/GB

E2SA599/15Feb52/GB

E2SA 600/7Mar52/GB

E2SA 601/11Mar52/GB

E2SA 602/10Mar52/GB: First owner Kenneth Crutch
entered this car in high-speed trials at Silverstone,
and was in 1953 6-Hour relay team of Alf Thomas.

E2SA 603/11Mar52/GB

E2SA 604/18Feb52/GB

E2SA 605/14Mar52/GB: Turquoise blue; b-460;
e-JUR25755N; SK4432; G.W. Bird.

E2SA 606/19Feb52/GB:

E2SAL607/11Feb52/USA

E2SAL608/11Feb52/USA

E2SAL609/11Feb52/USA

E2SAL610/11Feb52/USACa: White; b-449; e-E2 SAL
516R; H. Korner.

E2SAL611/13Feb52USA

E2SAL612/12Feb52/USA

E2SAL613/12Feb52/USA

E2SAL614/11Feb52/USA

E2SAL615/12Feb52/USA/Va: (1963)

E2SA 616/25Feb52/GB: NTJ998; possibly scrapped.

E2SA 617/4Mar52/S

E2SA 618/25Feb52/GB: Red; b-433A; e-R25108;
entrant Morecambe Rally, May1952; DS3131;
J.H. Jezard.

E2SA 619/27Feb52/GB: NPO5; possibly scrapped.

E2SA 620/26Feb52/GB: Red; b-349A; e-D9 PA 3066;
c-91704; FUD194; G.A. Mumby.

E2SA 621/26Feb52/GB:

E2SA 622/7Mar52/GB: RPF978; (1968).

E2SA 623/24Apr52/GB

E2SA 624/6Mar52/GB

E2SA 625/1Apr52/GB

E2SA 626/29Feb52/GB: Cream; b-431A; e-(ns);
c-H25; RAE850; J. Watkinson.

E2SA 627/28Feb52/GB

E2SA 628/25Feb52/GB

E2SA629/29Feb52/GB: Sand; PBH583; G. Duce.

E2SA 630/11Mar52/GB

E2SA 631/26Feb52/GB

E2SA 632/12Mar52/GB

E2SA 633/13Mar52/GB: Red; b-411A; e-20657;
MGD475; T.W. Miller.

E2SAL634/13Feb52/USA

E2SAL635/13Feb52/USA

E2SA 636/29Feb52/GB: BRG; b-408; e-E3 PE 23828;
c-25676; car adapted to take Ford V4 engine as
alternative; chassis cut. G. Mitchell.

E2SAL637/19Feb52/NL: Red; e-RGM16J; 15-98-GH;
G.B.J. Lubbers.

E2SA 638/11Mar52/GB: Green; b-316A; e-E2 SA 638R;
c-20682; BCW337; N. Hughes.

E2SA 639/24Mar52/GB: Green; b-315A; e-E2 SA 639R;
RPG231; W. Lock.

E2SA 640/4Apr52/GB

E2SAL641/22Feb52/B

E2SA 642/4Mar52/GB

E2SA 643/7Mar52/GB

E2SA 644/17Mar52/GB

E2SA 645/17Mar52/GB

E2SA 646/12Mar52/GB: Green; e-R5054; MOE 87;
(1981).

E2SA 647/14Mar52/GB: Red; b-357A; e-R6188;
RPG776; J.S. Ingleby

E2SA 648/18Mar52/GB: White; e-E2 SA 648; NRO964;
J.J. Tait.

E2SAL649/20Mar52/USA/Az: b-442A; e-2 SAL 649R;
c-20850; P. Teske and B. Hessemer.

E3SA 650/19Jun53/GB: Aubergine; b-400A; e-E3 SA
650R; c-691 G 26647; entrant 1971 Civil Service
M.A. Curtis-Bennett Rally, M.J. Smailes/M. Berrie.
Used in sprints, hill-climbs, HSCC races in mid
1970s. These low-numbered E3 cars were evidentally virtually completed in early 1952, but not
sold until 12 to 18 months later. M. Smailes.

E2SA 651/17Mar52/GB: Used rather unsuccessfully in
competition by first owner G.A. Dudley. NPO133;
G.E. Wilson.

E2SA 652/12Mar52/GB: b-418; e-E2 SA 652R;
KER437; M. Chevers.

E2SA 653/27Jun/GB: White; b-407A; NLX901;
J. Astill.

E2SA 654/23Jun52/GB/USA/NH: b-470A;
e-JUR26229N; c-92254; UK reg GKE445; H.
Chambers.

E2SAL655/7Mar52/B

E3SA 656/15May53/GB

E2SA 657/4Apr52/GB

E2SA 658/20Mar52/GB: Copper; b-475A; e-E2 SA
658R; MOC898; D. Parry Jones.

E2SA 659/7Apr52/GB: Poly-blue; e-E3 PE 24448; c-671
& 26995; FFE648; R.R. Whittle.

E2SA 660/23Jun52/GB: Maroon; b-466A; e-R017354;
c-17930; PFM606; J.E. Snelling-Colyer.

E2SA 661/12Mar52/GB

E2SA 662/5Sep52/GB: Red; b-484A; -E2 SA 662R;
c-21102; KRY170; (1969).

E2SA 663/9Apr52/GB

E2SA 664/25Apr52/GB: JS9660; M. Riley.

E2SA 665/10Apr52/GB

E2SA 666/7Apr52 GB

E2SA 667/3Apr52/GB; Dark blue; b-462A;
e-R026263N; c-91210; CBR99; Rev W.H.G.
Bristow.

E2SA 668/9Apr52/GB: VEV21; Mrs P. Young.

E2SA 669/1Apr52/GB: Badly crashed in 1965.

E2SA 670/27May52/GB/IRL: Yellow; e-JUR26150N;
c-24312; SW8769; taken to Eire in 1970; P.J.
Johnson.

E2SA 671/28May52/GB: NPT795; (1967).

E2SA 672/17Mar52/GB: MXP610; L. Richardson.

E2SA 673/2Apr52/GB: Grey; b-487; e-R015848N;
c-3244; FHS338; J.I. Phillips.

E2SA 674/18Jun52/GB: b-499; e-R2477; c-13761;
NLT331; T. Thorne.

E2SA 675/2Apr52/GB

E2SA 676/28Apr52/GB

E2SA 677/4Jul52/GB: b-477; e-E3 PE 24590; c-1033 &
27171; OJH161; M.J. Edgington.

E3SA 678/29Jun53/GB: b-481A; GBA743; J. Blazé.

E3SA 679/22May53/GB/IRL: b-469A; LMJ517; J.
Porter.

E2SA 680/2Apr52/GB: ECF494; J.F. Baker. Used in E.
Anglian MC Winter Rally (a 60-mile frolic),
24Jan54.

E2SA 681/23May52/GB/NZ: b-505 originally but now
removed. chassis in wreckers yard 1975.

E2SA 682/23Apr52/GB: White; b-493A; e-JUR25124;
c-92646; HDM949; G.V. Jackson.

E2SA 683/8Apr52/GB: White; e-E1 SA 541R; c-19947;
G.T. Walpole.

E2SA 684/23Apr52/GB: b-501A; EVG853; R.D. Laurie.

E2SA 685/3Apr52/GB: b-491A; FBA737; possibly
scrapped.

E2SAL686/19Mar52/SF

E2SA 687/20Jun52/GB: Aubergine; b-506A; e-E2 SA
687R; c-92675; JDM184; A.R. Malvin.

E2SA 688/1Apr52/GB

E2SA 689+/25Mar52/GB

E2SA690/3May52/GB: Red; b-474A; VN0118; G.M.
Mitchell.

E2SA 691/3Apr52/GB: Green; b-502A; ERN383;
F. Sharp.

E2SA 692/4apr52/GB: b-515A; GNJ756; W.T. Grayson.

E2SA 693/9Apr52/GB

E2SA 694/1Apr52/GB: Green; b-509A; e-JUR25535, but
E2 SA 751R on plinth; c-92321; NAT146; D.S.
Riley.

E2SA 695/16Apr52/GB: Bronze; b-430; e-E2 PE 22749;
c-24244; FJN326; C. Walmsley.

E2SAL696/19Mar52/BR

E2SA 697/10Apr52/GB: Cooper; e-E2 SA 697R;
c-21328; BHF308; J.C. Watkinson.

E2SA 698/21Apr52/GB

E2SA 699/21Apr52/JAP

E2SA 700/21Apr52/GB: Red; b-519A. KOY350; G.M.
Mitchell.

E2SAL701/19Mar52/BR

E2SAL702/20Mar52/USA

E2SAL703/21Mar52/USA/Ca: Probably scrapped by
M.C. Green in 1968; body parts survive.

E2SA 704/4Apr52/GB: Green; b-494; HUN428; R.
Wood.

E3SA 705/1Oct63/GB: b-511A; 143AMM; K. James.

E2SAL706/21Mar52/USA

E2SA 707/9Apr52/GB: b-513; believed to have MGA
engine, Wolsley grille in 1979; MEL96.

E3SA 708/16Jul53/GB: b-486A; BHG703; dismantled
to frame which is owned by D. Cox.

E2SAL709/21Mar52/USA/Ca: b-539 but car dismantled
– chassis and body frames abandoned behind a
filling station in San José. Car had covered 13,000
only.

E2SAL710/19Mar52/P/ex: To F.L. Archer, Germany.
UK reg HKW407.

E2SA 711/14Aug52/GB: KDA943; sold engine-and-gear-
boxless for £5 in 1968.

E3SA 712/8Jul53/GB: Originally supplied as E2 SA
712R in July 1952.

E2SA 713/24Mar52/GB: e-R025284; MVM488; R.
Cross.

E2SA 714/27Jun52/GB

E2SAL715/21Mar52/USA/Ca: No engine or
transmission. D. Howard.

E2SAL716/25Mar52/USA

E2SA 717/29May52/GB: Green; b-526A; e-JUR26063;
c-27198; extra headlamps faired into bonnet;
JWS95; J.A. Walters.

E2SA 718/20Jun52/GB: Raced by J.D. Lewis during
1953; HKY344; (1953).

E2SAL719/26Mar52/USA

E3SA 720/28May53/GB: Red; b-518A; e-E3 SA 679R;
c-475G; BHG501; F. Fearn.

E2SAL721/25Mar52/USA

E2SA 722/29May52/GB: Green; b-520; original reg
HS1 for first owner the shipbuilder Sir James
Lithgow; JHS365; J. Read.

E2SA 723/29May52/GB: Green; b-508A; e-E2 PE
23506; c-25235; KDA678; (1979).
724+ This chassis was made into car E2SAL938R

E2SA 725+/31Mar52/GB: White; FHC by C. Robinson
for P. Fotheringham-Parker; first owner John
Willment, Sr. e-R012981X; c-13254; 32 MMY;
E. Nankivell.

E2SA 726+/25Mar52/GB

E2SA 727/23Jun52/GB: b-471A; e- (ns); c-202 &
27033; KRK203; B.C. Robertson.

E2SAL728/27Mar52/USA

E2SA 729/16May52/GB: e-JUR25658N; D.G. Day.

E2SAL730/28Mar52/USA/Ca: Possibly dismantled.

E2SAL731/26Mar52/USA

E2SAL732/25Mar52/USA/Ca: b-546; e-E1 SAL 193R;
c-17050; F. Shirado.

E3SA 733/23Jul53/GB: b-503; BHG914; G.M. Mitchell.

E2SA 734/8Apr52/GB: Turquoise blue; b-533;
MYM925; D. Sparrow.

E2SA 735/1Sep52/GB: Light almond; b-468; e-R25104;
c-91731; JBL418; T. Brown of London.

E2SA 736/17May52/GB: Green; b-521; e-E0 PB 11039;
HBU900; J. Smith.

E2SA 737/10Apr52/GB: BEN197; (1966).

E2SA 738/20Aug52/GB: Red; b-467; e-JUR26376N;
c-91914; OJH778; B. Street.

E2SA 739/11Jun52/GB: b-559 but dismantled to chassis
frame which is owned by D. Cox. RPL519.

E2SAL740/27Mar52/USA/Ca: Black; b-529;
    e-E2SAL740R; c-21418; R. Burr and F. Jimenez.
E2SAL741/27Mar52/USA/Mn: Copper; b-548; e-E2
    SAL 795R; c-22010; L. Carlson.
E2SAL742/27Mar52/USA
E2SAL743/26Mar52/USA/Ca: Tan; b-514; e-E1SAL
    208R; c-20409; H.R. Aitchison.
E2SAL744/26Mar52/USA
E2SAL745/27Mar52/USA/Ca: b-538; R. Wise.
E2SAL746+/9Apr52/DK: Returned to factory, rebuilt
    as E3SA937R.
E3SA 747/30Sep53/GB: Red; b-561; 977AMC; D.
    Banks.
E2SA 748/11Jun52/GB: b-523; e-RGM1; first owner Ian
    Sievwright used it in motor sport in 1952; best
    result 5th Welsh Rally, Dec52. KDA937; S.
    Burgess.
E2SA 749/25Apr52/GB: b-542; e-JUN25727N;
    c-92423; YRE937; Higgs.
E2SA 750/26Jun52/GB
E2SA 751/1Jul52/GB: Chassis frame and tail only
    survive; NXH439; P. Quirk.
E2SA 752/23Jun52/GB: b-549; KGD967; R. McKinley.
E2SA 753/28May52/GB
E2SAL754/11Apr52/USA
E3SA 755/11Aug53/GB/NZ: Green; b-555; e-(ns);
    c-92000; UK reg DJX141; to NZ in 1971;
    FP9623; P. Furness.
E2SAL756/10Apr52/USA/Ca: Black; b-656; e-E1 SAL
    524R; c-X19577; body altered to make it look
    more like a Mk1a; J. Miller.
E2SA 757/13Jun52/GB
E2SAL758/10Apr52/USA/Ca: Red; b-566; K. Jerard.
E2SAL759/11Apr52/USA
E2SAL760/10Apr52/USA
E2SA 761/29May52/GB
E2SAL762/11Apr52/USA/Ca: b-560; e-E3 SCL 176R;
    (1977).
E2SAL763/11Apr52/USA/Ca: b-562; Olds mobile V8
    engine + automatic transmission. Triumph Herald
    suspension. Accident-damaged front. R. Allino.
E2SAL764/11Apr52/USA
E2SAL765/11Apr52/USA/Ca: b-500; had Volvo engine,
    F.W. Croft.
E2SAL766/11Apr52/USA/Ca: b-568; Ford 6 cylinder
    engine and gearbox had been fitted, MGA steering
    box. W.T. Johnson.
E2SAL767/10Apr52/USA
E2SAL768/24Apr52/USA
E2SAL769/11Apr52/USA
E2SAL770/11Apr52/USA
E2SAL771/25Apr52/USA
E2SAL772/24Apr52/USA
E2SAL773/25Apr52/USA/Ca: White; b-552; e-E3 SCL
    773R; c-26500; (1977).
E2SAL774/24Apr52/USA
E2SAL775/24Apr52/USA
E2SAL776/25Apr52/USA/Ca: b-572; R. Burr and F.
    Jiminez.
E2SAL777/24Apr52/USA
E2SAL778/25Apr52/USA/Az: b-531; e-E1 SA 266R;
    extra fuel tank in luggage locker. J. Kenna.
E2SAL779/25Apr52/USA

E2SA 780/16Jun52/GB: b-544; KBE595; may have
    been scrapped in 1967.
E2SAL781/24Apr52/USA
E2SAL782/24Apr52/USA/Ca: b-575; W. Johnson.
E2SA 783/27Jun52/GB: b-534 but scrapped in 1974.
E2SAL784/25Apr52/USA
E2SAL785/25Apr52/USA
E2SAL786/25Apr52/USA
E2SAL787/30Apr52/USA/Az: Mettalic green;
    e-E3SCL787R; c-25597; S. Samelik.
E2SA 788/15May52/GB: Blue; b-516; e-R/25406;
    c-92276; MOF554; J. Riley.
E2SAL789/29Apr52/USA
E2SAL790/18Jun52/GB
E2SAL791/29Apr52/USA
E2SAL792/30Apr52/USA
E2SAL793/2May52/USA/GB: b-581; e-E3SCL 817R;
    c-26072; returned to England 1978; J. Cochran.
E2SAL794/29Apr52/USA/Mn: b-586; e-E2 SAL 794R;
    T.V. Middough.
E2SAL795/30Apr52/USA/Ca; b-585; e-E2 SAL 759R;
    Jesse Parker.
E2SAL796/2May52/USA/Ca: J. Haggee.
E2SAL797/1May52/USA
E2SAL798/2May52/USA/Ca: (1968).
E2SAL799/30Apr52/USA/Ca: Light tan; b-591; e-E2
    SAL 799R; R. Allino.
E2SAL800/2MAY52/USA/Ok: Red; S. Durrett.
E2SAL801/2May52/USA
E2SAL802/2May52/USA
E2SAL803/2May52/USA
E2SAL804/2May52/USA
E2SAL805/3May52/USA
E2SAL806/3May52/USA: (1967)
E2SAL807/7May52/USA
E2SAL808/7May52/USA
E2SAL809/8May52/USA/Wa: Yellow; e-E2 SAL 809R;
    (1975).
E2SAL810/7May52/USA
E2SAL811/8May52/USA
E2SAL812/8May52/USA
E2SAL813/8May52/USA/Ca: R. Reinstedt. Pebble
    Beach Concours First Class Award 1969. Car very
    complete and original.
E2SAL814/9May52/D
E2SAL815/7May52/USA/Ca: b-604; K. Hammond.
E2SAL816/7May52/USA/Ca: White; b-606; e-E2 SAL
    816R; c-26486; J.W. Wooding.
E2SAL817/8May52/USA/Ca: Green; b-603; lacks
    engine, doors, bonnet, all interior; E.W. Miller.
E2SAL818/4Jun52/D
E2SAL819/18Jun52/S
E2SAL820/22Aug52/USA/Ca: b-608; e-(ns); c-23961;
    (1963).
E2SAL821/14Aug52/USA
E2SAL822/22Aug52/USA
E2SAL823/23Jul52/P/ex: HKW232.
E2SAL824/14Aug52/USA
E2SAL825/22Aug52/USA
E2SAL826/14Aug52/USA
E2SAL827/27Jun52/USA
E2SAL828/27Jun52/USA
E2SAL829/20Aug52/USA/Ca: b-619; e-E2 SAL 825R;
    R. Dodson.

E2SAL830(19Aug52/USA

E2SAL831/19Jun52/P/ex: b-620; e-E2 SAL 831;
c-22459; UK reg HKY225; (1968).

E2SAL832/22Aug52/USA

E2SAL833/13Jun52/F

E2SAL834/22Aug52/USA

E2SAL835/19Aug52/USA

E2SAL836/22Aug52/USA

E2SAL837/19Aug52/USA

E2SA 838/9Jul52/GB: e-(NS); c-92101; J. Webster.

E2SA 839/2Jul52/GB: b-628; possibly scrapped.

E2SA 840/1Jul52/GB/N. Ireland: Demonstration car
of Belfast agent, in which Jowett rep Bob McKee
died; PZ1007; Mrs E. Davis.

E2SA 841/7Jul52/GB: Claret; b-650; e-E1 PD 19933;
c-19961; NKD258; K. Clements.

E2SA842/7Jul52/GB

E2SA843/27Jun52/GB

E2SA844/21Aug52/GB: E. Tonner.

E2SA 845/4Jul52/P/ex: HKY226.

E3SA 846/20May53/GB

E2SAL847/5Jun52/F

E3SA 848/20Aug53/GB: b-636; 966AMC; P. Bell.

E2SA 849/2Sep53/GB: New to Holland 1Aug52,
returned to factory 19Sep52; b-647; XVW170 but
possibly scrapped.

E3SA850/19Aug53/GB: Original owner U.K. Fleming
active in SJCC events, NYM483; possibly scrapped
after crash in 1964

E2SA851/1Jan53/P/ex: JAK824.

E3SA 852/10Jan53/WAN

E3SA853/26Aug53/GB

E3SA 854/10Jul53/GB

E3SA 855/29May53/GB: b-642; burned in a fire in
1953, rebuilt with non-standard glass-fibre and
aluminium bodywork, original scuttle and doors;
potato-chip grille; hill-climbed in Scotland in mid-
to late-1950s by its rebuilder, L. Paladini.
KSG532; G. Stanley.

E3SA 856/Dec53/GB

E2SA 857/23Aug53/GB: b-655; OLK685; B.S. Cole.

E2SA 858/20Mar53/GB: b-661; YMP935; P. Ferguson.

E2SA 859/10Mar53/GB/B: Red; b-654; LBY254;
F.W. Woolley.

E2SA 860/9Jul52/GB: Cream; e-JUR26352N; c-12857;
HKG669; J.M. Dickie.

E3SA 861/18Aug53/GB: Red; b-653; RKO 10; C. Skipp.

E2SAL862/20Jun52/USA/Il: Ivory; b-652; e-E2 SAL
862R; c-23141; T. Ritter.

E3SA 963/23Jul53/GB: Beige; b-646; e-JUR25902;
c-929 & 27091; RTD111; at time of writing (Jan
1980) offered for sale by the Victoria Carriage Co,
London, at £3,750.

E2SA 864/24Jun52/P/ex: HKY227.

E3SA 865/29Aug53/GB

E2SA 866/22May53/GB: White; e-JUR25270; NXN866;
K. Latham.

E2SA 867/3Jul52/GB

E2SA 868/3Jul52/GB

E2SA 869/7Jul52/GB

E3SA 870/25Jun53/GB

E3SA 871/13Aug53/GB: Red; e-E33 SA 871R; 7881H;
K. Latham.

E3SA 872/7Aug53/GB: Green; b-658; e-R025567;
c-92223; GBA895; J. Gipe.

E2SA 873/10Sep53/GB: Red; b-662; e-26823; c-721;
SPB725; G.H. Massey.

E3SA 874/24Aug53/GB

E2SA 875/8Sep52/GB: Green; b-668; e-E2 SA 875R;
c-23525; UVW849; P. Hickling.

E3SA 876/8Jun53/GB: Green; b-664; entered in
'Griffiths Formula' inaugural event of the Historic
Sports Car Club in 1966, driver F. Mockridge;
FVG332; P. Dixon.

E3SA 877/22Jul53/GB: Grey; b-667; NYM671/; P.
Dingle.

E3SA 878/19Sep53/GB: Red; b-665; e-RGM22; c-2750;
956AMC; E. Hawthorne.

E3SA 879/18Aug53/GB

E3SA 880/30Oct53/GB: Green; b-670; e-R014527;
OGX224; J. Riley.

E3SA 881/10Aug53/GB: Green; b-669; e-El PD 19921;
c-19932; TPF601; P. Holliday.

E2SA 882/3Sep52/P/ex: HKY762. This car is believed
to be in Sri Lanka.

E2SA 883/2Sep52/GB: Turquoise blue; b-677;
LDG988; R. Doughty.

E2SA 884/13Mar53/GB: b-679; e-JUR25832N;
c-92226; BFL578; L.W. Daniells.

E3SA 885/21Aug53/P/ex: JKU945. Sold new to US
Army T/Sgt R.W. McDonald. It has turned up in
Tucson, Arizona (there is a US army missile-
testing range near), with apparently the Jupiter
body (b-676) clothing an Austin chassis. G. Hall.

E2SA 886/3Sep52/DZ: (originally rolling chassis 243)

E3SA 887/12May53/GB: b-687; e-R6627; c-91270;
JUN 68; G.M. Mitchell.

E2SA 888/16Sept52/GB: b-672; e-R026272N; c-25151;
FRJ132; M. Alston.

E3SA 889/21Jul53/GB: Red; b-671; e-(ns); c-92681;
RAU436; G. Gilliver.

E3SA 890/28Apr53/GB: White; e-E3 SA 890R;
c-23152; PWE755; J. Hopkinson.

E2SA 891/26Nov52/BR

E2SA 892/28Nov52/P/ex: JAK557

E2SA 893 1Apr53/GB: b-680; RUA893; G.M. Mitchell.

E3SA 894/24Jul53/GB: Green; b-689; e-R4134; c-8780;
NYM449; R. Walkling.

E2SA 895/3Sep52/DZ

E3SA 896/20May53/GB: White; b-695; TJO887; V.
Smithson.

E3SA897/20Apr53/GB

E3SA 898/30Jun53/GB: Red; b-694; JUN592: P.
Crosby.

E3SA 899/3Jun53/GB: Red; b-698; e-E3SA 899R;
c-91155; TPD543; R. Howard.

E3SA 900/1Jul53/GB: White; b-706; e-E2 PD 22212;
c-23470; GFR766; W. Meneely.

E3SA 901/14May53/GB: Red; e-E3 SA 901R; c-27237;
J.E. Snelling-Colyer.

E3SA 902/18Oct53/GB

E3SA 903/27Apr53/GB: Red; b-708; e-R8267; c-13865;
FVG87; J. Miller.

E3SA 904/20May53/GB

E2SA 905/10Oct52/GB: White; b-693; e-E2SA905R;
c-20948; NLA45; C. Lane.

E2SA 906/3Sep52/DZ

E2SA 907/26Nov52/BR

E3SA 908/3Jul53/GB

E2SA 909/1May53/GB: Ivory; e-JUR25717; OKC687; (1967).

E2SA 910/5Mar53/GB: BHG181; D. Marshall.

E2SA 911/11May53/P/ex: The engine from this car has turned up in the Republic of South Africa.

E3SA 912/16Apr53/GB:

E3SA 913/Jan54/GB: BRG; b-700; e-R025811N; c-92089; OLO429; A. Fewster.

E3SA 914 Apr53/P/ex: Now in RSA red; b-701; e-(ns); c-932 & 27100; UK reg JKU729; Otto.

E2SA 915/27Apr53/GB:e-E3SA915R; OKC941; A. McMullen.

E3SA 916/9Jun53/GB: b-699; GBA438; G. Wills.

E3SA 917/22Jun53/GB: b-681; e-E3 917 SA; c-24484; OKD725; S. Wilson.

E3SA 918/23Jun53/GB/USA/Mo: Red; b-720; e-JUR25491; UK reg PNK627; to USA in 1973; D. Hudgens.

E3SA 919/8Sep53/GB

E3SA 920/19Aug53/GB: b-709; possibly scrapped.

E3SA 921/29Jun53/GB: b-704; c-A23; NYM283; G.R. Smith.

E2SA 922/17Nov52/GB: b-715; e-R649; c-7483; sold 1961 to Budge Rogers, Bedford and England rugby player, who crashed it in France. HKY770; M. Barton.

E3SA 923/29May53/GB: Green; e-E3 SA 923; c-23539; FJR759; H. Morrison.

E3SA 924/23Jun53/GB: b-685; OKC950; dismantled; tail on 211, bonnet on 876; bodyframe on 246, chassis with G. M. Mitchell.

E3SA 925/23Jun53/GB/AUS: Green; b-721; e-R014844; UK reg NXX416, to AUS in 1971; F. de Pinna.

E2SA 926/16Mar53/GB

E2SA 927/19Sep53/GB/Bermuda: Blue; b-713; e-JUR25711; c-92585; to UK in 1957 on Queen Mary; TOW997; J.D. Rogers.

E3SA 928/24Apr53/GB: b-723; JSR964; in Myrton Museum, East Lothian, Scotland, as is the drop-head Javelin; they are owned by D. Cremer.

E3SA 929/20Jun53/GB: LJW979; rallied by first owner Ronald Harrison (class-won Concours of 1953 MCC *Daily Express*).

E3SA 930/25Jun53/GB: Red; b-716; MWU540; R.H. Simpson.

E3SA 931/14Apr53/ZA

E3SA 932/5Jun53/GB: BRG; b-714; e-JUR26241N; c-91172; BHG633; J. Ingram.

E3SA 933/24Jun53/GB: Blue; b-717; e-R016552N; c-17088; FVG634; C.P. Jackman.

E3SA 934/3Jul53/GB: Green; b-712; e-JUR26270N; c-H20; KWS137; C. Stemps.

E3SA 935/23Oct53/GB: Green; b-724; e-E3 SA 720R; c-725 G 26651; 189AME; W.H. Derbyshire.

E3SA 936/30Oct53/GB: b-725/; 980AMC; possibly scrapped.

E3SA 937/27Jun53/GB: Red; b-726; e-E3 SA 937; c-23460; originally chassis 746+ therefore metal-bushed front suspension retained; NYX763;

in collection of Lord Cranworth.

E2SAL938/22Aug52/USA: Originally chassis 724+.

E2SAL939/19Sep52/Jap: Originally chassis 244+.

E2SC 940/17Nov52/GB: Red; JAK76; b-SC1; probably the 1952 Motor Show exhibition car; H. Brierley.

E3SC 941/22Aug53/IRL: b-SC6; owned from new to 1960 by a brewer at Dublin's Guinness brewery; ZU120; P. Halion.

E2SC 942/21Oct52/GB: Red; b-2C; e-R25835; thought to have been the 1952 Motor Show demonstrator, as it was reg JAK74 for JCL Bradford. A.A.R. Pluckrose.

E2SC 943/9Dec52/GB: RVK105; N.H. Spawton.

E2SC 944/16Jul53/GB: b-8C; 2258E; G.M. Mitchell.

E3SC 945/23Jul53/GB

E3SC 946/19May53/GB: b-13C; JUN 70; S. Seabridge.

E3SC 947/20May53/GB: Brown; b-11C; e-JUR25937N; c-91078; NXH709; G. McAuley.

E3SCL948/13Jan53/USA/NY: b-12C; e-E2 SCL 948R; c-24193 G; (E3 in records but E2 on car); D.A. Sneddon.

E3SC 949/4May53/GB

E3SC 950/6Feb53/B

E3SCL951/3Jun53/USA/Il: b-30C; (1964).

E2SCL952/3Jun53/USA/Ma: A. Enders.

E3SC 953/20Aug53/Pex: JKW72.

E3SCL954/2Feb53/CO: b-33C; (1981).

E3SCL955/11Jan54/RSR

E4SCL956/15Feb54/P: b-40C; apparently not sold until 21Dec56.

E3SC 957/8May53/GB/WAL: Gree; b-26C; p/ex, so reg JKW925 by factory, returned 1957; G.M. Mitchell.

E4SCL958/5Mar54/A

E3SCL959/2Feb53/CO

E3SCL960/13Jan53/USA

E3SC 961/6May53/B

E3SCL962/7Jul53/P/ex: To Cuba, JKW539.

E3SC 963/3Jun53/USA

E2SC 964/3Dec52/GB/CH: e-JUR25627N; UK reg JAK592; in private collection of post-war sports cars. P. Strinati.

E3SCL965/3Jun53/USA

E3SC 966/15May53/GB

E3SCL967/3Jun53/USA/Mi: Green; b-46; e-E3 SCL 967R; c-25823 G; D. Cleavinger.

E4SCL968/26Feb54/P/ex/USA/Ca: Ivory; b-48; e-E1 SAL 529R; UK reg KAK775; E.W. Miller.

E3SCL969/25Nov53/USA

E3SCL970/3Jul53/P/USA/Md: Allegedly raced by first owner José F. Batista car sponsored by the Lisbon importer. Lt-Col A.S. Aitken bought the car in Lisbon in 1962, took it to USA in 1964, still had it there in 1968.

E3SCL971/28Nov53/USA/Ca: b-22C; e-E2SAL781; c-26502; the only Jupiter to have been sold by World Wide Import Inc; P. Clark.

E3SC 972/16Jan53/GB: Red; b-17; e-R017622N; c-9771; new to W.J. Tee, managing director of *Motor Sport*; JAK998; D. Liley.

E3SC 973/13Mar53/CY

E3SC 974/8May53/GB: Car was cannibalised to restore 1013.

E4SCL975/2Mar54/P/ex

E3SC 976/20Apr53/GB

E2SC 977/29Dec52/HK/GB: Black; b-91; engine and crankcase numbers removed; to GB in 1959; S. Keil.

E4SC 978/5Feb54/GB

E3SCL979/24Jul53/P/ex: JKW741.

E3SC 980/6Jul53/GB: Dark green; b-89; e-JUR25476; c-24557; GJN466; G.F. Henderson.

E3SC 981/22Jul53/P/ex/RSR: Silver; b-23; e-JUR26117N; c-24947; UK reg JKW679; first owner took car to RSR via Blantyre; RSD7501; F. Robinson (1970).

E2SC 982/24Dec52/: Green; e-E2 SC 982R; c-25625; G.R. Worn.

E3SC 983/9Apr53/S

E3SC 984/30Apr53/GB: Ivory; b-16; e-N25102; c-27486 & 91580; first owner T.A.G. Wright won novice award 1953 London Rally. Present owner has fitted overdrive; JJU655; K.J. West.

E3SC 985/2Jan53/GB: JNT230.

E3SC 986+/2Mar53/RL

E3SCL987/24Jul53/USA/Md: The building that housed this car was gutted by fire June 1977, car a total loss.

E4SCL988/7Mar54/P/ex/USA/NJ: Blue; e-E4 SCL 988RZ; c-91414 & 27423; M. Reinwald.

E3SCL989/14Aug53/P/ex

E3SCL990/13Nov53/F/USA/Va: J. Madden.

E3SCL991/3Jun53/USA: b-68.

E3SC 992/19Jun53/GB: Blue; e-JUR26313; c-92048; STN474; P.L. Ashworth.

E3SC 993/1Jul53/GB

E3SC 994/3Jul53/GB: Green; b-7; e-JUR25775N; c-23294; OPX494; K. Roberts.

E3SC 995/8Jul53/P/ex/GB: Green; b-77; e-R25148; c-92623; JKW560; B. Keil.

E3SC 996/3Nov53/GB: b-75 originally: now, bonnet 559, rear section and offside door hitherto unused set; b-81C; CEN154; D. Marshall.

E3SC 997/19Oct53/GB

E3SC 998/3Nov53/WAN

E3SC 999/5Nov53/GB: Metallic Sherwood green; b-100; e-E3 SC 999R; c-1004 & 27113; PKB 17; K. Latham.

E3SC 1000/12Nov53/GB

E3SC 1001/21Jan54/ZA: b-67, H. Moore.

E3SC 1002/21Jan54/ZA

E3SC 1003/21Feb54/Portuguese East Africa

E3SC 1004/4Dec53/GB

E3SC 1005/21Jan54/GB

E4SC 1006/13Mar54/GB: b-15; JRX663; possibly scrapped.

E4SC 1007/11Feb54/GB: b-65; e-8761, 3021; c-24782; GJT620; (1979).

E4SC 1008/3Feb54/JA

E4SC 1009/3May54/ZA

E4SC 1010/28Aug54/GB: Damaged in 1964.

E4SC 1011/13May54/ZA

E4SC 1012/13May54/ZA

E4SC 1013/27Aug54/GB: White; b-66; PLB310; K. Lees.

E4SCL1014/6Apr54/USA

E4SCL1015/1Apr54/SF: b-80; e-RGM36J; c-92123; UD-119; S.F. Borg but in a Finnish museum.

E4SCL1016/15Apr54/F: S. Espoury.

E4SCL1017/16Apr54/F/USA/NY: b-55; e-E4SCL1017R; c-91283 & 27432; F reg 632-AH-59; to USA in 1963. F. Whiting.

E4SCL1018/2Jun54/F: Red; b-95; H. Louis.

E4SCL1019/16Jul54/USA/Pa: b-36, (1979).

E4SC 1020/18Aug54/GB: Ivory; e-E4 SC 1020; KDN799; R.D. Laurie.

E4SC 1021/6Jul54/ZA: Ivory, b-74; e-E3 SA 911R; c-426 & 26584; TJ 94676; D. Kennedy.

E4SCL1022/26May54/F: Metallic grey; e-E4 SCL 1022R; c-1471 & 27450; (1973).

E4SCL1023/14Jun54/F

E4SCL1024/30Jun54/F

E4SCL1025/12Jul54/F: b-97; e-E4 SCL 1025; 1895-GR-75; (1973).

E4SC 1026/9Jun54/GB: White; b-71; e-R012901; c-21247; TTD88; K. Clements.

E4SC 1027/21May54/GB: White; b-92; e-E2 PD 21397; c-21916, OYE244; D. Toogood.

E4SC 1028/28Aug54/GB: 826DRE; abandoned at Harringay Arena, London, in 1967, known to have been vandalised.

E4SC 1029: No release date given, but its (export) invoice number is higher than that of 1031. Destination was Turkey: 'Sale or return' at the Izmir Fair.

E4SC 1030 27Aug54/GB: PGP 10; E. Wood.

E4SCL1031/23Jul54/F: Red; b-93; e-E4SCL 1031R; c-91492 & 27454; 5658-VH-75; (1973).

E4SC 1032/27Sep54/GB: Red, b-64; PLB552; J. Parker

E4SC 1033/4Nov54/GB: Blue; b-53, e-4 SC 1033; c-91524 & 27474; the last motor vehicle built by Jowett Cars Ltd, it is believed using the Show chassis (2), KKY155; J.W. Smith.

A Mk1a Jupiter was built from new spares in the mid-1950s by Robert Townend of Cottingham in Yorkshire. It was registered VWF99 on 10Jul58. The body is not a set; bonnet 84, boot lid 94, a door 87, etc. Original engine e-JUR25762; c-134; I. Anderson.

E1R1 1/6Jun51: Green; HAK364; entrant Le Mans, 1951, driven by Tom Wisdom and Tommy Wise; winner, Queen Catherine Monteur Cup, Watkins Glen 15Sep51; class 4th, Prix de Monte Carlo, 2Jun52, driven by Marcel Becquart; practice car Le Mans 1952; driven by Gatsonides/Nijevelt in race, from which it retired.

– R1 2 to R2 55 were not built.

E2R1 56/20May52: Green; HKY48; entrant Le Mans 1952, driven by Hadley/Goodacre – retired.

– R1 57 to R1 61 were not built.

E2R1 62/20May52: Blue; HKY49; class winner Le Mans 1952, driven by M. Becquart/G. Wilkins; present owners P. Dixon/D. Sparrow.

The R4 Jupiters were not entered into the factory records.

117 Peter Dixon takes E2R1 62 around Snetterton in a COMCC handicap race, October 1978

Epilogue:
Sir Hugh Bell Remembers

The car [EO/SA/25R] was the quickest and best-mannered car I had ever had. I did the Tees, Darlington to the Thames, Chelsea, door to door in 4 hrs 20 mins [approximately 245 miles at 55 mph] on Pool petrol diluted with 50 per cent alcohol, comfortably. There was no dual carriage-way north of Hatfield! Until the Mercedes 300SLR I thought it the best-mannered car in the world in the wet.

It seemed a lucky car and is the only car I never spun! I was only stopped once by the police – for doing 80 mph down the Seven Sisters Road; they let me off! It was about two o'clock in the morning.

I remember the Jupiter with the great affection one has for intelligent but difficult children on whom much thought is lavished and who make up for it by their intermittent brilliance.

I recommend the empty narrow twisting hilly roads of Scotland to know it at its best.

Index

A40 (Jensen body), 50, 69, 70, 82
Abbott, E.D., of Farnham, 80, 81, 107,
   127
Adams & Robinson, 106, 107
Allard, car, 48, 49, 52, 56, 58, 63, 68, 72
   Sydney, 52, 58, 93
Alpine Rally
   1951, 50-52
   1952, 56-7
   1953, 59
Angell Motors, 14, 120-21
Appleton-Jupiter special, 9
Appleyard, Ian, 48, 49, 52, 55, 56
Armangaud, 51-2, 57
Armstrong, J.J., of Carlisle, 107
Aston Martin, 34, 36, 83, 86
   DB1, 50
   DB2, 52
   DB3, 40, 66, 70, 72, 79
Autocar, 6-7, 127
Autosport, 18, 19
Auto Union, 10

Bancroft, Ken, 55, 56
Barnaby Body Builders, 107
Barton's Transport, 107
Bastow, Donald, 14, 79, 101, 102
Baxter, Raymond, 44-5
Becquart, Marcel, 60, 80, 109
   Le Mans, 6, 35-42
   Monte Carlo Rally, 52-4, 57-8
   RAC Rally, 50, 54-6
Bendall, James, & Sons, 107
Beutler, Gebruder, 107-8
Beverley Motors, 86, 108
Blackburn and General Aircraft Co., 16, 17,
   103
Boddy, William, 18, 25, 60, 67, 85, 93
Bolster, John, 18, 60, 63
Bonnet/Bayol, 37
Booth, Ted, 49-51, 52, 54-6, 64, 80, 107
Boreham, 74
Brearley, W.A., 68, 74, 75, 76-7, 80
Bremgarten, 63
Briggs Motor Bodies Ltd, 14, 15, 20, 57,
   101, 102
Brighton Speed Trials, 74, 78, 86
British Empire Trophy
   1951, 63-4

   1952, 72-3
Burke Mountain H.C., 63

Castle Coombe, 55, 59, 75, 93
Chiron, Louis, 44, 46
Cisitalia, 10, 109
Clarkson, Roy, 82, 107
Clore, Charles, 8, 10
Coachcraft of Egham, 108-9
Coffin, Dexter, 63, 64
Cooper-MG, 33, 34, 63-74 *passim*, 79, 85,
   99
Croft, 64, 74
Crouch, John, 108-9

DB, 37, 38
Delahaye, 44, 45, 46
Dundrod, *see* RAC TT
Dyna-Panhard, 40

Eberhorst, Robert, 8, 9, 10, 11, 18-19,
   19-21, 66, 113, 114
Ellison, Robert, 44-5, 53, 110
Emery, Paul, 104, 107
ERA, 8, 9, 10, 61
   -Javelin, 8, 11, 113
   Jupiter chassis, 9-11, 13, 113, 126

Farina, Pinin, 22, 109
   Stabilimenti, 13, 52-4, 57, 108, 109-10
Faroux, Charles, 39
   Charles Faroux Challenge Cup, 45, 53,
   58
Farr, J.E., & Son Ltd, 53, 110
Ferguson, Harry, 78, 119
Flewitt, 110
Floyd Bennet Trophy, 78
Ford, and Briggs, *see* Briggs
   Consul, 54, 60
   Pilot, 46, 48, 49
Foster, Bob, 58, 59
Fotheringham-Parker, Phillip, 60, 107
Foulds, Edward, 52, 80
Frazer Nash, 36, 38, 61, 63, 72-3
Fryer Scientific, 9, 89

Gatsonides, Maurice, 38-40, 50, 54, 60
Ghia Suisse, 53, 57, 110
Giants Despair H.C., 62

Gomm, Maurice, 17, 86, 108, 129
Goodwood, 68, 69, 74, 76, 77, 78, 79, 81
Gordini, Amédée, 35, 44, 54
   car, 38, 39, 79
Gordon, Alec, 50, 56, 60, 81, 82
Gott, John, in HRG, 48, 51, 52, 61, 84
   in Jupiter, 56-7
Grandfield, Charles, 11, 16, 38, 43, 54, 60,
   61, 78
Green, George, 16, 17, 101, 121-2, 123
Green, Phil, 38, 42, 102, 125
Grimley, Horace, 10, 11, 35, 38, 44, 46,
   53, 61
Grounds, Frank, 53, 58, 59, 60, 74, 82,
   110
Gurzeler, T., 63

Hackney, Hunter, 33, 76, 80, 81, 122
Hadley, Bert, 19, 32
   Le Mans, 34, 35-6, 39-41
   Prescott, 19, 71
   RAC Rally, 54-6
   RAC TT, 65-6
   Silverstone, 62, 68-9
Hartwell, George, 110
Hayward, Dick, 18
Healey, at Le Mans, 35
   Nash-engined, 39
   Saloon, 67
   Silverstone, 70, 72, 82, 104
   Sportsmobile, 13
Hepworth, Jack, 47, 78
Hill, Claude, 50, 78
Hodge, S.O., 108
Hodkin, David, 10, 113
Hoffman M.C.C., 11
Hoffman, Max, 37, 68, 109
Hotchkiss, 50
HRG, 19, 21, 32
   Aerodynamic, 74
   Meadows-engined, 18, 34
   Offenhauser-engined, 68
   races, 34, 38, 61, 62, 63, 68, 71, 84
   rallies, 48, 50, 51, 54-7 passim, 80

Imhoff, Godfrey, in Allard, 48, 56
   in Jupiter, 49, 50, 80
Ineson special, 9, 131
International Harvester, 16, 17, 42, 82
Iseran, Rallye de l', 52
Isle of Man, see British Empire Trophy

Jacobs, Dick, 61, 62, 63, 65-6, 68
Jaguar, 38-9, 61
   C-type, 88
   XK120, 22, 34, 35, 62, 72-6 passim, 91
   XK120C, 66
   XK150, 91, 92
'Jaguar Eater', 91-2
'Jehu', 9, 77, 78, 84
Johnson, Leslie, 10, 11, 32, 34, 39, 61,
   113

Jopling, Arthur, 8, 16, 78
Jowett Bradford CD, 15, 16, 21, 32, 33,
   78, 101, 104
   Cars Ltd, 8-17, 19, 22, 32, 33, 78, 82,
      101-3, 106, 112-13, 117
   Engineering Ltd, 17, 82, 117
   Javelin, 8, 19, 32, 33
      in races, 34, 61, 82, 84, 87, 88
      in rallies, 38, 43-60 passim, 80
   Jupiter, 12, 16, 22, 23, 25, 26
      chassis, 21, 22-3
      coachwork, 22-6
      colours, 27
      design, 20-27
      engine, 21, 26, 38, 39, 78, 104, 118-20,
         123
      gearbox, 27, 57, 85, 86, 91, 120
      handling, 18-21, 38, 86, 129-30
      hood (top), 25
      Mk2, 14-15
      performance data, results and records,
         27-31
      R1, 9, 21, 34, 37-8, 67, 91, 99, 139
         at Le Mans
            1951, 35-6
            1952, 6-7, 38-42
      R4, 9, 15, 16, 21-2, 34, 101-5, 120,
         123, 138
         tested by Autosport, 79
         in competition, 85-90 passim, 103-4
      scale model, 18
      special bodywork
         open, 9, 13, 51, 55, 65, 106-16 passim
         saloon, 9, 10, 13, 52-3, 59, 63-4, 85,
            86, 106-16 passim

Kanrell, Carl-Gustav, 110-11
Kelly, Joe, 72-3, 74
Klemantaski, Louis, 43
Korner, Reg, 10, 11, 20, 22
KW Bodies, 85, 111

Lancia, 22, 48-9, 51, 109
Latune, Jean, 53-4, 57, 58
Lazards, 8, 57, 58
Leacroft, 111
Le Mans, 6, 11, 32-42
Lester, Harry, 61, 65, 68
Lester-MG, 33, 34, 38, 63-74 passim, 89,
   99
Levegh, Pierre, 39, 46, 61
Lisbon Rally:
   1951, 48-9
   1952, 56
   1953, 59
Lloyd, Bill, 78
Lotus, 21, 84, 85, 88, 89, 103
Lund, Ted, in Jupiter, 78-9
   in MG, 61, 62, 63-4, 69-70, 72, 73
Lunn, Roy, 8, 9, 50, 54-5, 78, 79, 101-2

Marshall, John, 45, 68

Maserati brothers, 39
Mayers, 65, 68, 72
Mays, Raymond, 10, 43
MCC Rally, 52, 57, 60, 85, 87
Mead, Richard, 9, 84, 111-12
Meadows gearboxes, 120
Meccanix Illustrated, 18
Mercedes, 39, 40
MG, 48, 54, 62, 67, 68, 69, 77, 84, 85, 89,
    91, 100, 130
    A, 88, 89, 91, 99, 103, 104
    B, 99
    TC, 19, 61, 62, 72, 73, 76
    TD, 18, 19, 32-8 *passim*, 50, 51, 56,
        57, 62, 63, 78
    TF, 85, 92
Midnight Sun, rally to the, 50
Miles Aircraft Co., 10
Mitchell, Nancy, 50, 54, 55, 56, 88
Monte Carlo, 46
    Prix de, 38
Monte Carlo Rally
    1949 and 1950, 43
    1951, 33, 43-7
    1952, 52-4
    1953, 58
Morgan, car, 54, 55, 56, 69, 70, 90, 91,
    107
Morgan, Peter, 54, 75, 88
Morrison, Vic, 91-2
Moss, Stirling, 32, 38, 52, 61, 62, 63, 66,
    70, 73
Moston, New, Sheet Metal Co., 112
Motor Panels of Epsom, 112
Motor Show, 110
    Brussels, 11
    Geneva, 11, 50
    London, 8, 10, 12, 101, 102
    New York, 11-12, 22
    Paris, 12, 14
Motor Sport, 18, 93-6
Motor Sports World, 18

Nathan, 57, 75
Nijevelt, van, 38, 60
Nockolds, Roy, 11
Nogueira, Joaquim Filipe, 48-9, 56, 57
Norlander, G., 54

Odell, Les, 45
Oulton, 89, 99
OSCA, 39-40, 57

Pace, Ashley, 76
'Pacific Spot', 90-91
Padman, Leao, 21, 119
Palmer, Gerry, 8, 20, 43
Park, W.M., 112
Pebble Beach concours, 37
Peck, Cameron, 12
Peugeot, 52, 58, 60
Phillips, George, 19

in Jupiter, 69-70
in MG, 35, 61, 62, 65, 79
Pinn, Des, 76
Pomeroy, Laurence, 8, 10
Porsche, car
    in races, 37, 39-40, 42, 67, 68, 72, 76,
        77, 84, 86, 90
    in rallies, 33, 54-9 *passim*
Porsche, Ferdinand, 10
Prescott, H.C., 19, 71, 75, 78, 84, 87

Queen Catherine Monteur Cup, 37-8, 62

RAC Rally
    1951, 49-50
    1952, 54-6
    1953, 58-9
RAC TT
    1950, 62
    1951, 64-6
    1953, 78-9
Radford, Harold, 10, 112-14
Rawson, Lionel, 13, 103, 107, 114-15
Reece, 65-6, 67
Reilley, Calcott, 8
Rest and Be Thankful H.C., 50, 55, 59, 63,
    96
Rheineck-Walzenhauzen H.C., 63
Road & Track, 18, 62, 121
Robinson, Bill, 19
    in races, 63-4, 68, 72-3, 78-9
    in rallies, 44-8, 51-2
Rosier, Louis, 34

Sainsbury, Wilf, 8, 11
Salter, Frank, 101
Scragg, E.P., 73
Searcy & McCready, 112
Shelsley Walsh H.C., 74
Simca, 39, 44, 45, 46, 48, 51, 54
Simca-Gordini, 35-7
Silverstone, 77, 84
    Production Car race
        1950, 61
        1951, 62
        1952, 68-70
    RAC rally trials, 50, 55, 59
    Six-hour relay handicap race
        1952, 74
        1953, 77
        1954, 84
        1955, 86
        1957, 89
        1958, 89-90, 103
    other events, 64, 73, 75, 83-90 *passim*,
        99, 103
Skelly, Bill, 54, 65-6, 67, 69-70, 72-3, 111
Skelton, Red, 14, 129
Small, Newton, 18, 67
Smallhorn, Dr, 51-2, 54
Snetterton, 75, 77, 99, 108, 117
Sommer, Erik, 114-16

Spa, 10, 34
Stephenson, Phil, 9, 15, 36, 47, 101
Still, F.E., 54, 73, 74, 80, 81, 99
Sunbeam Alpine, and Talbot, 52, 60, 110
Sweet, Cyril, 18

Talbot, 34, 39, 46
Taylor, L.J.Roy, 19, 80, 126
Tew, Maurice, 54, 59, 60, 76, 82
Thomas, Alf, 64-5, 74, 75, 76,
    82-90 *passim*, 103-4
Thomas, Barry, 82-90 *passim*, 103
Torry Pines, 67, 76
Tour de France, 57
Triumph TR2, 83, 87, 90, 99, 102, 103,
    130
    TR3, 99, 104, 109
Tulip Rally, 38, 47-8, 60

Ulster TT, *see* RAC TT

Veritas, 38, 75

Veuillet/Mouche, 37, 39
Volta a Portugal, 56

Wansborough, George, 8, 10
Warblaufen, 115
Weaver, George, 37-8, 64
Wharton, Ken, 46, 48, 75
Whittet, Pat, & Co., 108, 115-16
Wilkins, Gordon, 6, 35-9, 44-7
Willow Springs H.C., 78
Wilson, Mike, 50, 54, 55
Winfield, 66, 76, 93
Wisdom, Tom, 34
    in Javelin, 10
    in Jupiter, 34-6, 62, 65-6
    in other cars, 39, 52
Wise, Tommy, in races, 34-8, 65-6, 67
    in rallies, 43-5, 49, 50-52, 54-7
Woodhead, Harry, 22, 78
Wylie-Javelin special, 87, 92

Ziegler, Henri, 50, 53, 58